MASS MEDIA
EFFECTS
ACROSS CULTURES

INTERNATIONAL AND INTERCULTURAL COMMUNICATION ANNUAL

Volume XVI   **1992**

INTERNATIONAL AND INTERCULTURAL COMMUNICATION ANNUAL
VOLUME XVI   1992

MASS MEDIA EFFECTS ACROSS CULTURES

edited by

Felipe KORZENNY
Stella TING-TOOMEY
with Elizabeth SCHIFF

Published in Cooperation with
the Speech Comunication Association
International and Intercultural Communication Division

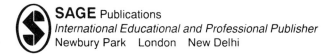

SAGE Publications
International Educational and Professional Publisher
Newbury Park   London   New Delhi

For information address:

 SAGE Publications, Inc.
2455 Teller Road
Newbury Park, California 91320

SAGE Publications Ltd.
6 Bonhill Street
London EC2A 4PU
United Kingdom

SAGE Publications India Pvt. Ltd.
M-32 Market
Greater Kailash I
New Delhi 110 048 India

Printed in the United States of America

Library of Congress Cataloging-in-Publication Data

International Standard Book Number 0-8039-4623-6

International Standard Book Number 0-8039-4624-4 (pbk)

International Standard Series Number 0270-6075

92 93 94 95 10 9 8 7 6 5 4 3 2 1

Sage Production Editor: Astrid Virding

Contents

Preface

The opportunity to assemble a volume that deals exclusively with media effects across cultures has been highly gratifying and unique. Few pieces on this topic exist in the available literature. The reliable and supportive work of Stella Ting-Toomey, coeditor of the series, has made the experience particularly fruitful and enjoyable. Elizabeth Schiff, associate editor of this volume, has been invaluable in making this book a reality. Her enthusiasm for communication scholarship and her fine eye for conceptual details constituted a major input. As a former student and as a current colleague, Elizabeth continues to shine when it comes to collaborating on academic endeavors. Without the contributions of Stella and Elizabeth, the present task would have been less rewarding and perhaps impossible.

San Francisco State University was highly instrumental in facilitating the editorship of this book. Nancy McDermid, Dean of the School of Humanities, continued her support for this series despite scarce resources. The institution, with the support of Dr. Marylin Boxer, Vice President for Academic Affairs, generously provided a sabbatical semester to complete the required work.

My appreciation goes to Sage Publications for their enthusiasm in supporting our field. Ann West deserves a special mention for her continued involvement with and contributions toward the progress of this series. The current volume is fondly dedicated to the memory of George McCune, who with his partner Sara made Sage Publications a reality.

Felipe Korzenny
San Francisco State University

1

Media Effects Across Cultures
Challenges and Opportunities

FELIPE KORZENNY ● *San Francisco State University*
ELIZABETH SCHIFF ● *San Francisco City and County,
Civil Service Commission*

The study of media effects across cultures has shown itself to be elusive and filled with frustration. From the time when communication scholars postulated the mass media as the panacea for national development (Lerner, 1958) to the present when a highly complex view of media effects prevails, there has been a vacuum in the literature which this volume partially attempts to fill. The historical period we presently witness is also ripe for the study of media effects across cultures because it involves the political upheaval in Eastern Europe and the Soviet Union, as well as unprecedented advances in electronic communication.

Great opportunities reside in the potential for using the knowledge we have accumulated up to this point to leap perhaps into an era of study of cross-cultural media effects that will bring about more conclusive and more relevant knowledge. The challenge is to comprehend the issues and difficulties that the contributing scholars report.

In discussing media effects across cultures one ought to consider the tradition of media effects research that leads us to the present. The paradigm bringing us to conceptualizing media effects as a subject of scholarly consideration derives from the tradition of Lasswell (1954). The classical question of "Who says what to whom, and with what effects?" has now passed to the annals of communication research history.

The assumption that media play a role in modifying human behavior has intuitive and empirical roots. But how mediated messages have an impact across cultures is largely undetermined. The level at which impact or effects are supposed to take place is blurred. Are we interested in long-term cultural change or in immediate individual change? Are we interested in how people of different cultures interpret messages or in the affective disposition the messages produce?

The casual observation of diverse contexts in international settings leads to immediate conclusions about effects as observed in the free market of television, music, film, and some of the print media. It can be extremely striking to hear John Travolta in an Andean market in Peru, or to look at audiences in remote villages in Morocco reacting to *Dallas.* It is also remarkable, and against common stereotypes of one-way flow of cultural influence, to be sitting in a café in San Francisco listening to the sounds of the Senegalese musician Youssou N'Dour coming over the stereo system. One cannot but infer effects.

Intuition would dictate that the current freedom or democratic movements and reforms in Eastern Europe, China, and the Soviet Union have something to do with the diffusion of information across borders and cultures. Ironically it is possible that the popular media of the West may have actually done in unsuspecting regimes. The political idealism of Eastern Europe and the Soviet Union, which attempted to pave the way to the final stage of history as predicted by Karl Marx, may have been eroded by entertainment from the West. A revolution of rising expectations may have taken place (Lerner, 1964).

Other casual observations lead to more direct inferences about effects. During the Allied war against Iraq, the diverse governments involved in the conflict established diverse types of censorship to protect their strategies. The effects so anticipated would be classified as incidental but certainly of great importance. CNN was attacked for providing too much information to the enemy.

Another type of inferred effect is that in which the media (e.g., CNN) provide diverse amounts of coverage to the different sources in the conflict. The more profuse and concentrated the coverage, the more the receivers of the information are likely to understand the source and potentially empathize with it. We worry about what is said and about what is not said in the media because we believe many others will have access to a powerful message. Almost anyone can blame the media for doing too much or doing too little, because the media is believed to be powerful.

Another interesting recent cross-cultural media event is that of the brutal police beating of Rodney King in Los Angeles. The fact that there was a visual record of the event and that the media repeatedly played it appears to be responsible for increased African American political and popular participation in decrying police abuse, and ultimately racism.

This volume encompasses a compendium of diverse perspectives on media effects. All the contributions found here are original pieces that attempt to represent thought, research, and ethics in the massive endeavor of understanding cross-cultural media effects.

In Chapter 2, Arthur Asa Berger provides a refreshing perspective on media analysis across cultures. He provides categories for focusing our attention when comparing "texts" from diverse cultures. Berger also looks at decoding media effects and cogently reflects upon the multiplicity of possible interpretations of particular sets of content. Individuals as cultures have unique experiences and perspectives and consequently decode text in diverse manners. The hypothesis of homogenization through media cultural imperialism is questioned and placed in a temperate perspective.

Akiba A. Cohen and Itzhak Roeh (Chapter 3) argue that the modification or "domestication" of media content becomes an issue of importance in determining media effects. These authors quote Lazarsfeld and Merton as suggesting that the search for mass media effects upon society is an ill-defined problem if the study of effects is not placed in the cultural/historical context of the society where effects are investigated. The proactive contextualization of media content calls for a "weak" view of effects. In essence, these authors argue for an etic approach to the study of effects as opposed to an emic perspective (Pike, 1966). In a sense Cohen and Roeh's perspective coincides with the "remediation" phenomenon endorsed by Yaple and Korzenny (1989). In Yaple and Korzenny's view, this chapter would fall into a "plural perspective" at its highest extreme. When the clear recognition of changed content and psycho-socio-cultural interpretation takes place, the researcher needs to switch analytical frameworks.

Chapter 4 by Steven H. Chaffee further emphasizes the importance of context in conceptualizing media effects. This chapter deals with the feasibility of conducting conclusive research founded on plausible conceptualization and a clearly delineated research design. Chaffee argues that because change-change studies are virtually impossible in the realm of international media effects, the study of change-state or state-change situations can offer appropriate tools for theory testing. Even state-state situations, when properly conceptualized and when the cultural context is carefully considered, can be used for the study of potential change under a theoretical paradigm. Chaffee argues that the combination of sound theoretical propositions, careful methodology, and the consideration of the cultural context can lead to the advancement of our understanding of media effects across cultures.

In his highly influential book, *Beyond Culture* (1977), Edward T. Hall emphasized the importance of "context" in the study of communication across cultures. Chapter 5 by Raymond Gozzi, Jr., is a premier attempt to specify the importance of context in media effects. Gozzi's chapter constitutes a heuristic set of hypotheses that provides a sense of understanding for the diverse effects similar media can have in dissimilar cultures. Gozzi's predictions include the propositions that certain media are most likely to lower context in high-context cultures, and that certain media are most likely to raise context in low-context cultures. Interesting implications of this line of thought are that, in the vein of Marshall McLuhan, the envisioned global village would be of "intermediate" context, as the convergence of contexts would be the most likely outcome.

Chapter 6 changes the pace of this volume. In it Kim Witte provides an insightful analysis of persuasion theory for cultural change. AIDS is the focus of Witte's analysis of variables that can be manipulated to induce changes in beliefs and behaviors. She provides a superb presentation of protection motivation theory, elaboration likelihood theory, and the theory of reasoned action, as conceptual bases for her message construction model. Her chapter is a needed contribution. She revitalizes the perspective of planned change across cultures with a solid foundation. AIDS messages need to be relevant to the culture they are directed to. While this chapter is mostly geared to message design it can also be read to understand how any messages can have an impact across cultures.

The empirical studies section of this volume contains ambitious, creative, and original pieces of research. Joseph D. Straubhaar and colleagues (Chapter 7) conducted an extensive study of news from diverse countries. Their content analysis had the central intention of testing *new world information and communication order* (NWICO) hypotheses with regard to the emphases of news stories. Key findings of this research suggest that news values are strikingly similar across nations. Development journalism, more likely to emphasize achievement and development, was found more predominantly in news from socialist countries. Diversity of approaches, however, even within political blocks, is more frequent than homogeneity. These trends signal the advent of diversity as the rule for thought and action in looking at media effects.

In Chapter 8, Renée Hobbs and Richard Frost conducted a sobering study dealing with comprehension of editing conventions. Their research calls into question the assumption commonly made that the grammar used in media productions needs to be learned to be understood. They showed that villagers who had had little or no exposure to Western media could understand reverse and forward chronological editing sequences. Although limited in some ways, this highly provocative study provides heuristic guidance in search of cross-cultural media principles.

Kate Madden (Chapter 9) uses the Inuit Broadcasting Corporation (IBC) as a case study in preserving cultural identity. Madden's analysis of selected messages produced by IBC lends credence to the notion that indigenous institutions more accurately reflect traditional cultural values and thus provide a sense of political and cultural "efficacy" or "reflexivity." Institutions like IBC that act with political and economic liberty can offer effective "mirrors" for cultures that aspire to survive the perils of global trends toward homogenization.

The multinational study by Bradley S. Greenberg, Linlin Ku, and Hairong Li (Chapter 10) constitutes an ambitious attempt to investigate parental mediation of media behaviors. Their comparison sheds light over cultural patterns in emerging technological societies. Child-rearing values can be detected in the ways in which diverse cultures deal with media discipline in the home. The results of this study, when studied in the gestalt of media effects across cultures, are likely to facilitate our understanding of information processing differences across cultures. Cultures that are highly sensitizing, or stricter in media supervision, may render offsprings who are more pragmatic in their approach to media learning than those individuals who are enculturated more inductively, or based on more reasoning and explanation (Korzenny, 1977). Inductive enculturation is more likely to result in higher degrees of self-monitoring.

In Chapter 11, Michael Morgan and James Shanahan provide us with interesting evidence substantiating a pluralistic view of media effects. When comparing cultivation effects across Taiwan and Argentina, the results point to the importance of context in mediating the effects the media can have. One of the cases in this study supports a cultural homogenization perspective, whereas the other case reinforces a view of heterogeneity of effects. Interestingly, the fact that both perspectives can be supported with a similar methodological approach substantiates the need for analysis of the cultural contexts where media effects are expected to take place.

With futuristic optimism and vision, L. Ripley Smith (Chapter 12) highlights the conditions and potential implications of global communication networks for sociocultural change. As the survival of the planet and the species becomes more and more dependent on cooperation and understanding, global networks have the potential for institutionalizing common symbol systems to facilitate this task. At a time when mass destruction is a matter of a few decisions made by a few individuals, diverse world constituencies can place increased pressure on decision centers when information and power are decentralized. A call for using media networks for the pursuit of survival and life enhancement goals is at the core of shared global meanings.

Following a futuristic view of the media, Thomas W. Cooper (Chapter 13) provides an ethical perspective that can be taken as a building block in a very long process. After a serious review of efforts to achieve a code of media ethics, Cooper concludes that three universals are at the head of the agenda: truth, responsibility, and freedom. This classical triad very much reminds the reader of the work of E. F. Shumacher (1977), in which he postulates that there are divergent and convergent problems. The question of media ethics is most likely a divergent problem, a problem without solution, a problem that can only be transcended. Truth and freedom can be antithetical in that the truth of one party can hurt the freedom of another. This type of problem can only be transcended and "responsibility" is a likely candidate for that job. Responsibility may be the force to reconcile the interest of truth when opposed to the freedom of others; responsibility may also be the key to reconciling the freedom of the individual when opposed to what is maintained as societal truth.

In the epilogue (Chapter 14), Fred L. Casmir presents a critical view of the articles in this volume. In the spirit of the ongoing academic dialogue we are engaged in, his analysis offers a challenging perspective. Diverse academic approaches may be promoted when reflecting upon his criticisms. This final chapter is a call for diversity in studying media effects in social, historical, political, and cultural contexts.

In looking at a scheme for the study of media effects across cultures, the work in this volume suggests a list of variable clusters that should be considered in future research:

Cultural Approach
etic versus emic

Antecedent
social, political, historical, cultural, and media contexts
cultural degree of context (i.e., high versus low)
demographic
enculturation factors
culture as modal personality, not as nation state

Interventing
audience activity: remediation and reflexivity
information processing styles
protection motivation, elaboration likelihood, and reasoned action
socialization and parental mediation practices
approaches to media use

Level of Analysis
individual
cultural collectivities or identity groups
heterogeneous nations

Type of Change
state-state
change-change
change-state
state-change

Dependent
changes in these domains:
cognitive
affective
connative
social
cultural

Type of Effect
intended versus incidental
immediate versus delayed
culturally relevant versus irrelevant
culturally desirable versus undesirable

There is no single methodology for the study of these processes; each problem calls for unique "ways of finding out." What seems to be clear is that methodologies must provide a sense of understanding for the effort to be considered fruitful. The study of media effects across cultures as a mechanical data collection endeavor cannot render insights. Rich data, collected through varied methodologies and taken seriously, have the best prospect for building knowledge. Successive approximations to studying change as the result of change is a worthwhile endeavor, but always in the light of "Why?"

REFERENCES

Hall, E. T. (1977). *Beyond culture.* New York: Doubleday.

Korzenny, F. (1977). *Styles of parent-child interaction as a mediating factor in children's learning from antisocial television portrayals.* Unpublished doctoral dissertation, Michigan State University, East Lansing.

Lasswell, H. D. (1954). The structure and function of communication in society. In L. Bryson (Ed.), *The communication of ideas.* New York: Cooper Square.

Lerner, D. (1964). *The passing of traditional society.* New York: Free Press.

Pike, K. (1966). *Language in relation to a unified theory of the structure of human behavior.* The Hague, the Netherlands: Mouton.

Shumacher, E. F. (1977, Sept.-Oct.). The nature of problems. *Quest/77,* pp. 77-84.

Yaple, P., & Korzenny, F. (1989). Electronic mass media effects across cultures. In M. K. Asante & W. Gudykunst (Eds.), *Handbook of international and intercultural communication* (pp. 295-317). Newbury Park, CA: Sage.

I

THEORETICAL AND METHODOLOGICAL REVIEWS

2

Texts in Contexts
Analyzing Media and Popular Culture
From a Cross-Cultural Perspective

ARTHUR ASA BERGER ● *San Francisco State University*

In analyzing mass media and popular culture from a cross-cultural perspective, it is suggested that regional and subcultural differences in countries be kept in mind. A list of various levels of analysis is provided, along with reasons for analyzing mass media, which, it is asserted, both reflect and affect a given culture and society. The argument about television as an instrument of cultural domination and cultural imperialism is discussed. A case study by Herta Herzog Massing of how Dallas *was decoded differently in America and Germany and work by semioticians on "aberrant decoding" of mass media are considered. A list of matters to deal with when analyzing televised texts (and by implication, other kinds of texts) from a cross-cultural perspective is offered, along with a recommendation that research by scholars dealing with various countries also be consulted. Finally, the matter of how one negotiates between hypergeneralizations and hyperspecificity is dealt with in the context of Durkheim's ideas about the relationship that exists between individuals and society.*

A STRANGER IN A STRANGE LAND

This chapter offers some suggestions about how one might analyze the mass media and popular culture from a cross-cultural perspective, pointing out some of the difficulties involved and offering a number of things to keep in mind when making such comparisons. The very notion of popular culture depends upon the existence of something else, that is, unpopular or "elite" culture. In the same way, the notion that there is such a thing as American culture only has meaning because there are other cultures, non-American and in some cases un-American and anti-American, with which we can compare and contrast ourselves.

As de Saussure (1966) wrote, "concepts are purely differential and defined not by their positive content but negatively by their relations with the other terms of the system" (p. 117). What de Saussure said about concepts we can say about cultures and subcultures. I say this because although there may be some generalizations we can make about American culture and society, and perhaps about that always elusive American "national character," we also must recognize that there are numerous Americas—different regions (the East Coast, the "arcadian" Pacific Northwest, the Deep South)—and within each of these regions there are great varieties of life-styles, belief structures, attitudes, values, and so on.

Let me put this matter of national, regional, and local cultures and subcultures in perspective by offering a chart showing the various possibilities that exist for comparative analyses:

Category	*Example (Level of Analysis)*
• universal	• humanity
• continental	• Asian, European, South American
• macroregional	• Western Europe, North American
• national	• United States, Canada, Japan, France
• regional	• East Coast, Pacific Northwest
• subregional	• California
• urban	• San Francisco
• urban district	• Pacific Heights, Mission District
• street	• Clement Street

This is our universe of possibilities; when making cross-cultural comparisons, we select areas, similar in level, to compare and contrast within this universe. Obviously, the larger the area, the more "glittering" the generalities we make about it. For example, at the universal level we can be sure that "all men and women are mortal." When we come to the bottom of the list, we can say "there are a lot of Chinese restaurants on Clement Street."

Even within California, for example, there are great differences between Northern California and Southern California and between San Francisco (and the Bay Area) and the Los Angeles area. This can be seen in the major industries found in the two cities, in the way people from the cities dress, in the number of miles devoted to highways in the two cities, and so on. San Francisco has hardly any freeways, whereas Los Angeles has hundreds of miles of freeways in it. There are also important differences between San Francisco and the areas surrounding San Francisco; within San Francisco, there are differences between

Pacific Heights and the Mission District or between the Mission District and the Castro District.

If it is dangerous, then, to offer generalizations about the culture of San Francisco or California culture or American culture; it is even more perilous to compare and contrast national cultures—yet we must do so (as de Saussure suggests) if we are to make sense of ourselves and others.

Let me speak from personal experience. A number of years ago I made a comparative study of comics in Italy and America. I tried to find strips that were similar in nature. I dealt with American and Italian comic strips that had the same kind of characters and appeared at approximately the same time. (I also made a study of Italian magazines. In the magazine press study, I focused my attention on Italian weekly magazines such as *Oggi* and *Epoca,* but I also offered a brief comparison of these magazines and weekly magazines in America.)

There are advantages for the culture analyst in being a "stranger" in a country, but there are disadvantages as well. You can see things that those socialized in the culture do not see, however, you do not always understand everything you do see. For example, in my study of Italian and American comics, I found that *Bonvaventura* (a "classic" children's comic strip) that Italians tended to see as "optimistic" was, in fact, "pessimistic." The strip's title means, roughly speaking, "Good Adventures," yet the hero of this strip is subjected to one catastrophe after another, surviving or triumphing only as the result of chance or good luck. Also, in the Italian strips authority figures almost always were dominant and their authority seen as valid. In this respect they differed considerably from American strips with the same kinds of heroes or heroines or lead characters.

Recognizing, then, that all generalizations are questionable (perhaps even this one), let me proceed.

WHY ANALYZE MEDIA AND POPULAR CULTURE?

We study the mass media and popular culture (which tends to be but is not always mass mediated, because popular culture also includes fads, fashions, material culture, etc.), because we assume that the media and popular culture will tell us something about the society being studied. We assume that the texts carried on the media reflect interesting things about the society (and country) in which they are created. We also assume that these texts affect their societies in various ways. (When I use the term *media* I really mean the programs or texts carried on the media, as contrasted with the technical aspects of the media or the patterns of ownership and control of the media.)

Those of us who look at things from an international perspective (or cross-national or cross-cultural or transnational perspective) are interested also in how the media, or, more precisely, how mass-mediated texts and popular culture from one country may affect people in other countries. Much media and popular culture is now international. Films, television programs, rock groups, folkdance groups, and folksinging groups now travel the world, and it is not unusual for any good-sized city to have English rock groups, Bulgarian choirs, Tibetan singers, French films, Russian ballet groups, Brazilian bands, Jamaican Reggae musicians, Chinese acrobats, German symphonies, and so forth passing through or, in some cases, performing at the same time. Many of these groups have records, appear frequently on television and the radio, and so cross whatever line exists (and some people believe that line is very faint) between popular culture and elite culture.

TELEVISION AND THE PROBLEM
OF CULTURAL DOMINATION

Let me focus attention now on television, which is the medium that has been the subject of most of the controversy between critics of the left and right (and some in the middle). For although there is an international cast to cultural and popular cultural flow, when it comes to television, things are different.

Programs from America and Western European countries are much cheaper for Third-World countries to buy than to produce, and some critics are worried that American and Western European cultural, social, and political values and ideologies will drive out supposedly less hardy and more fragile native or traditional cultural values. (Entertainment, it turns out, is the second biggest American export. Airplanes are first.)

This thesis is known as "cultural imperialism" or, in its American manifestation, "coca-colonization." Some critics, who tend to be Marxists or critical theorists, believe that American media will destroy regional and local cultures and lead to ideological domination by American "bourgeois" values and to a loss of cultural identity by people in other cultures. Mixing metaphors and food products, we might say that coca-colonization will lead to cultural homogenization. This is not looked upon with favor, let me add, by those who seem to believe (and there is an element of elitism here) that in society (as in bottles of milk) the cream should rise to the top.

THE CASE OF *DALLAS* IN GERMANY

Dallas is (or was, at one time) broadcast in something like 90 different countries and has been studied extensively by scholars. Recently, Herta Herzog Massing (1986) made a study of the way *Dallas* was viewed in both Germany and America and came up with some interesting findings. As she wrote in her article in *Society:*

> Critics of popular culture, and of things American in particular, have concerned themselves with the question of whether the worldwide diffusion of programs such as "Dallas" made possible by the growth of the new media technologies may eventually result in worldwide cultural assimilation at the expense of indigenous diversity. (p. 74)

As the result of her pilot study, she came to the conclusion that viewers in America decoded *Dallas* differently from viewers in Germany. Her conclusion to the article sums things up: "The answer to my initial question—do viewers in different countries read popular culture differently?—must be answered affirmatively" (p. 77). *Dallas* is not popular in countries such as Brazil, which has its own telenovelas, and various Asian countries. In many countries it gets very low ratings.

The notion that everyone decodes, interprets, gets the same things out of a text is very close to being a throwback to the old "hypodermic needle" hypothesis of media effects. The development of semiotics has shown that not only do people in different cultures and societies interpret texts differently, so do people in the same society.

As Umberto Eco (1972) has argued:

> Codes and subcodes are applied to the message [text] in the light of a general framework of cultural references, which constitutes the receiver's patrimony of knowledge: his ideological, ethical, religious standpoints, his psychological attitudes, his tastes, his value systems, etc. (p. 115)

What we can expect from the mass media, Eco says, is "aberrant decoding." We, as individuals and as members of subcultures and cultures, read texts through the prisms of our knowledge and understanding of the world. The situation in East Europe, where people were subjected to 40 years of propaganda by state-controlled radio and television stations (and the press) yet threw out their Marxist governments as soon as they realized the Russian army would not get involved, suggests that the power of the media is limited.

ANALYZING TELEVISION FROM A CROSS-CULTURAL PERSPECTIVE

Let me suggest a number of things one might consider in making an analysis of a televised text from a cross-cultural perspective. The very notion of cross-cultural analysis implies that some kind of comparison is being made between texts that are similar in nature, usually in terms of genres. In all of the matters listed below, there is an implicit notion that comparisons between similar kinds of texts in different countries are to be carried out. With that as a given, let us consider what we might focus our attention on.

Characters' Values

What values are espoused and what values are attacked, downplayed, or neglected in a text could be considered. Values are understood as general notions about what is good and what is bad, what is desirable and what is undesirable. Here one might think of the difference between the characters in *Till Death Us Do Part* and the American series based on it, *All In the Family,* and in particular between Alf Garnett and the "lovable bigot" Archie Bunker.

Characters' Social Class and Characteristics

Although it is difficult to be precise in many cases, the socioeconomic class of the various characters and how this affects their roles and their values can be considered. Is class membership an important consideration? In this regard, consider the difference between programs such as the English series *Upstairs-Downstairs* and American soaps such as *Dallas*. In *Upstairs-Downstairs,* class differences are all important (as even the title of the show suggests), whereas American soaps tend to have a classlessness about them (peopled by wealthy men and women who gain their status by achievement, not ascription).

Characters' Roles
(particularly gender roles)

What roles do the characters play? What roles do women play and what is suggested as normal and natural for women? Are certain socio-economic classes (and attendant occupations), sexes, ages, races, ethnic types (and so forth) over- or underrepresented? One topic that comes to mind here would be the use of sexuality in television commercials. English and French and other continental commercials tend to be much more risqué and overtly sexual than American ones, though we seem to be moving away from our relatively Puritanical style.

Plot Construction

How are the plots constructed? Is there, for example, a difference in the kinds of resolutions of plots that are found in texts from the countries being analyzed? Would societies that are hierarchical and see authority as "legitimate" (such as in England) tend to have solutions to story problems imposed from above, in contrast to an egalitarian society (such as in the United States) where this is not accepted?

Protagonists' Characteristics

What are the heroes and heroines, villains and villainesses like? What are the characteristics of the protagonists? What are their values, qualities, and characteristics? How do they function in the text? Are the characters rounded, three dimensional, believable, or do they tend to be two dimensional?

Dominant Themes

What are the dominant themes? Do texts that are similar in genre and plot have different themes? If so, what does that suggest? If not, what does that suggest? One would expect that American soap operas would reflect our dominant ideology that success is a function of willpower, because we live, supposedly, in a society where the playing field is "level" (where all have opportunity). The heroes of these programs therefore would be business and professional people who "prove" that our ideology is correct. One might expect in English shows, in contrast, aristocratic types whose values are quite different from American ones. This relates to another of our considerations mentioned below, involving ideological matters.

Stereotypes

What are the main stereotypes (if any) found in the text? If there are stereotypes in the text, what are they and what function do they have?

Ideology

Is there an ideological dimension you can find in the text? Is there some kind of ideology (a logically coherent, sociopolitical set of beliefs) that is found in the text? If so, what is it? How effective do you think the ideological message is?

Language and Dialogue

How would you characterize the use of language and the quality of the dialogue in the text? What role does language play in the text, as far as indicating class, identity, values, and so on? In the United States, accents do not reflect socioeconomic background the way they do in England. One might make a sampling of American and English news shows, situation comedies, and soaps and analyze the accents found in them (and the degree to which the "received pronunciation" is waning in English television). Many Americans find it almost impossible to understand what is being said in *East Enders,* an English show about working-class people who are quite far removed from the "Upstairs" people found on *Upstairs-Downstairs.*

Visual Style

What is the visual style of the text like? What is the camera work like? What kinds of shots are dominant? What is the lighting like? What editing techniques are used? How sophisticated is the text from a technical point of view? One might examine (from a visual perspective) the way in which English or French or German football (soccer) matches are televised and compare this with the way American football games are televised.

Humor

If the text has humorous elements, what techniques of humor are dominant? Humor, we know, varies considerably from country to country and from class to class (and gender to gender). One way it varies is in terms of the techniques used to generate the humor, and these should be elicited and analyzed. It also varies in terms of who (which occupations, ethnic groups, gender, kinds of people) is the "butt" of the humor—and how people use humor as a means of resistance against domination by those elements that control society. In this regard, one might compare American and English shows. Why is *Monty Python's Flying Circus* popular in America—or, more precisely, with whom is it popular and why?

COMPARING MASS MEDIA FINDINGS TO OTHER STUDIES

It is useful to see what sociologists, cultural anthropologists, political scientists, and other scholars have to say about the countries, societies, and cultures being studied. Do your findings correlate with those by others who have investigated other aspects of the country being studied? In 1963, when I made my study of Italian and American comics and found that they differed considerably in terms of attitudes toward authority, I also made use of research by Italian sociologists who argued that the Italian family was authoritarian.

In recent years, cultural anthropologists have become interested in the mass media and popular culture and have done some extremely interesting work. An example of this is Conrad Kottak's (1990) recent study of television in Brazil, *Prime-Time Society*—a work that makes a number of important methodological advances (and has a cross-cultural perspective). In studying the media and popular culture, we should make use of work by those in other disciplines as much as possible. Some argue that communications is not a discipline, but an area where scholars trained in a number of different disciplines congregate, a crossroads where, as Wilbur Schramm put it, "few tarry.")

The goal of cross-national studies is to gain insights into such matters as national character, social and political values, belief systems, and related concerns. It is assumed that the mass media and popular culture help reinforce certain dominant values by focusing attention on them and by neglecting other values. Every country is involved, I would argue, in a dialogue with itself, as groups with different perspectives, ideologies, belief systems, and so forth contend for power and control of things. In our analyses of the media and popular culture, we should pay attention to both sides of this dialogue.

We should also consider how the media and popular culture help people gain and consolidate a sense of identity. In particular we should investigate how national ("I am French"), gender ("I am a French woman"), class ("I am a working-class French woman"), and ideological ("I am a working-class French woman and a Communist") identities are created. How do we explain the creation and persistence of subcultures in societies where the media are designed to reflect some kind of a national sense of things or are controlled by a small group of people? Or where the state runs the media and uses it as an instrument of propaganda? And how do resistant subcultures make use of media in these various societies?

BETWEEN SCYLLA AND CHARYBDIS

Somehow we must find a way to negotiate between hypergeneralizations and hyperspecificity. When talking about the effects of the media, for instance, some scholars suggest that all we can say with any certainty is that "in some cases some people are affected in some ways." On the other side of this polarity are those who make statements about "the English" or "the French" or "the Japanese" based on studying sampling of the mass media in these countries.

The solution, I believe, is to learn to narrow our focus and qualify our assertions and to recognize how complex cultures and societies are. As I write this, a number of countries are experiencing difficulties holding themselves together. In Canada, for example, there is talk of the French-speaking province of Quebec leaving Canada and becoming a nation. Here language (and culture connected to that language) is the issue. In the Soviet Union, the Baltic states, Georgia, Muslim territories, and other regions are trying to set themselves up as autonomous states. Here, it is language, religion, ethnicity, and race (and combinations of these factors) that are the major factors. The same applies to other countries, as well.

One thing seems to be certain. The mass media in these nations have not "homogenized" the people and the various ethnic, religious, and linguistic groups or subcultures have kept hold of their identities. And it is increasingly difficult, then, to make generalizations about "the Russians" that are useful. Even generalizations about the Soviet Russians, the people of Great Russia, are fraught with danger, as anyone who has read Geoffrey Gorer's remarkable book, *The People of Great Russia,* knows.

And yet, we are social animals and are affected, in profound ways, by the societies in which we live and the cultures in which we grow up. As Durkheim (1965) wrote in *Elementary Forms of the Religious Life:*

> Collective representations are the result of an immense cooperation, which stretches out not only into space but into time as well; to make them, a multitude of minds have associated, united and combined their ideas and sentiments; for them, long generations have accumulated their experience and their knowledge. A special intellectual activity is therefore concentrated in them which is infinitely richer and complexer than that of the individual. From that one can understand how the reason has been able to go beyond the limits of empirical knowledge. It does not owe this to any vague, mysterious virtue but simply to the fact that according to the well-known formula, man is double. There are two beings in him: an individual being which has its foundation in the organism and the circle of whose activities is therefore strictly limited, and a social being which represents the highest reality in the intellectual and moral order that we can know by observation—I mean society. This duality of our nature has as its consequence in the practical order, the irreducibility of a moral ideal to a utilitarian motive, and in the order of thought, the irreducibility of reason to individual experience. In so far as he belongs to society, the individual transcends himself, both when he thinks and when he acts. (p. 29)

Somehow, in dealing with the mass media from a comparative cultural perspective, we must find a way to negotiate between two extreme conceptions—the oversocialized "robot-like" individual and the undersocialized, anarchic individual. If we focus our attention on specific texts that are similar in nature and, to some degree "representative," I think we can escape overgeneralizations and extreme narrowness of focus.

We have to find a way to navigate between two simplistic notions of what individuals (and societies) are like and how they are reflected and affected in texts (and the mass media) without being too reductionistic or too broad. It is a very dangerous calling—but think how exciting it is when we succeed.

REFERENCES

Berger, A. A. (1965, Feb.). I settimanali italiana di attualita. *Il Mulino*, pp. 173-193.

Berger, A. A. (1966, Dec.). Authority in the comics. *Transaction*, pp. 22-26.

Berger, A. A. (1976). *The TV-guided American*. New York: Walker.

Berger, A. A. (1980). *Television as an instrument of terror: Essays on media, popula* *culture and everyday life*. New Brunswick, NJ: Transaction.

Berger, A. A. (1991). *Media analysis techniques* (revised edition). Newbury Park, CA Sage.

Berger, A. A. (1989). *Signs in contemporary culture: An introduction to semiotics*. Salem WI: Sheffield.

Berger, A. A. (1990). *Agitpop: Political culture and communication theory*. New Brunswick, NJ: Transaction.

de Saussure, F. (1966). *Course in general linguistics*. New York: McGraw-Hill.

Durkheim, E. (1965). *Elementary forms of the religious life*. New York: Free Press.

Eco, U. (1972). *Towards a semiotic inquiry into the television message* (Working Paper in Cultural Studies). Birmingham, UK: Centre for Contemporary Cultural Studie University of Birmingham.

Gorer, G. (1962). *The people of Great Russia*. New York: W. W. Norton.

Kottak, C. P. (1990). *Prime-time society: An anthropological analysis of television an culture*. Belmont, CA: Wadsworth.

Massing, H. H. (1986, Nov.-Dec.). Decoding *Dallas*. *Society*.

3

When Fiction and News Cross Over the Border
Notes on Differential Readings and Effects

AKIBA A. COHEN ● ITZHAK ROEH ● *Hebrew University of Jerusalem*

The present chapter has three interrelated objectives. First, it discusses how the two most prevalent kinds of television texts—fiction and news—are differentially mediated and modified as they cross international and cultural borders. Second, it cautions against the temptation to overgeneralize from studies of fiction to studies of news with regard to the way these two categories of texts are "read" by audiences around the globe. Third, it considers some of the implications of these phenomena in a more general context for the perennial discussion on the nature and magnitude of media effects.

MEDIATION AND MODIFICATION
IN BORDER CROSSINGS

It goes without saying that every border crossing involves some need for adjustment and acculturation. Just as visitors often find the need to adopt the "manners" and "customs" of their host country, so do texts. Texts transmitted across borders cannot escape some form of transformation. Moreover, we wish to suggest a continuum that can manifest the different levels of mediation and modification in the process of the importation of texts across borders. At the minimal level, a text crosses the border without undergoing any change, and it is up to the consumer to use it in a way that is particularly meaningful to himself or herself. At the maximal level, the text goes through one or more processes of change prior to reaching its potential consumers. These processes of active mediation and modification involve intervention by various social institutions and relate to factors such as production, marketing, scheduling, and censorship.

What we have just indicated can be said about all forms of texts. In the present chapter, however, we wish to focus on television. In some locations, television texts might be metaphorically considered as being "smuggled" across borders in the sense that they can be "picked up" on the other side without any institutional intervention. This can occur among neighboring countries as well as across vast distances, thanks to recent advances in telecommunication technology. In such border crossings only the viewer serves as mediator. On the other hand, in "legal" crossings, when television texts are bought and paid for, as when one station purchases a program produced by another, active institutional mediation is evident, albeit in varying degrees. It is the latter kind of border crossing that is the focus of our discussion.

In what follows we concentrate on the different characteristics of fiction and news as far as border crossing is concerned. We suggest that fictional programs lie closer to the minimal intervention end of the continuum, whereas news tends to reside closer to the other pole and exhibits a greater measure of mediation and modification.

Let us begin with fiction. The main audiences for most fictional television programs, which are produced especially for television—dramatic serials, situation comedies, and made-for-television movies—reside in the countries where the programs are produced. And yet, much of the television repertoire of several Western countries, mainly those of the United States and the United Kingdom, is produced with the knowledge that it could be made available to audiences in a variety of cultures, often very soon after being aired in their respective countries of origin.

Given this situation, a question arises as to whether or not such American and British programs are designed, created, and produced with their potential foreign audiences in mind or whether they are mainly designed for their respective domestic audiences. In the present chapter we do not attempt to answer this question. We do assume, however, that for the most part such programs are produced primarily for the domestic audience, even though some consideration might be given by the producers to foreign markets as well. It should be noted, for instance, that the price paid by television stations in the nonproducing countries for the right to air the programs is relatively low, depending on the size of the audience, thus it seems reasonable to argue that profit is the main incentive for marketing the programs outside their respective countries of origin.

What is of concern to us here, however, is what kind of intervention occurs when such fictional television programs are exported from one country to another. A distinction should be drawn between two groups of importing countries, based on whether or not the language spoken in the exporting and importing country is the same. If the program is imported by a country whose population speaks the same language as the exporting country, virtually no change is necessary. Thus, for example, an American program being aired in Australia might be shown as is.

In most cases, however, where the spoken language is different, linguistic translation is required, allowing for one of two options: dubbing or subtitling. Dubbing is the more common practice in larger countries, as it is a more expensive process and hence requires a larger audience to make it economically viable. It also alleviates the necessity of requiring the audience to read a considerable amount of text, at what is often a fairly rapid and hence difficult pace. Subtitling is more commonly utilized in smaller countries as it is much cheaper to produce.

Both forms of linguistic translation naturally modify the text to some extent. Technical considerations regarding the length of utterances and the need for audiovisual synchronization are often a problem, leading to cutting the translations short and the omission of parts of the text. There is also the ever-present danger of changing the meaning of the text, given different nuances or the difficulty of translating certain words or terms that might be unavailable in the importing culture. Finally, some errors in translation are almost inevitable. And yet, other than the linguistic translation, the text as presented in the importing country might remain relatively unchanged.

But, then, this is not the end of the story. For in addition to linguistic translation, some other forms of institutional intervention might take place. Thus, for example, the commercials that were shown in an original American program will be omitted, and others might or might not be substituted, depending on whether the importing country presents commercials altogether. If there are no commercials at all, the various program segments (or "acts") will be linked together. In addition, the importing station might, for a variety of cultural, religious, or political reasons, discard certain segments of the program—sometimes very brief segments, sometimes longer segments. In other words, some form of censorship might be implemented. Finally, the scheduling policy of the station in the host country might be different from that of the originating country. Thus, for example, in one country the program might be aired in "prime time" and in another it might be shown late at night. Prime time might not even be the same in both places.

And yet, even if we add up the various modifications that occur regarding fictional programs, the resulting changes typically are significantly fewer than those that occur with regard to news. The transfer of news, or what has often been referred to as the "international news flow" presents a totally different situation. We refer here mainly to "foreign news," that is, news items concerned with issues and events that deal with and originate in one country. Although the primary interest in such items is naturally in the country of origin, television stations in other countries—sometimes in virtually all countries—will present a story about the same issue or event. The reasons why this happens is not central to our discussion; suffice it to say that it has been investigated by numerous scholars (e.g., Galtung & Ruge, 1965). It should be noted, though, that sometimes such foreign news items constitute a considerable proportion of the newscast (for a recent example, see Wallis & Baran, 1990). But the point we wish to argue is that when such stories are shown outside the country of origin, they are hardly ever presented as is, above and beyond the necessary linguistic translation. We wish to suggest that such stories are almost always modified or "domesticated" by the importing station in ways that make them more relevant and meaningful to the audience of the importing country.

An excellent illustration of this process can be found in the operations of several news exchange services. These regional organizations provide mechanisms by which "raw material" on news events is provided from a station or a TV news agency (e.g., Visnews or World Television News) to stations in other countries in a way the materials could be used to create a news item or story. Thus, for example, if a television news crew filmed an event, say on the Temple Mount in Jerusalem, the material is then transmitted, via satellite, to a central switching point (Brussels, in the case of the European Broadcasting Union's [EBU] News Exchange Service), and from there it can be relayed to many stations in the region or even around the world.

What is central to our thesis is that the raw material is rarely, if ever, simply put on the screen as it is provided by the Exchange. Instead, it goes through the entire process of editing and production, just like any other domestic news item, resulting in a story that the foreign news editor (or some other functionary in the news department) feels is an adequate way of presenting the particular event to viewers in his or her country. In other words, virtually by definition, the story about the same event, say the rioting and killings on the Temple Mount, would be shown in a different manner in each station, hence there would be many versions of that story. By the same token, when two reporters, each representing a different station, file a report from the country of location to their home audience, the stories shown would not be identical, even if they are sometimes based upon identical or very similar footage.

Our recent research illustrates this with several stories. In studying the television coverage of the Intifada (the uprising of the Palestinians in the West Bank and Gaza), we examined 10 accounts of the same incident as reported in five countries (the United States, the United Kingdom, France, West Germany, and Israel). In a confrontation between Israeli security forces and Palestinians that occurred on April 14, 1989, in the village of Nahalin, four Palestinians were killed (a fifth died of wounds the following day). The same raw material was clearly used by most of the stations, and many of the stations referred to the event as "one of the bloodiest Intifada days." Although many of the same visuals were presented, meaningful different stories were told, some relatively "open" and others relatively "closed" (Roeh & Cohen, in press). A detailed analysis (Cohen & Roeh, 1990) shows, for example, how the French networks (TF1 and A2F) followed the chronological time flow, but also clearly demonstrates that time order does not guarantee a "true" presentation of the events. TF1's story begins two seconds after A2F's and ends first. Consequently we see on TF1 a stone-thrower that seems to be the trigger—perhaps the cause—for what will follow: two Israeli soldiers on a jeep enter the frame, jump from the jeep, capture a Palestinian, and drag him to the jeep. Cut! A2F's story begins later with a jeep entering the frame, with no preceding cause (only those who might have also seen the TF1 rendition, as we did, know that a stone was thrown in the direction of the jeep). The two Israelis jump from the jeep, capture the same Palestinian, drag him to the jeep, and at the point where TF1 cut the footage, A2F shows the Palestinian being pushed on the jeep and beaten by the Israelis with a rifle. Only then, cut! Now certainly these stories suggest a different view of the Israeli soldiers. They are quite brutal on A2F and less so on TF1. The Palestinian on A2F is presented more as a victim who deserves empathy, but less so on TF1.

In another example (Gurevitch, Levy, & Roeh, in press), four reports—one (CBS) from America, one from France, one from Belgium, and one from England—on the Irish parliamentary elections of 1987, aired on the night before the actual balloting, present four different themes of the expected event. The American version refers to the powerful impact of the Irish famine and the subsequent wave of immigration to the United States. This theme is the central motif of the present story, focusing on the dire economic situation in Ireland, the high rate of unemployment, and implying that many Irishmen will once again hit the American shores. The French story expresses a different cultural resonance. It is told from a rather "Catholic" point of view. Many references are made to the similarities and differences between French and Irish Catholicism. There is a sense of ambivalence: both nostalgic and ideological motives were implied. Irish Catholicism, it is suggested, is pure, innocent, and naive as traditional Christianity is usually perceived. This fundamentalist view is countered by a somewhat detached and critical attitude when the fragile economy of Ireland is referred to. Ireland pays a price for its innocence. So many young people have to emigrate, whereas those in France stick with the motherland. The Belgian story also adopts an involved Catholic point of view, but there is less ambivalence and tension between the Irish and Belgian versions of Christianity. The British story, it goes without saying, is closer to being a domestic story. It is a practically straight political report referring to concrete current political issues that face Ireland and one of particular importance to the relations between the United Kingdom and the Republic. Four stories, four "domesticated" versions of the same event.

Even in those rare cases when news stories from one country are shown in another country exactly as they were shown in the country of origin, without editing or deletion—with full credit naturally given to the station of origin—even in such cases the text of the anchor or news reader, by way of introducing the story, would probably not be the same, nor would the position in the line-up be identical, hence the context in which the story is presented is different and the story cannot be perceived as the same.

To sum up the discussion thus far, our basic argument is that there is a major conceptual and operational difference in how fiction and news are transmitted and presented across national and cultural boundaries. Fictional programs, for the most part, are transferred and subsequently broadcast as they are originally produced, with minimal modification by the host country, whereas news inevitably goes through a more elaborate process of mediation and modification to make it relevant and appropriate for the audience of the importing country.

THE READINGS OF FICTION AND NEWS:
SAME OR DIFFERENT?

Does this differential treatment of fictional and news texts make a difference for the viewing audience? Does it influence the way audience members read, interpret, makes sense of, or understand the messages?

Thus, for example, when the thrilling intrigues of J. R. and Bobby (in *Dallas*) or Adam and Blake (in *Dynasty*)—or for those who might prefer to fantasize along with Sue Ellen and Pam or Crystal and Alexis—are exposed, they remain essentially the same scenes no matter where they are presented and in whatever language they are spoken, except for some slight possible modifications relating to the hour of broadcast and perhaps some minor "cultural" censorship.

This does not mean, of course, that viewers in different cultures would "read" or interpret the exploits of the Ewings or Carringtons in an identical manner. In fact, audience members in different cultures might interpret the episodes differently (see, for example, Katz & Liebes, 1986).

On the other hand, when dealing, for example, with news reports about a meeting between Presidents Gorbachev and Bush or the adventures of Saddam Hussein as they are aired in different countries, these news items, which might deal with the same basic issues and events— perhaps even the same basic "facts"—are most likely to be portrayed differently in the various places. Hence, when considering news, given the presentation of intrinsically nonidentical stories, "readings" or interpretations of the news are bound to be different, not only because of the different social, cultural, and political contexts of the different countries, but also because the stories are presented in a different manner in the first place.

Put another way: all texts, both fiction and news, are mediated. But whereas in the case of fiction the mediation is done mainly by the viewers, the mediation in the case of news is in many ways accomplished for the viewers by different social mechanisms, including the television organization. And in the course of this process, the organization does not only reflect journalists' attitudes and interpretations but also the position of other cultural agents, such as politicians, civil servants, the clergy, and other power holders in the society.[1]

Now, this situation is bound to create problems for researchers in attempting to isolate the factors responsible for the specific differential interpretations in a cause-and-effect sense. We recall in this connection an important methodological distinction drawn by Miller (1970) between the so-called *investigational* and *experimental* paradigms in communication research. Although Miller was referring to research in the controlled laboratory setting, we believe the points he makes are pertinent for less rigorously controlled research settings as well.

The investigational paradigm, in which the same stimulus is presented to two (or more) groups of people who differ on at least one variable, is most relevant to our discussion of cross-cultural differences in the reading of fictional programs. Following exposure, differences in relating to the stimulus can then be attributed to the differences characterizing the groups. Thus, for example, if a specific television program, say a particular episode of *Dallas,* is shown to a group of Americans and to a group of Australians, or even to a group of Russians (with the imperative linguistic translation, of course), and the groups judge the program differently on some variable (say, the justification for some interaction between Bobby and Pam), then one might attribute the differences to the fact that one group consisted of Americans (including everything that this distinction entails) and that the other groups consisted of Australians and Russians (including all implications of this). We emphasize the term *might,* because it is also possible that some other factor associated with nationality, and not nationality in and of itself, could be the cause of the different judgments. The same logic follows when presenting the same program to a group of highly educated people and a group of people with little education, for example. Thus, something about being educated or lacking education might determine how audience members would evaluate the identical program or issue.

In the case of the experimental paradigm, in which two (or more) different stimuli are shown to randomly created groups (hence assumed to be a priori equivalent), variation can be clearly attributed to the difference between (or among) the stimuli. Thus, for example, if two different (say an American and a Russian) versions of a news story about a summit meeting between Bush and Gorbachev are presented to two groups of Americans, then differences in interpretation between those who saw the American and the Russian versions could be attributed to the different nature of the reports. The same logic would follow, of course, if the two reports were shown to two groups of Russians. However, this kind of situation, in which an American story is presented to a Russian audience, or a Russian story to an American audience, is highly unlikely. Hence the analogy to a true experiment is all but irrelevant.

The third possibility, according to Miller's taxonomy, is one that occurs all the time in the framework of television news. It is what Miller would call the *mixed model* in which the Russians are shown a Russian version of the summit, and the Americans are presented an American version (or of one of its multiple networks). To what can the differences in judgment between the Russians and Americans be attributed in such a case? The differential interpretation of the readings in this case are the most complex. Part of the variation in judgments might be attributed to the difference in the nature of the audiences (Americans versus Russians) and part may be due to the different nature of the stimuli (the American versus the Russian versions).

Why is all this of importance and why have we gone into such detail regarding these well-known methodological paradigms? We believe it is important because there is a growing trend among media scholars to focus on and to study so-called "universals" of media contents and the "globalization" of media markets and processes. In so doing there is a growing interest in conducting cross-cultural research to test hypotheses generated from these concepts (Gurevitch, 1989).[2] Yet, as we have already intimated, what may be the case for fiction is not necessarily the case for news.

IMPLICATIONS FOR THE STUDY OF MEDIA EFFECTS

In this final section we wish to discuss some broader implications of our present thesis in a historical context of the traditions of studying media effects.

The study of media effects seems to have been obsessed even to this very day with a perception of "powerful media." This perception is rooted in the Lasswellian linear model of communication. The die-hard "stimulus-response" model, according to which effective messages flow from a source to a recipient, seems to get its vitality from an urge in the social sciences to model themselves after the natural sciences. To be able to determine causal relations between observable (and if possible, "measurable") "facts" out there is a central paradigm in science, and for social science it is a powerful rhetorical tool (or strategy).

More than 40 years ago, Paul Lazarsfeld and Robert Merton (1948) referred ironically to the "magical belief" widely held at the time that "the power of the radio can be compared only to the atomic bomb." It was "the ubiquity of the mass media [that] lead[s] many to an almost magical belief in their enormous powers." In their seminal study, Lazarsfeld and Merton suggest that "to search out the effects of mass media upon society is to set upon an ill-defined problem" unless we locate the study of effect in cultural/historical context and thus critically question its "universalistic" or "essentialist" character.

Even though *universalism* and *essentialism* are not typically their vocabulary, it is noteworthy that Lazarsfeld and Merton's observation pertains to our main argument in the present chapter, which seeks to locate effect (or efficacy) in cross-cultural contexts and thus to critically question its productive explanatory power. Today's academic vocabulary has changed considerably and we readily tend to, as they say, "read into" them such current notions as (the commendable) contextualization and (the denounced) universalism. Also, Lazarsfeld and Merton would not feel the need to use the term *ideology*. It should be noted that the end of ideology (Bell, 1961) was a viable intellectual option at the time, which seems quite relevant to us. Moreover, their emphasis on concrete structural social conditions is easily "translated" by us into an emphasis on the ideological, our main argument being that the international flow of news does by no means indicate universal reception.

To the contrary, our studies of foreign news on television lead us to suggest a clear "post-Babel" hypothesis: Journalists, and the press in general, despite modern technologies that many predicted would create a global village, have not reached the point where "the whole earth was of one language and of one speech" (Genesis, 11:1), but rather, they speak the language of their respective culture/tradition/audience. Comparative study of foreign news clearly suggests that "the same" story tends to be presented differently to different societies, that is, it is "domesticated," or adopted to particularistic societal contexts.

We can speak here of two kinds of domestication in the process of television production and reception as a cultural agent. One form of domestication takes place in the framework of the news where social institutions are actively involved. From the start and throughout all stages of the process there is organized and institutionalized mediation, which is reflected in the operations of the various individual newsrooms vis-à-vis the "global newsrooms" of the news exchange services (such as that of the EBU). Although the global market applies pressure toward uniformity, by providing the same materials to all its subscribers, the individual stations press for parochialism in terms of language, culture, ideology, politics, and censorship. In the world of fictional contents, domestication is of a lesser scale. Active social intervention does take place as in the case of linguistic translation, scheduling, and processes of selection. However, the main burden of domestication here is borne by the recipients. Viewers interpret the messages according to their predispositions, schemas, repertoires, social locations, and life histories.

In a sense we are trying to provide a tentative answer to the question of how culture works, raised by Schudson (1989), and to suggest the relevance of cultural studies (Geertz, 1983) and of the *interpretive turn* (Rabinow & Sullivan, 1979) to the study of the meaning of news. It is important to note that in the growing literature on the interpretive processes of television texts, most of the attention by researchers has been on fiction, and very little on news, as two recent reviews (Carragee, 1990; Evans, 1990) suggest. When the interpretation of news was studied, it was rarely done in a comparative framework, where different cultural ecologies were taken into account.

To conclude, what we are faced with is a continuum of mediation types where news is at the "strong" pole and fiction at the "weak" pole. What we are advocating is that instead of the old classical "strong" media effects approach, implicitly based on a stimulus-response model, one should take a rather "weak" culture-bound "circular" view, where the processes of media production and consumption are necessarily contextualized. Message analysis, both in fiction and in news, must be done in a dynamic contextual framework, taking into account the sociocultural ecology where meaning is produced and reproduced. Without this broader context the discussion of media effects seems to be rather limited and unconvincing.

NOTES

1. It should be noted, though, that even with regard to fiction, Carragee (1990) and Gripsrud (1990) persuasively argue that contextual factors must be taken into account, such as the reason that the particular program was produced and/or broadcast in the first place in a given culture.

2. In a recent issue of the *American Behavioral Scientist* (Cohen & Bantz, 1989) dedicated to future directions in television news research, various questions that are normally found in the framework of the study of fiction (e.g., content and meaning, journalism as storytelling, and comparative news research) are applied to the study of news.

REFERENCES

Bell, D. (1961). *The end of ideology.* New York: Collier.

Carragee, K. M. (1990). Interpretive media study and interpretive social science. *Critical Studies in Mass Communication, 7*(2), 81-96.

Cohen, A. A., & Bantz, C. R. (1989). Where did we come from and where are we going: Some future directions in television news research. *American Behavioral Scientist, 33*(2), 135-143.

Cohen, A. A., & Roeh, I. (1990). A five-version tale of one jeep, one Palestinian and two Israelis: Some secrets of TV news editing that only comparative viewing might reveal. *Feedback.*

Evans, W. A. (1990). The interpretive turn in media research: Innovation, iteration, or illusion? *Critical Studies in Mass Communication, 7*(2), 147-168.

Galtung, J., & Ruge, M. H. (1965). The structure of foreign news. *Journal of Peace Research, 1*(1), 64-91.

Geertz, C. (1983). *Local knowledge.* New York: Basic Books.

Gripsrud, J. (1990). Toward a flexible methodology in studying media meaning: *Dynasty* in Norway. *Critical Studies in Mass Communication, 7*(2), 117-128.

Gurevitch, M. (1989). Comparative research on television news: Problems and challenges. *American Behavioral Scientist, 33*(2), 221-229.

Gurevitch, M., Levy, M. R., & Roeh, I. (in press). The global newsroom: Convergences and diversities in the globalization of television news. In P. Dahlgren & C. Sparks (Eds.), *Communication and citizenship.* London: Routledge & Kegan Paul.

Katz, E., & Liebes, T. (1986). Mutual aid in the decoding of *Dallas:* Preliminary notes from a cross cultural study. In P. Drummond & R. Paterson (Eds.), *Television in transition* (pp. 187-198). London: British Film Institute.

Lazarsfeld, P. F., & Merton, R. (1948). Mass communication, popular taste and organized social action. In L. Bryson (Ed.), *The communication of ideas* (pp. 95-118). New York: Harper & Row.

Miller, G. R. (1970). Research settings: Laboratory studies. In P. Emmert & W. D. Brooks (Eds.), *Methods of research in communication* (pp. 77-104). New York: Houghton Mifflin.

Rabinow, P., & Sullivan, W. M. (1979). The primacy of meaning: Culture as context. In *Interpretive social science.* Berkeley: University of California Press.

Roeh, I., & Cohen, A. A. (in press). One of the bloodiest Intifada days: A comparative analysis of open and closed news.

Schudson, M. (1989). How culture works: Perspectives from media studies on the efficacy of symbols. *Theory and Society, 18,* 153-180.

Wallis, R., & Baran, S. (1990). *The known world of broadcast news: International news and the electronic media.* London: Routledge & Kegan Paul.

4

Search for Change
Survey Studies of
International Media Effects

STEVEN H. CHAFFEE ● *Stanford University*

Change, either in mass media or in the people reached by them, is central in testing hypotheses of effects of mass communication. This chapter reviews four low-budget survey studies on international communication issues and analyzes the role of change in their research designs. Study 1 shows effects of attention to international news on the structure of affect toward other nations during the period when China was becoming independent of the Communist bloc. Study 2 shows that Chinese career women heavily exposed to Communist government influences held strongly state-oriented values, whereas those exposed to new Western media held more individualistic values. Study 3 shows that television plays a "bridging" role in political socialization of people moving from Korea to the United States. Study 4 provides evidence that the introduction of international television to Belize stimulated adolescents' desires to emigrate to the United States.

Students of international mass communication lack paradigmatic models for empirical research. The two most popular effects designs, the controlled experiment and the correlational survey, do not serve very well, each for a different reason.

The idealized experiment is almost never a feasible international design. To assign entire peoples randomly to exposure versus control conditions simply cannot be done. The correlational approach offers a substitute, but usually a poor one. The researcher faces enormous difficulties in attempting to measure and control statistically for all the relevant variables that

AUTHOR'S NOTE: Authors of studies described in this chapter include Dr. Chang-Keun Lee, Gwangwoon University, Seoul, Korea; Dr. Clifford Nass, Stanford University; Dr. Connie Roser, University of Denver; Dr. Leslie Snyder, University of Connecticut; Dr. Seung-Mock Yang, Choongnam National University, Daejun, Korea; and Dr. Xiaoyan Zhao of Louis Harris & Associates, Inc. The author is also grateful to Dr. Debra Lieberman for a review of an earlier manuscript.

might make different people even roughly comparable. If they are not comparable—as are the exposure and control groups in an experiment—any interesting differences that might be found can too easily be attributed to factors such as differential history and self-selection.

This chapter is nonetheless dedicated to the assumption that we can design correlational survey studies that will help in establishing a plausible case on behalf of a theory of international media effects. This assumption rests upon more assumptions, the most important of which is that we can build research around phenomena of change. Also important are the general research assumptions regarding theory and its amenability to testing.

Change is central. Given that almost anyone's general conception of "media effects" involves some kind of change, the study should be set in a context where one can reasonably assume that either the media or the people they are affecting are undergoing a process of change. This chapter will review four studies that embody, in various ways, one or another of these two general categories of change.

A theoretical premise, generalizable beyond the immediate circumstances of the study, and some way of testing it, are also essential. Comparisons that conform to the outlines of the theory should be built into the data collection design so that tests of hypotheses cannot be explained away by history or selection (Campbell & Stanley, 1966; Chaffee, Roser, & Flora, 1989). These may be comparisons between people, or between media. As a rule of thumb, the comparison should match the change; if people are changing, compare groups of people, and if media are changing, compare different media.

One's results should not be vulnerable to easy dismissal as artifacts of third-variable factors, such as simple demographic differences between groups. In survey research this means controlling statistically, or possibly by research design, for such factors. One's design, and hence one's inference, will be stronger when the control factors are selected for their relevance to the process of interest. When media change is at stake, controls should relate closely to media; when change in people is being examined, the control variables should represent extraneous factors that might explain differences between people.

In the end, results should conform more to the theory in question than to rival theories. This is the ultimate evidentiary test of the construct validity of one's measures, design, and inferences. The scholar whose findings contradict a favored theory should be willing to abandon it in favor of a formulation more consonant with the evidence.

These broad homilies do not require prohibitively laborious or expensive research procedures. With thoughtful planning they are within the reach of any investigator. The studies reviewed in this chapter all meet these general requirements, some with greater success than others. Three of the four are, as is most commonly the case in field studies, cross-sectional sample surveys. The other (Study 1, below) employs a successive cross-sections design. Only the latter study involved major data collection expense, and it is a secondary analysis of archived data that cost the authors virtually nothing beyond computer data runs. The other studies were conducted by either a single investigator using field contacts or a small team of collaborating researchers. None required extensive funding. These studies, then, are models for the student of international communication to whom potential personnel and cost factors may at first seem enormously imposing. Carefully planned designs can yield useful theoretical results, one's investment being primarily in thinking through rather than in paying for a project.

VENUE AND THEORY

Researchers study effects of mass communication between nations in either of two general venues, which one might call "Here" and "There." Usually the researcher has a homebase country (Here) and is interested in communication to or from another country (There). In the four present studies, "Here" is the United States—although apart from this author most of the researchers involved were from the other countries in question. In all four studies, "There" is a developing nation. These two perspectives of venue, the United States (Here) and developing countries (There) are associated with two quite different kinds of media effects hypotheses. We will refer to these as *media imperialism* and *cognitive effects* theories.

Media Imperialism

In the case of communication from the United States to a developing nation, one of the most durable theories has been the critical formulation often called *media imperialism* or *cultural imperialism* via the mass media (Lee, 1980; Schiller, 1976). American media products, the argument runs, undermine the indigenous culture of a less developed society. In importing Western television signals, to take one popular variant of this thesis, a country is also importing Western value systems and encouraging its young people to envy and seek to join the alien culture they are viewing.

Although plausible on its face, the media imperialism thesis has rarely been tested empirically. One reason is that empirical research is part of the Western culture that critical theorists criticize. But even setting aside that ideological factor, it is very difficult to identify the conditions under which the process in question might operate. There is rarely much change to be studied, and when radical changes in international communication and culture are afoot, developing countries do not often welcome social survey researchers of any political stripe. Perhaps for these reasons, even the handful of empirical studies on the issue yield rather little evidence that would support the media imperialism thesis. Two of the exceptions are described in this chapter (Studies 2 and 4; below).

Cognitive Effects

The two studies (Studies 1 and 3) that were done in the United States have an entirely different emphasis. Like so many media effects projects of recent decades, they are built around cognitive rather than affective or behavioral concepts (Becker, McCombs, & McLeod, 1975). They represent two of the strongest kinds of cognitive dependent variables, learning of information (Study 3) and the organization of perceptions (Study 1). Specifically, one study looks for effects of communication on information about American politics among internationally mobile people, and the other examines changes in American citizens' perceptions of the structure of international relationships.

Information in the sense of amount of knowledge held is a common study topic in media research. But effects of mass communication on the structure of knowledge or perceptions are rare, and are even more rarely recognized as a distinct kind of study. Amount of information is usually indexed by a simple tallying of the number of correct answers the average person gives to a series of informational questions. The hypothesis is equally simple, normally taking the form, "The greater the exposure to media, the greater the knowledge." This is a very sensible criterion for evaluating news media, whose primary task is to inform, and for evaluating campaigns designed to educate people about a health topic, promote a technological innovation, or disseminate cultural content.

Structure of knowledge, by contrast, consists in the relation between, as distinct from the amount of, a set of cognitions. Factor analysis, based on correlations between items, is the most widely used method of ascertaining structure. This chapter includes one study that uses changing factor structures as the dependent variable in media effects analysis (Study 1).

SPECIFYING THEORIES OF STATE AND CHANGE

As stated, change is at the heart of traditional concepts of communication effects. A media effect is thought to have occurred when a change in the media, such as a new channel or novel content, is introduced and a subsequent change is observed in members of the audience. The task of theory is to specify the linkage between these two changes. Methodologically, this change-change model corresponds to the laboratory experiment, where a manipulation (change in media) is performed, and then the hypothesized outcomes (change in person) are measured. But experimentation, presumably the optimal method for testing change-change theories, is not a practical alternative for most media effects of interest to students of international communication.

A correlational survey of media and persons at one point in time is a state-state design. It fails to capture change in either the independent or the dependent variable, so it cannot tell us much about media effects. Cross-sectional surveys can, of course, tell us a good deal about the media audience. One fact that has emerged from a half-century of such studies is that people's patterns of media activity tend to be highly stable over time. This means that there is not going to be much change to study if one waits for a change in audience behavior. The media tend to be quite stable institutions. Hence research must be designed around periods of unusual instability if we are to analyze media effects in terms of change.

Short of change-change studies, there are many situations where either the media or the people are changing, although not both. These venues can be capitalized upon by the resourceful researcher, but it is important to bear in mind the onesidedness of change when interpreting media effects. Change-state and state-change studies might be thought of as make-do designs. They are more satisfying as tests of media hypotheses than static correlational (state-state) research but never as conclusive as a true experiment (change-change).

State-change designs are perhaps least obvious as media effects research. Here one must find people who have changed or are changing in some way, and find out about their media habits. The hypotheses are as often postdictive as predictive. Studies of businessmen, for instance, have inquired into their media use patterns and found marked differences from the typical citizen (Bauer, de Sola Pool, & Dexter, 1963). Whether the media use (state) accounts for their business success (change) always remains arguable. As is the case with basketball players' height (a state) and achievement (a change), state-change relationships ordinarily represent necessary, but not sufficient, conditions to explain an outcome. Two of the studies here (3 and 4) focus on a process of migratory change in some individuals' lives, in the context of stable media, and are therefore state-change surveys.

Change-state designs are much more common. When there is change in the media, a cross-sectional survey of people with differential exposure to that change can provide rather strong evidence of effects. Successive cross-sections drawn from the same population are even more persuasive (although twice as expensive for the researcher). Study 2 represents a very common research situation, where a change-change theory is tested with data that are at best of a change-state character.

Changing Media

Two general classes of change in mass media need to be distinguished. One is a change in content, such as occurs where there is an innovation in television programming or a marked shift in the character of news. The other change is the addition of a new medium to a locale. Both are quite possible in today's world arena, where dramatic shifts in international political and economic relations are occurring (hence changed media content), and where countries are abruptly opening their borders to previously barred media from elsewhere.

A number of projects have been built around the introduction of new media, especially television, to a community. Usually there is enough advance warning that these media innovations can be treated as a quasi-experiment. What has generally been found is a considerable shifting of audience behavior in terms of time allocation but little net change in people's underlying attitudes or values (Schramm, Lyle, & Parker, 1961).

Two studies described below (Studies 2 and 4) were planned to make use of the introduction of new media into a country. In both cases, that change had begun but was not yet complete when the survey was conducted. This design has its own problems, although it clearly has a better chance of capturing change than would a static survey conducted either before or after completion of the diffusion of a new medium. Both studies suggest that there is some value in arriving early rather than late in the process of a media intrusion into a society. A third study (1) is built around changes in international alignments that altered the structure of news about the world. It is a secondary analysis of successive cross-sections of the American public, from before to after China's shift away from the Communist bloc and toward a more independent role in world politics.

Changing People

This chapter will also examine in two studies (3 and 4) that most palpable form of international change at the individual level, migration from one country to another. When a person moves physically, the attendant shift in media may produce effects even though the media themselves remain quite constant both There and Here.

One media imperialism criticism has been that Western media encourage emigration from developing countries to the more attractive life they see depicted on the screen. That is, one international media effect may be to stimulate undesirable (from the developing country's perspective) migration. Study 4 examines that feared media effect.

Once the person has migrated to a new land, for whatever reason, there arises the problem of resocialization to the new political environment (Study 3). This too is a task that falls largely to the mass media. Even though mass communication Here did not cause the migration from There, media can be essential to the process of learning about life Here. Only a few social scientists have so far explored this important function of the media for immigrants (Subervi-Velez, 1986).

The studies reported here were conducted by, or in collaboration with, my graduate students and colleagues at Stanford University and the University of Wisconsin-Madison during the 1980s. Each has been reported more fully elsewhere, and the reader interested in precise details of any single project is referred to those publications. Portions of the findings will be summarized here mainly to illustrate certain points about the design of international media effects research.

STUDY 1: AMERICANS' PERCEPTIONS
OF SHIFTING BLOCS OF NATIONS

Much of the international news that reaches the American audience is not so much about single countries as about sets of countries. It is common to read about supranational entities: Islam, NATO (North Atlantic Treaty Organization), Black Africa, democracies, the Third World, and so forth. A strong affective component runs through these groupings. Allied powers and groups that share language or political features with the United States are generally considered by Americans to be good. Most prominent among those thought of as bad has been the Communist bloc, long presented as "the evil empire," although it was changing well before the recent dramatic collapse of socialist regimes in Eastern Europe. To see international communism as a unit, and to respond affectively to its member nations in a consistent fashion, was commonplace among Americans a few decades ago. The question in this study is whether this homogenization of perception and affect breaks down when there are shifts in international alignments. More specifically, Study 1 asks whether the news media helped in breaking down that monolithic picture of the world.

Given a world that is portrayed (a) in good-bad terms and (b) as supranational blocs rather than discrete nations, it makes sense to examine the factor structure of people's feelings toward other countries. Those that are apprehended as part of a common whole should be highly correlated (McNelly & Izcaray, 1986; Robinson, 1968). Attitudes toward New Zealand should be similar to those toward Australia, for example, and these should be different from attitudes toward Ecuador and Peru, or Sweden and Denmark, or Lebanon and Syria. World events can disrupt these perceptions. Today there is little reason to group Japan, Germany, and Italy, but during World War II they were the Axis powers. Many Americans today might group India and Pakistan together—unless a new war were to break out between them.

Sensitivity to shifting alliances and enmities around the globe is scarcely characteristic of the "typical" American citizen. Surveys often show the United States below European nations in the average level of public knowledge of world events. Around this low norm, though, there is wide variation in the American media audience, between those who follow international news and those who do not. Only the former group has the immediate means to keep track of changes in the structure of international relations. The person who follows one international event or story as a rule follows the others. These habits are stable, and do not provide much change for the study of media effects.

Although attention to international news tends to be a constant individual difference in people, shifts in international alignments are by definition not a constant factor. Chaffee and Lee (1989) designed

TABLE 4.1 Factor Structures of Feelings Toward Selected Countries (Study 1)

| | 1978 Factor Loadings | | 1982 Factor Loadings | |
	I	II	I	II
Total sample	(N = 645)		(N = 678)	
USSR	+++		+++	
Cuba	+++		+++	
China (PRC)	++	+	+	++
Poland		+++		++
Canada		++		++
Low news attention	(N = 186)		(N = 179)	
USSR	+++		+++	
Cuba	+++		+++	
China (PRC)	+++		++	
Poland		+++		++
Canada		++		+++
High news attention	(N = 194)		(N = 239)	
USSR	+++		+++	
Cuba	+++		+++	
China (PRC)	++	+		++
Poland		++		++
Canada		++		++

NOTE: Data are based on U.S. national sample surveys, as analyzed by Chaffee and Lee (1989, Tables 1 & 2). Entries indicate strength of factor loading: + = .3, ++ = .4, +++ = .6.

their study around a period of years, 1978 to 1982, in which there were major changes in the international picture. The most dramatic in historical retrospect was the departure of Communist China from close alignment with the Soviet Union and its client states.

Was this breaking away of China comprehended by the American people? The answer, according to this study, was partly yes, partly no. The parts in this instance refer to those who pay attention to international news and those who do not.

Table 4.1 summarizes some of the results reported by Chaffee and Lee (1989) on this question. These findings are summarized from a factor analysis of ratings of five countries on a "feeling thermometer" scale. Two of these countries, the USSR and Cuba, were selected because of their close political alliance during this period. As expected, in all factor analyses in Table 4.1, these two Communist nations loaded strongly on the first factor. To provide a contrasting anchor, Canada was included in the analysis. As a neighbor with close similarities and ties to the United States, it should provide the greatest contrast with the Communist bloc. As expected, it loads on a second factor in each analysis.

The other two countries are Poland and China. Poland had already in the late 1970s demonstrated considerable independence from the Soviet Union and this fact was not lost on the American public. In every analysis, feelings ("warmth" or "cold") toward Poland correlate primarily with the second factor, which is to say with Canada rather than with other Communist countries.

The USSR-Cuba and Canada-Poland linkages, in terms of evoking similar feelings in Americans, are stable in Table 4.1, in that the data for 1978 and 1982 are very much alike. What changes is the position of China. In 1978, China evoked variable "warmth-cold" ratings, but for most people was seen as part of the Communist bloc. By 1982 this had changed; China, which was by 1982 going its own way in international politics, aroused reactions of warmth that were more strongly associated with feelings toward Canada and Poland.

These overall results can be seen more clearly in the lower portions of Table 4.1, showing the factor structures for the low- and high-attention subsamples of the 1978 and 1982 national samples of American adults. For the low-attention group, China arouses the same emotions as do Cuba and the USSR—and it does so in 1982 almost as consistently as it did in 1978. It is as if for these Americans, who remain oblivious to international news, nothing had happened to the legendary Communist bloc. High consumers of international news, by contrast, account for the overall shift in the perceived location of China in the world structure. By 1982 they responded affectively to China in ways more similar to Canada than to the USSR.

The substantive point of this study is that changes in world political alignments are only understood by people who follow international news in some measure—and that many Americans do not fit that description. A sensible U.S. foreign policy must rest on a general public consent, and that in turn must rest on a general public understanding of international alignments. When those alignments change, the public's perception changes too, but more slowly as word of the real-world change for a time only reaches those who are paying attention to international news events.

For the researcher, this study points up the usefulness of concepts of perceived international structure and of methods for eliciting structure from people's affective responses in survey research.

STUDY 2: CHINESE WOMEN'S CHANGING VALUE PRIORITIES

The opening to the West that China undertook in the early 1980s provided an opportunity for a second study, this one by Xiaoyan Zhao 1989), a teacher at the Beijing Broadcasting Institute, who came to the United States for graduate study but returned to China to conduct her dissertation.

China, the world's largest and oldest continuing culture, is an imposing venue for the study of changes in people's values. The longstanding family-oriented Confucian tradition has been, however, forcibly disrupted since 1950 by the Communist government's attempts to replace it with allegiances to the state. One communication influence of interest, then, is that of the government's media. Does exposure to these centralized state sources predict a decline in family-level values, as has been intended in Beijing?

More international in nature is the further question of cultural imperialism, which is to say the erosion of Chinese values by media influences (both news and entertainment) from the West. Although it is difficult to say in an era of internal cultural revolution whether Chinese values are family centered or state centered, they are clearly not individualistic. The self, not a featured concept in traditional Confucian teaching, has been openly rejected by statist Communist doctrine. Western media, however unknowingly, transmit messages that prize the individual self, presumably fostering such Western values as independence, privacy, equality, and freedom.

Western media only minimally crept into China until the 1980s, and the same could be said of survey research. Indeed, the opening has been rather brief to date. The study summarized here was conducted in 1986. It consisted of a survey of career professional women in three locales: Beijing, Nanjing, and Shenzhen. The latter is an industrial "new city" near Hong Kong and thus reached by many western media sources. By contrast, those living in the capital city of Beijing were most heavily exposed to government sources.

Values were conceptualized at three levels: the family level, the state or social level, and the self or individual level. Examples of values, which each respondent was asked to rank in priority order, include "family harmony and joy" and "helping husband and children" (family level); "contribution to national development" and "opportunity for social contribution" (state level); and "displaying self-worth" and "developing

TABLE 4.2 Chinese Women's Values at Three Levels, by Sources of Communication Influence (Study 2)

Influence	Family Values	State Values	Individual Values
Traditional sources	++	0	0
Government sources	– – –	++++	– –
International news	0	0	++
Foreign entertainment	0	0	+++

NOTE: N = 990. Entries are based on regression equations reported by Zhao (1989, Table 2) predicting value priorities at the levels of the family, the state, and the individual. Entries are zero (0) if the beta was nonsignificant, plus (+) if it was significantly positive, and minus (–) if significantly negative. The number of plus or minus signs indicates approximate strength of the relationship. In regression, effects of all other sources listed are controlled when testing the effect of each source.

own expressive world" (individual level). Factor analysis confirmed the a priori clustering of the three value levels, each represented by 3 items among 12 in a forced-ranking measurement procedure.

Communication influences that Zhao (1989) hypothesized would affect these value priorities were also measured by self-report. *Traditional influences* were represented by questions about the home the person had grown up in. *Government influences* were covered by a large number of items, including reading a national news magazine, reading the central government's newspaper and television news program, knowledge of state propaganda, membership in the Communist Party, and city of residence. *Western influences* were divided into news and entertainment. The news measure included exposure to foreign news magazines, syndicated international television news, and reprinted items from foreign press sources. The entertainment index was based on watching foreign series, films, and performing arts on television.

Zhao's main results are summarized in Table 4.2. Essentially she found what she predicted. First, a traditional family upbringing is associated with giving high priority to family-centered values. Heavy exposure to Communist anti-Confucian influences is a strong negative predictor of family values, as the Chinese government has intended.

Indeed, Table 4.2 illustrates just how successful a sustained propaganda program under a Communist regime can be. Government influences are strongly associated with high priority for state-level values, and a correlatively low priority for individual as well as family-level values. These findings are not simply mirror-image results. They are based on regression analyses in which other sources of influence, and other value levels, are controlled statistically when calculating the strength of a particular value-communication association. Neither traditional influences nor the two indices of international influence affect more than one value level.

The latter two measures provide a rather strong case on behalf of the media imperialism theory. Exposure to international news, and especially to foreign entertainment, are both associated with prizing individual-level values. To set the individual above the family and the state would be, respectively, un-Confucian and un-Communist. Western media do indeed appear to be having these Westernizing effects on the women in this survey.

The fear that Western media would also undermine a culture's traditional values cannot be examined very clearly in China, where the government itself has for decades attempted to do just that. It is noteworthy in Table 4.2, though, that neither international news nor foreign entertainment is associated with any decrement in either family-level or state-level values. What seems to be happening is that these external media sources encourage individualism, without particularly attacking any alternative value structure.

The focused nature of this apparent effect makes sense, in that Western media only indirectly project individual values. The self may be more central in a passionate love story, say, than in a White House newscast via Cable News Network (CNN). The statistical link of international news to individual values in this study is notably weaker than that of foreign entertainment.

Why are we able to see evidence of media imperialism so clearly in this study, when it has proven so elusive in most empirical work on the theory? The People's Republic of China can be viewed, for these purposes, as a massive quasi-experiment without much of a control group. One third of the world's people are in a "treatment condition," subjected to a sustained internal propaganda campaign aimed at building state-level values and suppressing individualistic and family values. This communication program has on the whole worked, although some traditional influences and, more recently, Western media influences have crept in and had their specific effects, at the family and individual levels, respectively.

STUDY 3: POLITICAL SOCIALIZATION
OF KOREAN-AMERICANS

Traditionally "a nation of immigrants," the United States has continuously served as host country for millions of people seeking a better life.

When they arrive, immigrants encounter two interrelated features of life in the United States: mass media and democracy. Studies linking the two date back to the earliest empirical research (Lazarsfeld, Berelson, & Gaudet, 1944). Mass communication has been examined as a factor in political socialization of young people for 25 years (Chaffee & Yang, 1989). The study summarized here is, however, one of the first to focus on the socialization to American democracy of immigrants from another political system.

In 1987, a group of Korean and American scholars at Stanford University conducted a mail survey of Korean-Americans in the San Francisco Bay area of California, where there are Korean-language newspapers and television news programs as well as a rich supply of conventional American mass media. Thus they were able to study "dual" socialization, a process wherein an immigrant does not simply assimilate to the host culture, but may also maintain Korean political identity and knowledge. In several papers (Chaffee, Nass, & Yang, in press; Chaffee & Yang, 1989; Yang, 1988) these investigators have traced some important patterns of Korean-American political socialization via mass media. Only a few of these will be highlighted here.

American politics presents a jumble to the newcomer. Voters are offered candidates for executive, legislative, and even judicial offices, at the federal, state, county, and municipal levels. In California, dozens of initiative propositions clog the ballot. There is a lot to learn. In this study, indices were created of knowledge both of American political leaders and issues, in terms of the conventional liberal-conservative dimension—a form of information one can glean from the news media.

The issue raised here, though, is not about the media in general but the specific difference between newspapers and television. Television news gets a lot of criticism from academics (and others), one of the complaints being that people do not learn much from it. Correlational surveys might seem to bear this out, in that people who rely on television for their news are not as well informed about politics as are newspaper readers (Becker & Whitney, 1980; Culbertson & Stempel, 1986; Kennamer, 1987). Newspaper reading, though, is not for everyone. Television news has proven a strong source of public affairs knowledge among adolescents, many of whom do not read a daily newspaper. The question arises, does television news similarly serve new immigrants, who may lack the English-language skills and community attachment associated with newspaper use?

TABLE 4.3 Korean-Americans' Knowledge of American Politics, by Immigrant Experience and Exposure to News Media (Study 3)

| | Little Experience | | Strong Experience | |
	Weak English	Short U.S. Stay	Strong English	Long U.S. Stay
Television exposure				
Knows leaders	++	+++	0	0
Knows issues	++	+	0	0
Newspaper exposure				
Knows leaders	++	+	+++	+++++
Knows issues	0	0	+	+

NOTE: $N = 277$. Entries are based on regression equations reported by Chaffee, Nass, & Yang (1990, Tables 4 & 5) predicting knowledge of American political leaders and issues. Entries are zero (0) if the beta was nonsignificant and plus (+) if it was positive. The number of plus signs indicates approximate strength of the relationship. In regression, the following additional factors were controlled statistically: age, education, socioeconomic status, citizenship, intent to stay in United States, social contacts with Koreans and Americans, and self-identification as a Korean or an American.

The answer seems to be yes, according to the results summarized in Table 4.3. Here we have divided the Korean immigrant sample into subgroups based on their English-language skills and the number of years they have been in the United States. On the left-hand side of the table are results among those with weak English, and those who have been here only a short time. For these newcomers, television is clearly the stronger medium for learning about liberal-conservative differences among political leaders and issue positions. This pattern resembles that found in more conventional political socialization studies of American adolescents, who also rely on television for much of their news (Atkin, 1981; Chaffee & Schleuder, 1986; Conway, Stevens, & Smith, 1975).

The television-newspaper contrast reverses when we look at the right-hand side of Table 4.3, which represents those Korean-Americans with strong English and those who have been in the United States for some years. For them, the newspaper is a major source of political information, and television is not. These results are similar to those typically found among adult Americans.

The point here is that it is change in the person, not in the media, that accounts for the result. When an individual moves from Korea to the United States, television provides a temporary bridge to the new political culture that is to be learned. As the person acquires more years of experience here and develops greater facility with English, television news no longer suffices. The newspaper takes its traditional role as the informative medium of the adult citizen.

STUDY 4: YOUNG PEOPLE'S DESIRE
TO EMIGRATE FROM BELIZE

Broadcast television was introduced to the small Central American nation of Belize in early 1982. Although pirated signals were retransmitted from telecasting systems in Mexico and other Spanish-language sources, the most popular by far were those broadcast in English—Belize's national language—from the United States. We (Snyder, Roser, & Chaffee, 1991) recognized this as an exceptionally good setting for a test of the media imperialism hypothesis. Emigration from Belize to the United States is fairly easy and quite common. Young Belizeans, educated in excellent schools established when the country was a colony (British Honduras), often find career opportunities in the U.S. Gulf states. If international broadcasting has the alluring effect imagined by media imperialism theorists, it should manifest itself in adolescents' responses to the new influx of foreign television.

To get at this issue empirically, Snyder et al. (1991) conducted a modest survey of teenagers in Belize City and two regional centers in the summer of 1982. The results were, as with all surveys, complex and involve many exceptions. At least one major finding, however, squares clearly with the criticisms lodged by the media imperialism school.

Table 4.4 summarizes results of multiple regression equations in which the young person's degree of desire to emigrate from Belize to the United States is analyzed in terms of various communication sources. The dominant factor clearly was interpersonal communication. That is to say, those young Belizeans who had contact with family members and friends in the United States were much more likely to want to go there themselves. This makes good sense, but mass communication, not interpersonal, is at issue in the media imperialism debate. Hence, interpersonal communication is statistically controlled, in two different ways, in Table 4.4. In the first column it is controlled as one of the predictor variables in the multiple regression equation; effects of all media sources listed are represented with the variation due to interpersonal contacts held constant. The other two columns of Table 4.4 show the media effects for those who either had or did not have extensive interpersonal contacts with the United States. This enables us to see the

TABLE 4.4 Desire to Emigrate From Belize, by Communication Sources (Study 4)

| Source | Total Sample | Interpersonal Sources | |
		Low	High
Interpersonal sources	++++		
Entertainment television	++	+	++
Newspaper reading	0+	+++	0–
Television news	0	0	0
American movies	0	0–	0
Entertainment magazines	0	0+	0–
Books (nonschool)	0–	0	0–
News magazines	– –	0–	– – –
	(*N* = 339)	(*N* = 201)	(*N* = 138)

NOTE: Entries are based on multiple regression equations reported by Snyder, Roser, & Chaffee (1991, Table 1) predicting desire to emigrate to the United States, in a sample of Belizean youth. Entries are zero (0) if the beta was nonsignificant, plus (+) if it was positive, minus (–) if negative. The number of plus or minus signs indicates approximate strength of the relationship. This table shows all variables entered into each regression equation. In the columns to the right, level of interpersonal contact with the United States was partitioned.

effect of international media in both the presence and the absence of interpersonal contacts.

The newly introduced entertainment television from the United States was, as we had suspected in line with media imperialism reasoning, positively and significantly associated with desire to emigrate. This tendency was, if anything, reinforced by interpersonal contacts (and vice versa).

What is at least equally noteworthy in Table 4.4, however, is that this pattern did not hold for any other mass medium. Reading an American newspaper predicted a desire to emigrate among those lacking interpersonal contacts, but the newspaper-emigration relationship was if anything in the opposite direction for the other (high interpersonal sources) group. For the five other kinds of mass media covered in our survey, there was either no relationship or a negative one.

News magazines produce the findings in Table 4.4 that run most clearly opposite to the media imperialism thesis. It may be that the traditional emphasis on "bad news," including violent crime, disasters and political impasses, projects a negative and repellent image of the United States to youth abroad. In our survey we also found (data not shown) that our young respondents thought murder was the most common crime in the United States, whereas they knew that in Belize the most common crime is "stealing things from people."

These results remind us that a very general argument like media imperialism can be overly broad even as it contains a kernel of truth. The introduction of television into Belize did, it seems likely, exacerbate that tiny nation's problem of young people emigrating to the United States. But at the same time some international media seem to have had the opposite effect, discouraging immigration to the "scary world" of the United States as portrayed in featured news accounts.

CONCLUSION

These four studies are set forth here as much for what they suggest about research strategies as for what they say about international mass communication. Certainly they illustrate that effects of mass media in the international realm can be demonstrated empirically through survey research. Further, they remind us that one need not have a huge reservoir of research funding to get a study in the field that addresses questions of academic interest.

But there are some lessons here for study design too. Not every survey will yield evidence of media effects. If, for example, Study 1 had been conducted only in 1978 (or in 1982) there would have been no evidence of an effect. Study 2 would have been much more equivocal if the author had studied only one set of communication influences, or one domain of values, instead of building a thoroughly comparative design. Had Study 3 been a survey only of longtime U.S. residents, it would have shown nothing different about Korean-Americans than we find among other adult American samples. Study 4 capitalized on the recent introduction of television in Belize, finding evidence on behalf of the media imperialism thesis for that new medium—and that medium only.

The emphasis in this chapter on these changes is intended to alert researchers to the need to find such venues when planning research. A survey that examines a wholly static situation, where neither the media nor the people under study are changing, is likely to yield disappointing results. It is not that there are no effects under such conditions, but simply that effects are hard to detect when all variables are highly stable.

Testability is a most relevant concern in study design. Static correlations without comparison groups have too many possible explanations—media effects aside—to provide a very convincing test of a dynamic hypothesis. Comparisons between time points (as in Study 1) or between groups that are similar except that they differ in terms of time (as in Study 3) provide an essential element of testability. Comparisons between media, examining a channel that is central to one's theory while holding other media sources constant statistically (as in Studies 2, 3, and 4), likewise help in specifying testable hypotheses.

Control variables should match the kind of change in question. For example, in Study 1 where changes in relations between nations constitute the independent variable, the authors included "control nations" such as Cuba and Canada in the factor analyses that show the effect of change. In Study 3 where the person is changing by virtue of immigration, variation in the immigrant experience (e.g., length of stay) is controlled. In Studies 2 and 4 where new media are being introduced into a country, other more stable sources of influence are controlled in the regression equations.

The causal ideal of change-change research has to be balanced against practicality each time a project is undertaken. Causal theories relate change to change conceptually, but this is rarely possible in a literal sense operationally. By building features of change into each design wherever possible, we strengthen the literature as a whole. Change-state evidence and state-change evidence, or studies of change in people and those of change in media, can in combination tell us more than the sum of the parts. All studies have their limitations, but not the same limitations. For example, the role of mass communication in Study 1 is based on a change in media, whereas in Study 3 it is the people who are changing. Study 4 uses only state-state data, and yet it can be assumed in that setting that both the media (with the introduction of television) and the people (youth anticipating emigration) are undergoing potential changes. What is most important perhaps is to recognize where one's particular study fits into this overall picture.

Ultimately, a study is judged for what it contributes to the larger literature. This is a problem of theoretical integration, and the clearer the theory the greater the potential contribution. For example, the two media imperialism studies here are likely to find a ready purpose in the literature on international mass communication effects. No single study stands on its own, its results self-representing. Each of the projects described here takes its place in a continuing procession of related research.

REFERENCES

Atkin, C. K. (1981). Communication and political socialization. In D. Nimmo & K. Sanders (Eds.), *Handbook of political communication* (pp. 299-328). Beverly Hills, CA: Sage.

Bauer, R., de Sola Pool, I., & Dexter, L. A. (1963). *American business and public policy.* New York: Atherton.

Becker, L., McCombs, M., & McLeod, J. (1975). The development of political cognitions. In S. Chaffee (Ed.), *Political communication.* (pp. 21-63). Beverly Hills, CA: Sage.

Becker, L. B., & Whitney, D. C. (1980). Effects of media dependencies: Audience assessment of government. *Communication Research, 7,* 95-120.

Campbell, D. T., & Stanley, J. (1966). *Experimental and quasi-experimental designs for research.* New York: Rand-McNally.

Chaffee, S. H., & Lee, C. K. (1989). Impact of media information on the structure of affect toward other nations. *Shinmun Hakpo, 24,* 363-384.

Chaffee, S. H., Nass, C. I., & Yang, S. M. (1990). The bridging role of television in immigrant political socialization. *Human Communication Research, 17,* 266-288.

Chaffee, S. H., Roser, C., & Flora, J. (1989). Estimating the magnitude of threats to validity of information campaign effects. In C. T. Salmon (Ed.), *Information campaigns: Balancing social values and social change.* (pp. 285-301). Newbury Park, CA: Sage.

Chaffee, S. H., & Schleuder, J. (1986). Measurement and effects of attention to media news. *Human Communication Research, 13,* 76-107.

Chaffee, S. H., & Yang, S. M. (1989). Communication and political socialization. In O. Ichilov (Ed.), *Political socialization, citizenship education, and democracy* (chap. 7). New York: Columbia University Teachers College Press.

Conway, M., Stevens, A. J., & Smith, R. (1975). The relation between media use and children's civic awareness. *Journalism Quarterly, 51,* 531-538.

Culbertson, H., & Stempel, G. (1986). How media use and reliance affect knowledge level. *Communication Research, 13,* 579-602.

Kennamer, J. D. (1982). Debate viewing and debate discussion as predictors of campaign cognition. *Journalism Quarterly, 64,* 114-118.

Lazarsfeld, P. F., Berelson, B. B., & Gaudet, H. (1944). *The people's choice.* New York: Columbia University Press.

Lee, C. C. (1980). *Media imperialism reconsidered: The homogenizing of television culture.* Beverly Hills, CA: Sage.

McNelly, J. T., & Izcaray, F. (1986). International news exposure and images of nations. *Journalism Quarterly, 63,* 546-553.

Robinson, J. (1968). Perceptual maps of the world. *Public Opinion Quarterly, 32,* 273-280.

Schiller, H. (1976). *Communication and cultural domination.* White Plains, NY: International Arts & Sciences.

Schramm, W., Lyle, J., & Parker, E. (1961). *Television in the lives of our children.* Stanford, CA: Stanford University Press.

Snyder, L., Roser, C., & Chaffee, S. (1991). Foreign media and the desire to emigrate from Belize. *Journal of Communication, 41*(1), 117-132.

Subervi-Velez, F. (1986). The mass media and ethnic assimilation and pluralism: A review and research proposal with special focus on Hispanics. *Communication Research, 13,* 71-96.

Yang, S. M. (1988). *The role of mass media in immigrants' political socialization: A study of Korean immigrants in Northern California.* Unpublished doctoral dissertation, Stanford University.

Zhao, X. Y. (1989). Effects of foreign media use, government and traditional influences on Chinese women's values. *Revue europeenne de sciences sociales, XXVII*(84), 239-251.

5

Mass Media Effects in High- and Low-Context Cultures

RAYMOND GOZZI, JR. ● *Bradley University*

This chapter explores the rich concept of communication "context," as elaborated by Edward T. Hall, and applies it to form a theory of mass media effects. In high-context cultures such as Third-World countries, the theory predicts that mass media will generally act to subtract context, by relativizing the local context and rendering it less able to confer meanings. In low-context countries such as the developed, industrial nations, mass media are seen as generally adding context, by filling in the sparse contexts available. The theory also suggests that in some cases, in high-context cultures, decentralized and local media may reinforce, or add, context. In some cases, in low-context cultures, conflicting media messages may act to lower context further.

A powerful theoretical concept invites us to re-examine familiar information in its new light. Such a concept is communication "context," as elaborated by anthropologist Edward T. Hall (1977).

In its generic definition, "context" is environment, that which surrounds something and helps give it meaning. Hall notes that the context surrounding any message may be relatively dense, or relatively sparse, with consequences for the style of communication. Certain cultures, which Hall calls "high-context" cultures, typically have denser contexts surrounding their messages; others typically have less context and are called "low-context" cultures. Hall places cultures along a continuum from high context to low context.

By distinguishing between low-context cultures like the United States and other developed and urbanized nations, and high-context cultures mostly in the Third World, we produce a theoretical tool of great usefulness. This conceptualization will allow us to theorize differing mass media effects in high- and low-context cultures. Often the results of mass media research conducted in the United States or Europe are applied without major modification to Third World countries. Yet the differing cultural context can crucially influence the effects media may produce (see Beltran, 1976).

55

This chapter will use Hall's elaboration of *context* to specify how mass media will have different effects in low- and high-context cultures. Specifically, in terms that will be explained later, mass media in a high-context culture will tend to subtract context, moving the high-context culture more toward the low-context end of the continuum. In a low-context culture, mass media add context.

The purpose of this chapter is to provide theoretical guidance for further research in mass media effects, as well as to correct some unclear assumptions regarding media effects across cultures. Because the basic concepts are of great generality, they will need to be applied carefully to specific cases. The so-called "Third World" is, in actuality, incredibly diverse. Mass media systems also vary greatly from country to country. No disrespect is intended by grouping such diverse phenomena under a few terms, such as "high-context" and "low-context" cultures. Suggestions for specific research approaches using the theoretical insights presented here will be given later in the chapter.

HIGH- AND LOW-CONTEXT COMMUNICATION STYLES AND CULTURES

Hall (1977) distinguishes between code and context in communication. The *code* is the explicit, formulated content of the communication. The *context* is the situation, the relational aspect, which includes the unexplicit, unformulated rules governing how information is handled and how people interact. At times, Hall uses *context* as a verb, *to context*, which is to integrate information into a pattern.

Hall's special insight is that some messages may carry more of their information in the explicit, coded content of the communication, whereas other messages may carry more information in the context, situational, relational aspect.

> A high-context (HC) communication or message is one in which most of the information is either in the physical context or internalized in the person while very little is in the coded, explicit, transmitted part of the message. A low-context (LC) communication is just the opposite, i.e., the mass of the information is vested in the explicit code. (Hall, 1977, p. 91)

Hall then distinguishes cultures as typically high- or low-context. Low-context are Scandinavians and Germans, with the U.S. WASP (white, Anglo-Saxon, Protestant) culture considered somewhat less low-context. High-context cultures would be Chinese and American Indian. It is clear from his usage that "context" is a relative term—within cultures some situations can be relatively high context, others relatively low context. Hall's primary example of this disparity is Japan, where family relationships are high context, but relationships with strangers or foreigners are very low context (Hall, 1977, p. 66).

Communications in high-context cultures are typically short, pithy, and poetic. They can be understood by a member of the "in-group" but are puzzling to outsiders, who do not get enough information from them. When dealing with touchy issues, high-context communications are not specific about them, but instead weave a web of inference around the issue, which, it is assumed, both parties are aware of and can draw conclusions from. Low-context intruders often see this as indirection and untrustworthiness (Hall, 1977, p. 113).

Communications in low-context cultures, on the other hand, must be longer, more elaborated, and explicit. Touchy issues are dealt with directly, openly, which high-context viewers see as impolite and clumsy.

In high-context cultures, the sign for something is seen as closely connected with its referent. At its extreme, this is "magical" thinking, where the manipulation of a sign is thought to affect the thing the sign represents. In low-context cultures, by contrast, the sign is thought of as only arbitrarily connected to its referent.

High-context cultures tend toward "closed systems" of thought that are self-validating and discourage fundamental questioning (Horton, 1967). Again, magical thinking is a primary example, often cited in the anthropological literature. Low-context cultures tend toward "open systems" of thought, more readily admitting indeterminacy, more often questioning the received cultural patterns.

High-context art forms tend to be participatory, such as village dances (Lomax, 1977). Low-context art forms tend to be performed by a few talented artists and watched by most people.

High-context cultures also tend to function on what Hall calls "polychronic time," as opposed to the "monochronic time" of low-context cultures. Monochronic time is "one-thing-at-a-time," being "on time" for appointments, and "getting the job done" by a deadline. People used to monochronic time become very frustrated by polychronic time cultures, where many things are handled at once, in no particular order; where appointment times are relative at best; and where it is more important to be courteous, kind, and sociable to others than to finish a particular job (Hall, 1977, p. 150).

This leads to a final point about high-context cultures. To maintain a high context for communication means that people must spend much time together, must talk with each other, must pay attention to each other. Context is not a given; it is an achievement, constantly being constructed. In low-context cultures people spend less time together and more time alone.

It is worth noting, in passing, that the relationship between communication and context can be studied on other levels than that of the whole culture. Bernstein's (1972) work on English families led him to posit in working-class families a "restricted code" of family communication, which is similar to high-context communication in its reliance on context. In middle-class families he found an "elaborated code" that is similar to low-context communication in its reliance on specific message content. Also, Hopper, Knapp, and Scott (1981) found that American couples developed their own personal idioms—a kind of high-context communication style—over time.

MASS MEDIA EFFECTS IN HIGH-CONTEXT CULTURES

This section will explore the ways that mass media in high-context cultures may act to lower context. It will claim that media lower context through relativizing the local culture, changing the focus of people's attention from each other to the media, separating the sign from its referent, turning participatory art forms into performances, and imposing a monochronic sense of time.

As noted earlier, high-context cultures are extremely varied, and it is difficult to generalize about them all. Therefore the predictions in this section should be taken as theoretical guides for further research, rather than as ironclad rules. However, on the theoretical level we are discussing in this section, it is difficult to escape the conclusion that mass media will have the overall effect of moving a high-context culture more toward the low-context end of the spectrum. Mass media will act to subtract context.

Let us recall that context is that which surrounds something and helps give it meaning. When context is coherent, or at least is directly related to personal experience, then meanings can be subtly expressed and polyvalent meanings are possible to communicate. The resulting high-context communication is rich, indirect, allusive, and personalized to a high degree.

When context becomes less coherent, and is less related to direct experience, then meanings must be made more explicit and monovalent in order to be communicated. This occurs when mass media, with their distant messages, intrude upon a high-context culture. The local context becomes relativized. It is no longer the context but one context of many. Even though more material is being added to the local context by the media, loss of context occurs because the overall context is thereby rendered less able to impart meaning.

This relativization of the local context may threaten local leaders, which explains their often-reported tendency to limit access to media or publicly interpret media messages in their own interest (Bordenave, 1976; Lerner, 1958).

More generally, relativization will tend to pry open the closed systems of thought on which high-context cultures rely. By illustrating different cultural systems or life experiences, media implicitly pose epistemological questions that simply are not present in more monocultural situations. Such questions may not be actively formulated but may be contributors to a tendency to question local authorities or customs and a willingness to migrate to the cities.

Research could study migrants to cities and attempt to determine what role mass media played in people's decisions to migrate. Interviews, questionnaires, and tabulations of amount of media use could be used. The theoretical prediction here would be that migrants were heavily influenced by mass media images, more so than those who stayed in the villages or rural areas.

More generally, research could study whether the authority of local value systems is challenged by mass media imagery. Extended interviews or case studies could attempt to discover instances where local authorities or concepts are called into question by being relativized by media-promoted concepts. Even more basic would be studies of people's capacity to make sense of events: What criteria would they use? Would the criteria be from local value systems or from media-promoted systems?

Another way that mass media can subtract context from a high-context culture is simply by taking more of people's attention. As noted earlier, a high-context culture exists because people are paying attention to each other, talking about and to each other, and spending time with each other. This flow of attention will become disrupted by mass media. Especially as the number of radios and televisions increases in a given high-context culture, people will pay less attention to each other and more attention to the media.

Sometimes this loss of community interaction can be quite striking, when each household gets a television set, for example, and the street life virtually disappears for hours at a time (as described of a Brazilian fishing village by Good, 1984, personal communication). In other cases it is more subtle and harder to measure. Yet it should be possible to measure amounts of time spent interacting with others and amounts of time spent with the media, and compare different areas with different amounts of media available. This was done in a case study of New Mexican Indians and Hispanics by Kent (1985), who found the presence of television significantly altered interaction patterns in families. The theoretical prediction here is that as media availability and use rises, interpersonal attention will decline.

The quality of interpersonal interaction will also change, according to our theoretical predictions, in a direction toward the low-context end of the spectrum. This third prediction states that because context is becoming relativized, and because people are paying less attention to each other due to mass media intrusions into the high-context culture, then communication styles will become more low-context in nature. Explicitly coded content will become more important than the implicit context for carrying messages.

Another aspect of this low-contexting of communication styles will be the tendency to see signs as separate from their referents, as opposed to the former high-context assumption that signs were intimately linked to their referents. Mass media will suggest this theory of sign-referent relations simply by their presence, for what could be clearer than the fact that a television, for example, does not really contain Bruce Lee, or that a transistor radio does not really contain the National Orchestra? Although at first such media effects are seen as "magical," with routine use will come the acceptance of the separation of the sign from the referent, and the interpretation that they are connected arbitrarily.

The predicted low-contexting of communication can be studied by observing communication styles over time, or perhaps by asking residents of high-context cultures affected by media about how people "used to talk." Assumptions about sign-referent relations could be discovered by interviews or questionnaires.

Another way that mass media may push a high-context culture more toward the low-context end of the spectrum is by turning its art forms into performances. High-context art forms tend to be participatory, such as communal dances. Crafts tend to be performed by many members of the group. Yet specific media attention to certain people, dancers or craftspeople, will single them out for particular attention. By implication, a skills hierarchy will be imposed that will encourage a few and discourage many from participation. Katz (1977) notes that the dance-drama in Bali may have become Westernized as a result of the demand of tourists for performances.

Research could focus on art forms of various types and attempt to discover changes that were media related. Interviews with craftspeople or dance leaders could compare past and present practices. The copying of patterns seen on the media should be noted, as well as any tendencies away from participation by the group as a whole. The prediction is that media will influence high-context art forms away from participation by the many and toward performances by the few.

Finally, media may undermine high-context cultures by imposing a new sense of time. As Hall noted, high-context cultures tend to run on polychronic time, where many things get attended to at once and the pace is usually according to natural rhythms. Media, particularly broadcast media with their linear and inflexible programming schedules, will tend to impose monochronic time on these cultures. Even if it is the case of an entire village gathering around the one television for an evening or weekly broadcast. a monochronic time has been imposed on the entire community. As Hall (1977) says, "if there is anything that can change the character of life, it is how time is handled . . . [it is] one of the most basic organizing systems of life, for all situational behavior has a temporal and spatial . . . dimension" (p. 136). Research could study how time is handled in communities with media and without media, and residents could be interviewed to discover their views about whether time usage has changed or not since the introduction of new media.

On this very general theoretical level, then, the theory that mass media will tend to lower context in a high-context culture leads to at least five predictions. First, the high-context culture's certainties and closed systems will be relativized by mass media intrusions, making them less able to confer meaning and leading to more questioning of the local cultural systems and greater willingness to move. Second, as people pay more attention to mass media, they will pay less attention to each other, weakening the bonds of context.

Third, as context weakens, the communication styles will become more low-context in nature, relying more on the explicit, coded portion of the message. Signs will be viewed less magically, and will increasingly be seen as only arbitrarily connected to their referents. Fourth, communal art forms will weaken if mass media selectively shows only the performances of a talented few. And fifth, and perhaps most pervasively, a new sense of mechanical, monochronic time will take hold in the culture.

MASS MEDIA EFFECTS
IN LOW-CONTEXT CULTURES

Although mass media act to subtract context in high-context cultures, they act to add context in low-context cultures.

In low-context cultures, people have relatively little shared experience that can be called upon in communicative interaction. The mass media often provide a background of shared stories, symbols, and characters that people will have in common, thus increasing context.

Low-context communications place most of their emphasis on the explicit, coded part of the message. Yet because low-context theories of the sign assume only an arbitrary connection between sign and referent, the content of a message must be closely examined to decode it. Mass media provide illustrations for the arbitrary signs, providing, in the case of television and photography, more information that is not, in popular opinion, arbitrarily related to the sign but is essentially connected with the referent. By illustrating the alienated sign, media provide context. And by providing signs that seem connected in a necessary manner to their referents, media move the low-context theories of the sign toward the high-context end of the spectrum.

Three major research traditions in low-context countries demonstrate the tendency of media in these cultures to provide context: cultivation research, agenda setting, and spiral of silence. In all of these approaches, low-context people are found making generalizations about the entire society from patterns they have picked up from the mass media.

The fact that people do use media representations to fill in their pictures of social reality is vividly demonstrated by the cultivation research of Gerbner and his colleagues (Gerbner, Gross, Morgan, & Signorielli, 1980). The perceptions of heavy television viewers about their society are shown to be distorted in the same ways that media representations are distorted: heavy viewers of prime-time action dramas believe the world is more violent than it really is, and that there are more police than there really are; heavy viewers of soap operas believe there are more divorces, deaths in childbirth, and other soap opera maladies than there really are (Buerkel-Rothfuss, 1981).

Another line of research that illustrates the process of media providing context is agenda setting, begun by McCombs and Shaw (1972). In this research, correlations were found between the amount of media treatment of an issue and the rankings of importance that voters gave to that issue. In this case, it is political context that is being provided by the media.

A third line of research that supports the hypothesis that media provides context comes from the work of Elizabeth Noelle-Neumann (1974) in Germany, another low-context country. Her studies document the influence of media in creating a "spiral of silence." By emphasizing certain opinions, media can create the impression that most people have that opinion on an issue. This in turn creates a tendency for people who oppose that opinion to remain silent, even if they are a majority. Here again, media has provided context in a low-context situation.

REFINEMENTS OF THE THEORY

The basic predictions of the theoretical approach developed here have been stated and illustrated. Because we are dealing with terms of such generality, and phenomena of such variability, a note of caution should be sounded. These predictions should not be applied blindly to every situation, but should serve as research hypotheses, to be tested in specific cases.

In fact, to give the present theoretical approach more flexibility, it is possible to theorize situations where, contrary to the previous predictions, mass media may subtract context from an already low-context situation, and where mass media may add context to an already high-context situation.

In a low-context cultural situation, if mass media increase ambiguity and uncertainty by delivering conflicting information, or incomplete information, then they will have the effect of subtracting context. As part of the context, they will detract from the context's ability to confer meaning. Researchers will need to determine whether low-context media increase uncertainty or increase information before they can judge whether context is decreased or increased.

In a high-context cultural situation, it is possible for mass media to reinforce or raise context. Research will have to determine whether the low-contexting effects of the mass media are outweighed in specific cases by the following configurations:

If mass media are configured so that they act as accessories to already existing interpersonal communication channels, they may act to increase context. If mass media themselves are used as two-way channels for communication with outside authorities, they may reinforce local contexts and authorities. And if mass media provide channels for all of a community's artistic endeavors, they may encourage participation in art rather than discourage it.

If media are used to augment interpersonal communication, then instead of interrupting contexting activity, they will reinforce it. People from high-context cultures all over the world are most interested in people they know directly. Cassirer (1977) notes that Canadian Eskimos wanted satellite communications to allow them to communicate among the tribes themselves. Powdermaker (1962) notes that a popular use of radio in Africa involved messages sent between villages and mine workers far away. This use of mass media implies that in order to be supportive of local, high-context cultures, media will have to be "small" and have local bases. The use of decentralized "small" media has been increasingly called for by development communication researchers (Lent, 1979).

If the mass media are used to provide two-way channels between local high-context cultures and the larger institutions that impinge on them, they may also reinforce the high-context culture. By providing the ability to "talk back" to government departments, international agencies, and so forth, the media may increase the viability of the local culture. Cassirer (1977) tells the story of Senegal's Rural Educational Radio, which encouraged villagers to write letters that would be read on the air. The letters exposed government agencies' corruption and incompetence and moved the president to deal with the abuses.

A third way mass media may reinforce high-context cultures is by acting as a channel for all local arts and performances, not just a few. Lomax (1977) notes that electronic communication is intrinsically multichanneled and can carry many different cultural expressions. When local high-context cultures see themselves recognized by mass media, they will continue their artistic traditions. In this way, mass media can encourage local arts, rather than discouraging them by only focusing on a talented few.

In fact, we may expect considerable innovation in the media itself from Third-World cultures, if the experience of anthropologist Sol

Worth (Worth & Adair, 1970) with Navajo filmmakers is any guide. The Navajos learned the equipment easily and soon were making unique films using new shooting and editing techniques.

SUMMARY

This chapter has explored the rich concept of "context" as it applies to studies of the mass media in the Third World. The mass media come from low-context countries, as do most of the research techniques to study the media. If nothing else, this chapter will have accomplished its goal if it has demonstrated that the mass media function differently in a high-context culture than a low-context culture and that it will need to be studied by different means.

On the most general level, mass media will tend to subtract context in high-context cultures, by relativizing the local context and rendering it less able to confer meanings. Other structural aspects of the media will also tend to lower context, such as its requirement for monochronic time and its diversion of attention away from interpersonal interaction.

However, in the previous section, three hypothesis were listed that suggest that, properly configured, media may reinforce context in high-context cultures, somewhat countering its inherent low-contexting tendencies. If media are decentralized and local, allowing for two-way communication between people and between localities and larger governmental units and for showcasing local arts, it is possible that local high-context cultures will not be as adversely affected by media as they otherwise would be.

Specific research that is designed to discover both the media-induced subtraction of context and media's possible reinforcement of context will be necessary to fully understand the complex effects of media in any particular situation.

Meanwhile, in low-context cultures, media can generally be seen as adding context, conferring greater meanings on the sparse contexts of those cultures. However, if media provide conflicting information, they may reduce context's ability to confer meaning and thereby subtract context from an already low-context situation. Research will need to be sensitive to the contexting implications of media content. If the research techniques in low-context cultures are conceived as studying "context effects," some theoretical unity may be achieved by those diverse approaches.

REFERENCES

Beltran, S. (1976). Alien premises, objects, and methods in Latin American communication research. *Communication Research, 3*(2), 107-134.

Bernstein. B. (1972). Social class, language, and socialization. In P. Giglioli (Ed.), *Language and social context* (pp. 157-178). New York: Penguin.

Bordenave, J. D. (1976). Communication of agricultural innovations in Latin America. *Communication Research, 3*(2), 135-154.

Buerkel-Rothfuss, N. (1981). Soap opera viewing. *Journal of Communication, 31*(3), 108-115.

Cassirer, H. (1977). Radio as the people's medium. *Journal of Communication, 27*(2), 154-157.

Gerbner, G., Gross, L., Morgan, M., & Signorielli, N. (1980). The mainstreaming of America: Violence profile no. 11. *Journal of Communication, 30*(3), 10-29.

Hall, E. T. (1977). *Beyond culture.* Garden City, NY: Anchor.

Hopper, R., Knapp, M., & Scott, L. (1981). Couples' personal idioms. *Journal of Communication, 31*(1), 23-34.

Horton, R. (1967). African traditional thought and Western science. *Africa, 37*(1, 2), 50-71, 155-187.

Katz, E. (1977). Can authentic cultures survive new media? *Journal of Communication, 27*(2), 113-121.

Kent, S. (1985). The effects of television viewing: A cross-cultural perspective. *Current Anthropology, 26*(1), 121-126.

Lent, J. (1979). *Topics in Third World mass communication.* Hong Kong: Asian Research Service.

Lerner, D. (1958). *The passing of traditional society.* New York: Free Press.

Lomax, A. (1977). Appeal for cultural equity. *Journal of Communication, 27*(2), 125-138.

McCombs, M., & Shaw. D. (1972). The agenda-setting function of the mass media. *Public Opinion Quarterly, 36,* 176-187.

Noelle-Newmann, E. (1974). The spiral of silence. *Journal of Communication, 24*(2), 43-51.

Powdermaker, H. (1962). *Coppertown.* New York: Harper & Row.

Worth, S., & Adair, J. (1970). Navajo filmmakers. *American Anthropologist, 72*(1), 9-34.

6

Preventing AIDS Through Persuasive Communications
A Framework for Constructing Effective Culturally-Specific Health Messages

KIM WITTE ● *Texas A&M University*

Although some AIDS prevention campaigns appear to be effective (specifically, those targeted toward urban, white, gay men), most have been marked by a lack of clear theoretical bases and a lack of appropriate design given specific population and cultural characteristics. A persuasive health message framework for mass media use designed to remedy these deficiencies is presented based on three major persuasion theories—protection motivation theory, elaboration likelihood model, and theory of reasoned action. The methods discussed for creating effective preventive health messages are different in that they focus on the actual information and content of the message. The preventive health message framework described focuses on creating AIDS-prevention mass media messages that are salient to a cultural group's beliefs, knowledge, attitudes, and subjective norms. Because the goal is to persuade members of a cultural group to change AIDS-related risk behaviors, the message content must focus on attitudes and beliefs toward the risk behaviors, as well as attitudes and beliefs toward AIDS. By doing this, optimal behavior change is hypothesized to occur. The methods to creating effective preventive health messages are described step-by-step and illustrated with the specific case of Hispanic men.

With no known cure, the best method to prevent the spread of AIDS (acquired immunodeficiency syndrome) is to change risky behaviors and attitudes. Prevention programs targeted toward white gays have been relatively successful in stemming the rise of AIDS in that population (Coates, 1990; Stall, Coates, & Hoff, 1988). Although AIDS has devastated the gay community, the proportion of white gay men with

AUTHOR'S NOTE: An earlier version of this chapter was presented at the Speech Communication Association preconvention conference on "Communication Research and the AIDS Crisis," November, 1989. I am grateful to Dale Brashers for his helpful contributions to this manuscript.

67

AIDS is slowly decreasing, partly due to changes in risky behavior (Shilts, 1989). Stall et al. (1988) documented the dramatic reduction i risky behaviors for urban white gay and bisexual men due to an increas in knowledge about AIDS, personal efficacy in reducing risky behavior perceived vulnerability to risk of AIDS, and changes in social norms in th white gay community. These authors hasten to add that these results ar not generalizable to minority gays, rural gays, or gays who have nc publicly stated their sexual orientation. Although not all prevention pro grams reduce risky behavior consistently, many have been shown to b efficacious when designed for and targeted toward a specific populatio (i.e., urban white gay men).

Prevention programs targeted toward other population groups hav been less successful, partly because of a lack of appropriate design fo specific population characteristics (Brooks-Gunn, Boyer, & Hein, 1988 Mays, 1988; Mays & Cochran, 1988; Peterson & Marin, 1988). To b effective, prevention programs must be tailored to the specific psy chosocial and cultural characteristics of different population group (e.g., women, ethnic minorities, adolescents). Mays and Cochran (1988 found a marked lack of concern about AIDS transmission from nearl 50% of black women college students who were sexually active. Th authors hypothesize that the reason for this lack of concern is that AID is depicted by the media and some prevention campaigns as a whit disease (e.g., white spokespersons). Similarly, Hispanic or black me who engage in high-risk sexual activities with other minority men ma not believe themselves to be at risk for AIDS because they also vie AIDS to be a white or gay men's disease (Peterson & Marin, 1988 Poor black or Latina women may not perceive the threat of AIDS to b severe compared to other more immediate threats such as lack c shelter, food, money, or protection for their children (Mays & Cochran 1988). Compared to other risks in their lives, "AIDS may be of rela tively low concern" (p. 951). Finally, adolescents may not perceive th threat of AIDS to be real because its consequences are in the distan future, and many adolescents believe themselves to be personally in vulnerable to injuries and disease (Brooks-Gunn, Boyer, & Hein, 1988 For these groups, a "generic" AIDS prevention program probably woul fail, because it most likely would not address the beliefs and attitude salient to these different cultures.

In addition to a lack of tailored prevention programs, AIDS preven tion programs have been marked by a lack of clear theoretical bases. A

Flora and Thoresen (1988) stated when speaking of AIDS prevention programs in schools:

> The vast majority of curricula are not well grounded in theory that integrates the information, understanding, and skills training needed to bring about change in sexual activities. Very little attention has been paid to date about possible ethnic, racial, or gender differences concerning how material is presented, different meanings that information may have for various groups, and possible barriers to understanding and behavior change that may be involved. (p. 965)

An integrated theoretical approach from which to launch AIDS mass media campaigns is sorely needed but often neglected. With the exception of urban white gay men, AIDS mass media prevention programs appear to have failed to ascertain the salient beliefs, attitudes, and behaviors of a targeted population and have neglected to integrate all of these elements into effective prevention messages. Persuasive communications should be theoretically based and utilize information (such as data on culture, social norms, beliefs, and behaviors toward AIDS) gathered by multiple disciplines (e.g., epidemiologists, psychologists, anthropologists). Following a brief review of three persuasion theories, a persuasive health message framework for mass media use will be presented.

FEAR APPEALS

Some of the first attempts at persuading people to change their health-related behavior was through fear appeals. A fear or threat appeal is hypothesized to arouse fear in order to motivate people to change their behavior.

Early researchers thought the relation between threat and message acceptance was curvilinear (Janis, 1967). That is, they believed too much fear interfered with message acceptance and resulted in defensive avoidant reactions. However, this position has been "overwhelmingly rejected" by subsequent research (Rogers, 1983, p. 156). Most research during the 1970s and 1980s demonstrated that higher levels of fear produced more change (Boster & Mongeau, 1984; Rogers, 1983; Sutton, 1982). However, fear appeals occasionally boomerang, most notably when perceptions of threat are high and efficacy beliefs are low (Kleinot & Rogers, 1982; Rogers & Mewborn, 1976).

Leventhal's (1970) work focused on cognitive processes, as opposed to fear arousal and reduction processes. His parallel response model distinguished between emotional reactions and cognitive reactions to message. Leventhal (1970) posited that protective behavior stemmed from attempts to control the danger (cognitions), not from attempts to control the fear (emotions). Thus, danger reduction was the important behavior change variable, not fear reduction. Rogers (1975) extended Leventhal's cognitive processing outlook by specifying the components of a fear appeal in protection motivation theory (PMT).

PMT further deemphasized the role of fear arousal in favor of cognition. Rogers (1983) proposed that cognitive appraisals of threat and efficacy are what lead to attitude and behavior change. PMT consists of four components: (a) perceived susceptibility to the threat; (b) perceived severity of the threat; (c) perceived efficacy of a recommended response; and (d) perceived self-efficacy (Maddux & Rogers 1983; Rogers, 1975, 1983).[1] Each of the PMT components is hypothesized to cause a corresponding cognitive mediating process whereby protection motivation response is elicited (Rogers, 1975, 1983). Perceived susceptibility leads to the cognitive appraisal of expectancy of exposure ("What are my chances of getting AIDS?"). Perceived severity of threat leads to the cognitive mediation process whereby a person decides whether the threat is severe or not ("How severe is AIDS?"). Response efficacy leads to the cognitive appraisal where a person decides whether the recommended response will reduce the threat ("Condoms prevent AIDS transmission"). Self-efficacy leads to the cognitive process where one's ability to perform the recommended response is appraised ("I can use condoms"). The intention of a person to adopt a preventive health communication's recommendation is hypothesized to be a function of how much protection motivation is aroused by these cognitive appraisal processes. Protection motivation "is an intervening variable that has the typical characteristics of motive: it arouses, sustains, and directs activity" (Rogers, 1975, p. 98). If an adequate amount of protection motivation is elicited through the cognitive appraisal of a persuasive communication, then acceptance of the message is expected to occur.

Overall, protection motivation theory appears to have explained much in how fearful persuasive messages promote attitude and behavior change. Susceptibility to threat and response efficacy have usually been predictors of behavioral intention change (e.g., Maddux & Rogers 1983; Wurtele & Maddux, 1987). However, given that most main effects account for less than 20% of the total variance explaining behavioral intentions (e.g., Stanley & Maddux, 1986; Wurtele & Maddux, 1987), PMT appears to be missing some important persuasive processes.

Specifically, PMT lacks reference to two important persuasive properties crucial to the health message framework presented here: message processing and content. First, PMT fails to specify how people process information. It describes cognitive appraisal processes people undergo (e.g., susceptibility to threat leads to expectancy of exposure evaluations) when confronted with a persuasive message, but it does not specify the specific cognitive processes (e.g., exactly when and under what conditions do people make their decisions) nor does it address the different attitudes people end up with given the same persuasive message. In the most recent depiction of his model, Rogers (1983) does state that costs and rewards are weighed in terms of threat and coping (efficacy) appraisals, but these variables are just beginning to be explored empirically. By adding elements from information processing models, which explain the information processing strategies people adopt when presented with a persuasive message, these weaknesses of PMT can be addressed.

MESSAGE PROCESSING

One of the most well-known information processing theories is the elaboration likelihood model (ELM) (Petty & Cacioppo, 1986). Given the same message, two people may process the information in very different ways because of their cultural background, prior experiences, personalities, mood states, and so on, and come up with very different decisions (i.e., behavioral intentions). According to the ELM, when people are involved and interested in an issue, they are more likely to think about, evaluate, and elaborate on the arguments. This central route process takes considerable cognitive exertion and is used only when issues are of the utmost importance to a person. Attitudes formed through the central processing route are more likely to be persistent, predictive of behavior, and resistant to change (Petty & Cacioppo, 1986). When people have little interest, ability, and/or motivation to process a message, they rely on peripheral cues such as simple associations, inferences, or heuristics (Petty & Cacioppo, 1986). For example, "I usually agree with people who are like me" is a heuristic device that takes relatively little cognitive work and is an efficient way to make a decision. Attitudes changed via this route are unstable and relatively easy to change.

The ELM states that variables can serve as cues, arguments, or they can affect the extent or direction of information processing by influencing motivation and/or ability to process the message (Petty & Cacioppo, 1986). Variables also can serve multiple roles depending on whether they are issue relevant or irrelevant. Dozens of experiments have been conducted to test the ELM, and many appear to support the theory (for review, see Petty & Cacioppo, 1986). However, other studies have yielded results contrary to the model's predictions (e.g., Gibbons, Busch, & Bradac, 1989; Mongeau & Stiff, 1989). In addition, the ELM has been criticized on theoretical grounds (Stiff, 1986; Stiff & Boster, 1987) and lacked support in a meta-analysis (Johnson & Eagly, 1989).[2] Even though the ELM may have difficulties as a model, the information processing notions of central versus peripheral route processing are useful for the persuasive health message framework. Other information processing models offer similar distinctions (e.g., Chaiken's [1980] heuristic model).

MESSAGE CONTENT

Missing from both PMT and ELM is a focus on the actual details of the persuasive message content. Rarely have actual message content characteristics been experimentally analyzed. Hundreds of studies have been conducted analyzing such factors as argument type, organizational patterns, or intensity (Burgoon, 1989; McGuire, 1985). However, the message content, the actual items of information, have yet to be thoroughly explored in relation to persuasive processes (Fishbein & Ajzen, 1981). On what specifically should severity or efficacy statements focus?

Often messages created for persuasion research are based on intuitive appeal, rather than sound methodology (Fishbein & Ajzen, 1981). For example, in creating the messages for testing PMT, it appears the content of the message, beyond the general specifications of severity, susceptibility, response, and self-efficacy, was largely up to the individual researcher. PMT is not the only study to have this deficiency. In fact, in most persuasion studies, messages appear to be created the same way (Fishbein & Ajzen, 1981). Petty and Cacioppo (1986) also acknowledge that "we too have ignored the specific qualities that render some arguments cogent and others specious. . . . [We have] postponed the question of what specific qualities make arguments persuasive" (p. 32). This state of affairs led Fishbein and Ajzen (1981) to conclude that "the general neglect of the information contained in a message and its relation to the dependent variable is probably the most serious problem in communication and persuasion research" (p. 359).

Fishbein and Ajzen (1975, 1981) suggest specific message construction techniques based on their theory of reasoned action (TRA). In TRA, Fishbein and Ajzen (1975) propose that a person's behavior is predicted by intentions, which in turn are predicted by attitudes toward the behavior and subjective norm. Attitudes are predicted by behavioral beliefs and evaluations of those beliefs. Subjective norms are predicted by normative beliefs and the motivation to comply with those normative beliefs. Fishbein and Ajzen (1975) state that two sets of beliefs must be altered prior to behavior change: (a) beliefs about the consequences of performing a certain behavior and the evaluation of those consequences (attitude), and (b) beliefs about what other people or referents think about the behavior to be performed and the motivation to comply with those referents (subjective norm). Only when a message targets the salient beliefs of these variables do attitudes and subjective norms, and, subsequently, behavioral intentions and behavior, change.

Table 6.1 illustrates how the TRA may be used to analyze a specific cultural group's behaviors in terms of AIDS prevention. Table 6.1a indicates one person's hypothetical attitude toward condom use. This person may believe that condoms are uncomfortable, prevent AIDS, interfere with spontaneity, and are expensive. The strength of these beliefs (from .00 to 1.00) is indicated in the second column and the evaluation (ranging from −3 [unfavorable] to +3 [favorable]) of these attributes is indicated in the third column. These belief strengths and evaluations are multiplied individually and then summed to create the overall attitude. For example, this person strongly believes that condoms interfere with spontaneity (.90) and this interference is evaluated unfavorably (−2). In addition, he does not believe very strongly that condoms prevent AIDS (.3), but anything that prevents AIDS is evaluated very highly (+3). It is clear, however, that the predominant attitude toward condom use is negative at −3.10.

Table 6.1b is a hypothetical example of a Roman Catholic man's subjective norm toward condom use. His specific referents include his girlfriend, his best friend, his church, and his mother. His normative beliefs reflect what he thinks each of these specific referents think about

TABLE 6.1 Hypothetical Attitudes and Subjective Norms Toward Condom Use

a. Hypothetical Attitude Toward Condom Use

Beliefs	Behavioral Beliefs	Evaluations	Beliefs × Evaluations
Uncomfortable	.70	−3	−2.10
Prevents AIDS	.30	+3	+.90
Interferes with spontaneity	.90	−2	−1.80
Expensive	.10	−1	−.10
			Attitude = −3.10

b. Hypothetical Subjective Norm Toward Condom Use

Referents	Normative Beliefs	Motivation to Comply	Beliefs × Motivation to Comply
My girlfriend	−1	+2	−2
My best friend	−3	+3	−9
My church	−3	0	0
My mother	−1	+1	−1
			Subjective norm = −12

him using condoms (ranging from −3 [should not use] to +3 [should use]). His motivation to comply with each referent is indicated on a scale from 0 (not at all) to 3 (strongly). In each case, the normative belief and the motivation to comply is multiplied to yield a product. The sum of these products is the subjective norm. This person's subjective norm toward condom use is negative (i.e., −12).

Fishbein and Ajzen (1981) argue that to change a behavior, the total set of primary (or salient) beliefs must be changed or shifted. In the examples of behavioral and normative beliefs (Table 6.1), note that if one belief changed, the whole attitude or subjective norm probably would not change. Fishbein and Ajzen (1975) state that salient beliefs must be altered to effect change because they are, in essence, what cause behavior.

When constructing persuasive messages, Fishbein and Ajzen (1975) note that it is crucial to choose the "right" target variable. What is the specific goal of the persuasive message—to change attitudes, intentions, or behaviors? Exactly which behaviors are to be targeted for change? Likewise, there must be precise correspondence in specificity between the persuasive message and the targeted goal. For example, a message arguing that AIDS should be prevented will only persuade people that AIDS should be prevented. However, more often than not,

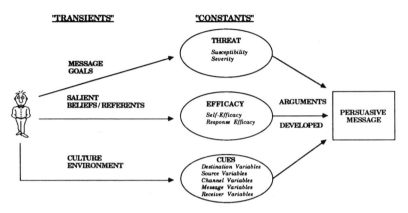

Figure 6.1: A Framework for Developing Culturally Specific Health Messages

practitioners will use such a message in which the arguments focus on AIDS when their goal is to persuade people to use condoms to prevent AIDS. The presumption is that people will infer that condoms prevent AIDS, simply because the end of the message states this. Note that there is a lack of correspondence between the message (attitudes toward AIDS) and the behavioral goal (attitudes toward use of condoms).

The three major theories discussed thus far, protection motivation theory, elaboration likelihood model, and theory of reasoned action, all have offered valuable insight into persuasion processes. An effort to integrate these theories into a preventive health message framework that is applicable for health communication mass media campaigns is offered next.

A PERSUASIVE HEALTH MESSAGE FRAMEWORK

The framework developed here borrows elements from the three theories reviewed. Specifically, the message components from PMT, the processing routes of ELM, and the message construction techniques offered by Fishbein and Ajzen will be used. This framework is designed with both theoretical and practical application issues in mind.

Figure 6.1 depicts the framework. The "constant" components of the framework serve to structure the content and features of a persuasive message. The "transient" elements of a message are those that change given different populations and message goals. Salient beliefs, salient referents, culture, environment, and message goals are all transient elements that determine the actual message content and features of the constant components. In other words, the transient elements feed information about the targeted population into the constant structural components, which are then used to develop the arguments for the persuasive message.

The first two constant components deal with message content structural issues. For example, in terms of the threat component, arguments should always address salient beliefs about susceptibility and severity, regardless of the goal or target population. Likewise, for the efficacy component, arguments should always address salient beliefs about response and self-efficacy. Although the topic of the message is transient (e.g., AIDS, breast cancer, exercise), the focus of each constant component is stable. Both the message goal and focus must be clearly defined (Ajzen & Fishbein, 1980). Threat arguments should target beliefs about the health threat (e.g., AIDS, heart disease). The efficacy arguments should target beliefs about the consequences of performing the recommended response (e.g., using condoms, exercising more). Note that arguments from the threat component focus on the health threat, and arguments from the efficacy component focus on the recommended response—regardless of the message topic.[3]

Threat and efficacy arguments are hypothesized to serve as key motivators in persuading people to process the message and to adopt the recommended response. If both threat and efficacy arguments are strong, it is believed that they will be cognitively appraised and will elicit a protection motivation response. It is critical that the cognitive appraisals of threat are sufficiently balanced by strong response and self-efficacy perceptions. That is, the recommended response must be perceived as efficacious enough to eliminate or substantially reduce the threat (Job, 1988). The arguments based on this persuasive health message framework should persuade people from targeted population or cultural groups that they are susceptible to AIDS, that AIDS is severe, that condoms prevent transmission, and that they are able to use condoms.

An additional persuasive motivator is the use of salient beliefs, which are transient elements. The transient elements of the framework serve two functions. First, they increase involvement in and personal relevance of the message to the targeted population by increasing salience. Recall that increased involvement in a message leads to central processing of the message (Petty & Cacioppo, 1986). Central processing also is desirable because it leads to lasting and stable attitude change. If salient beliefs are targeted in the message, then the motivation and/or ability of members of the population to process the message also should increase. For example, because the message targets the salient beliefs of a group of people, the message becomes personally relevant, and members of the group become motivated to process it. Likewise, if cues (discussed below) are tailored toward a specific cultural or population group (e.g., language, education level, social class), then the ability of members of the population to understand the message should be heightened. Thus, surveying for salient beliefs/referents and incorporating these beliefs into a persuasive message should increase cognitive processing of the message, which will, in turn, lead to lasting and stable attitude and behavior change.

The second function of the transient elements is to develop correspondence between the audience's salient beliefs, the persuasive message, and the desired outcome behaviors. An increase in correspondence is likely to yield a greater change in behavior or attitude (Fishbein & Ajzen, 1975). For example, a population's salient beliefs about the efficacy of condoms in preventing AIDS should be targeted in the persuasive message if the desired behavioral outcome is increased condom use.

The third constant component of the framework is based on the peripheral cues portion of the ELM (Petty & Cacioppo, 1986). Although the salient beliefs of a targeted audience should cause them to care and think about the message, sometimes audiences may be preoccupied or tired and fail to process the persuasive message through a central route. Thus, elements serving as cues should be included in the message. This strategy should lead to a message that influences nearly all of the audience, including those who do and do not care about the message.

In a review of the persuasion literature for public communication campaigns, McGuire (1984) designed a checklist in which he grouped five types of variables that influence persuasive processes. Many of these variables appear to affect behavior change as cues. *Destination variables* reflect whether a message affects knowledge, attitudes, or action; whether the message is to be processed immediately or in the future; or if the message is intended to cause change in behavior or resistance to change. *Source variables* include communicator credibility, attractiveness, power, and number of communicators. *Message variables* refer to message style, type of appeal, type of argument, inclusions/omissions, message organization, and repetition. *Channel variables* relate to type of channel used, direct versus mediated, verbal versus nonverbal, and context in which the channel is used. Finally, amount of participation, demographics, personality, and abilities all pertain to *receiver variables.* Many studies have shown a relation between these variables and a persuasive message's effectiveness. Because it is unlikely that subjects will consciously think about a communicator's attractiveness or the channel through which the message came, it is postulated that these variables affect the persuasive process through peripheral routes. An exception to this is if the cue is *issue relevant* (Petty & Cacioppo, 1986). Then a cue may serve as an argument or a variable that increases motivation and/or ability to centrally process the message.

As many of the cue variables (e.g., source, channel variables) as possible should be addressed in the persuasive mass media message. Transient cultural, environmental, and demographic factors influence the selection of appropriate cues variables. The inclusion of cues in a communication is an attempt to make the "whole" message salient to a population.

CONSTRUCTING PERSUASIVE MESSAGES: THE CASE OF HISPANIC MEN

The steps for constructing persuasive messages based on the persuasive health message framework will be illustrated with the case of Hispanic men. First, the transient (or changeable) elements of the persuasive message must be determined (see Figure 6.1). This transient information can then be integrated with the constant (or structural) elements to create the persuasive message.

The first transient elements to be determined are the specific message goals. The message goal must be the specific behaviors that are to be changed. In this case, let the message goal be to prevent AIDS by using condoms (Koop, 1986). In addition, a specific population must be selected to further define the message goals. One group that has been disproportionately hit by the AIDS crisis is Hispanics (Marin, 1989). Hispanics are almost twice as likely to have contracted AIDS than whites (Marin, 1989). Because of the large gender differences between male and female Hispanics, one should be chosen as the targeted population. In this example, let Hispanic males, aged 15 to 44 years, be the targeted population. Therefore, the specific message goal is to prevent AIDS among Hispanic men aged 15 to 44 years through increased condom use.

After the message goals have been specified, the salient beliefs and referents need to be determined. To ascertain salient beliefs about the components of the framework (i.e., threat and efficacy), one should survey for modal salient beliefs from a representative sample of the population—in this case, Hispanic men. Likewise, to determine salient referents, modal salient referents would have to be determined.[4] For example, the salient beliefs of Hispanic males about the consequences of using condoms to prevent AIDS need to be discovered. Specific questions might include, "Will you contract the AIDS virus? Why or why not?" (susceptibility), or "What will happen to you if you get AIDS?" (severity). In terms of beliefs about efficacy one may ask, "Why are you able, or not able, to use condoms?" (self-efficacy), or "Do you think condoms prevent AIDS? Why or why not?" (response efficacy). Other efficacy questions should center on the consequences of the targeted behavior, "What are the advantages or disadvantages of using condoms?" Salient referents are solicited by asking "Are there any people or groups who would approve or disapprove of you using condoms?" or "Are there any people or groups who would approve or disapprove of you using condoms to prevent AIDS?" Note that these last two questions may yield different answers so both should be used. Great cultural sensitivity must be used in formulating these personal sexual questions. For example, it is preferable to have a same-sex member of an in-group ask the questions using the appropriate colloquialisms or slang (i.e., a male Hispanic ask the questions), because some Hispanics have been found to resent questions about their sexual lives (Longshore, 1989; Navarro, 1989). Ideally, Ajzen and Fishbein's (1980, chap. 6) techniques for gathering information about salient beliefs and referents should be used.

If practitioners are unable to conduct a survey, much information about Hispanics' salient beliefs toward AIDS and condoms already exists. For example, researchers have found that Hispanic males in general perceive little susceptibility to AIDS (Navarro, 1989; Peterson & Marin, 1988). Hispanic men do not think they are engaging in risky behaviors—even if they have unprotected anal intercourse with other men (Carrier, 1976; Marin, 1989; Peterson & Marin, 1988). In addition, because strong cultural and religious taboos exist against homosexuality (Carrier, 1976; Marin, 1989), messages targeted toward homosexual actions are likely to be ignored or seen as irrelevant to many Hispanic men. Hispanic men's perceived severity of AIDS is unknown. Hispanics in general know less about AIDS and its prevention than non-Hispanics (Marin, 1989). In one survey, over half (53%) of the participants admitted knowing little or nothing about AIDS (Marin, 1989). Typically it is assumed that most people "know" that AIDS is a severe disease. However, this assumption may be erroneous.

In terms of perceived efficacy beliefs toward condoms, a great deal is known about Hispanic men's self-efficacy beliefs, but little is known about their response efficacy beliefs. Recall that self-efficacy is one's perceived ability to perform a given behavior. In the case of using condoms to prevent AIDS, it appears that many variables influence Hispanic men's perceived ability or willingness to use condoms. First, condoms are used relatively infrequently by Hispanics (Marin, 1989). Hispanics associate condoms with uncleanliness and prostitution and think that they reduce pleasure, virility, and are inconvenient and uncomfortable to use (Carrier, 1989; Marin, 1989; Marin & Marin, 1987). Additionally, using condoms may be seen by Hispanic men as admitting that they are at-risk for AIDS (Marin, 1989). Furthermore, instructions about how to use condoms are typically difficult to read and often in English only (Richwald, Schneider-Munoz, & Valdez, 1989). In terms of response efficacy, it is unknown whether Hispanic men think that condoms prevent AIDS (Marin, 1989).

Salient referent groups are transient elements that also need to be ascertained. Salient referent groups for Hispanic men are likely to be other Hispanic men, significant others, family members, and the Roman Catholic church (Carrier, 1976; Navarro, 1989; Thompson, 1987). Members of some of these groups strongly disapprove of Hispanic men using condoms (i.e., the Roman Catholic church) (Navarro, 1989). However, there is some evidence that suggests the church is not as strong a referent group for Hispanics as is generally thought (Amaro, 1988). It is important to find out which groups are the strongest referents for Hispanic men, as well as what members of these groups believe about the threat of AIDS and the efficacy of condoms.

In sum, the existing literature has enabled us to determine many of Hispanic men's salient beliefs and referents about using condoms to prevent AIDS. We now know that Hispanic men perceive little susceptibility to AIDS and probably feel little self-efficacy about using condoms. We do not know whether AIDS is perceived as severe or whether condoms are seen as effective by Hispanic men. These are the specific beliefs that need to be targeted by the arguments in the persuasive message.

The final transient information to be gathered is the specific cultural and environmental data of the targeted population. This information is used to devise the cues or "extra-message" features of the communication (i.e., receiver, channel, message, source, and destination variables). McGuire's (1984) checklist may be utilized in determining which cues to include in the message. Each of these cues variables will be discussed and illustrated, in turn. A composite description of the "typical" subject in the target population may be helpful in isolating receiver characteristics. Based on anthropological, psychological, and sociological data provided by Carrier (1976), McKenna (1985), Marin (1989), and Villareal (1986), the "typical" (admittedly stereotypical) Hispanic male speaks Spanish at home and prefers medical information in Spanish (two thirds of Hispanics prefer to communicate in Spanish; 15% prefer their information to be in English), has a relatively low literacy level, lives in the Southwest, is in his twenties (median age 22.8), retains many elements of his Hispanic culture, and is likely to be economically and medically disadvantaged.

Other receiver variables include certain cultural values that influence Hispanic men's sexual behaviors (Marin, 1989). The value of *machismo* is characterized by a need to demonstrate virility. Prostitutes may be seen as a way of confirming machismo (Marin, 1989). This is problematic in that Hispanic prostitutes have high rates of the human immunodeficiency virus (HIV). Other cultural values include *familialism* (i.e., sense of obligation to support extended family); *respéto* (i.e., respect for others, allowance of face-saving strategies); *simpatia* (i.e., politeness, discouragement of confrontation); *personalismo* (i.e., the notion that relationships with others should be personalized and involve trust); and *cooperacion* (i.e., the prevailing notion that social interactions should be without competition) (Ehling, 1987; Marin, 1989). These cultural values may be used in public health campaigns to promote behavior change. For example, if AIDS prevention campaigns are framed in terms of cultural values (i.e., "prevent AIDS to preserve our families"—familialism), then cultural members may be more willing to make changes in their behaviors to uphold these values.

The best mass media channels to reach Hispanic males appear to be radio or television (Marin, 1989; Mays & Cochran, 1988). Hispanics may not want to be seen reading newspapers or magazines about AIDS prevention strategies (Peterson & Marin, 1988). In terms of message variables, messages must use appropriate words and referents for such terms as "anal intercourse," "oral intercourse," and "active sexual life."

Marin (1989) reported a study that found the Spanish equivalents of these words were misinterpreted by Hispanics. In addition, the message must be presented in a "culturally appropriate way" when it is "about behaviors that are considered to be private (sexual)" (Marin, 1989, p. 414). A member of the Hispanic man's most salient referent group may be effective as the source of the message. Source credibility and attractiveness need to be determined from the Hispanic man's point of view. The destination variables have already been determined by the message goals (i.e., the message is intended to cause behavior change).

CONSTRUCTING THE PERSUASIVE MESSAGE

After the determination of transient variables, the persuasive message can be constructed. Although the usual focus of mass media persuasive messages has been on changing beliefs, Burgoon (1989; McGuire, 1985) notes that there are two additional roads to persuasion. A message can also reinforce existing attitudes or induce resistance to future persuasive attempts. After surveying for salient beliefs, an investigator can decide whether the population's salient beliefs need to be targeted for change or for reinforcement, or whether resistance to other persuasive attempts should be included, and adjust the persuasive message accordingly. In the case of Hispanic men, it appears that susceptibility and self-efficacy beliefs need to be targeted for change, and that severity and response efficacy beliefs need to be either introduced or reinforced.

The persuasive message should contain arguments that specifically correspond to the goals of the persuasive message. In other words, the threat arguments should target the salient beliefs about susceptibility and severity of AIDS outlined earlier. Likewise, the efficacy arguments should target salient beliefs about response and self-efficacy of using condoms to prevent AIDS. Factual evidence should be included to support the arguments. For instance, Hispanic men's beliefs that they are not susceptible to AIDS must be countered with the fact that they are at increased risk for AIDS. Likewise, because Hispanic men believe that condoms reduce virility, arguments must be generated to counter this misconception. Arguments may be developed using members of salient referent groups as advocates of condom use to prevent AIDS (if this is accurate). Ideally, each salient belief described earlier should be refuted or reinforced in the persuasive message. However, if the persuasive message is limited by space or time, only the most salient beliefs may be targeted for change.

CONCLUSION

A comprehensive framework for constructing effective persuasive messages has been presented and applied to the specific issue of AIDS prevention among Hispanic men. Persuasive health messages based on this framework are particularly appropriate for mass media channels. Persuasive communications through mass media may reach individuals at risk for AIDS who would not be reached through mainstream prevention programs (Mays & Cochran, 1988). The framework outlined in this chapter offers a relatively easy method for creating a highly persuasive preventive health message for a variety of audiences. Perhaps some of the devastation caused by AIDS can be prevented through the use of culturally appropriate mass media persuasive health messages.

NOTES

1. Readers will notice similarities between PMT and the Health Belief Model (Becker et al., 1977); some consider PMT to be an experimental variant (e.g., Leventhal, Safer, & Panagis, 1983).

2. Johnson and Eagly (1989) suggested in a meta-analysis that studies by Petty, Cacioppo, and colleagues (the "Ohio State" research group) were more likely to obtain predicted results than studies conducted by "other" researchers (p. 304). See the 1987 issue of *Communication Monographs, 54,* for the exchange between Stiff, Stiff, and Boster, and Petty and Cacioppo.

3. Ajzen and Fishbein (1980) state that the message should focus on the consequences of the recommended behavior (e.g., using condoms), as opposed to the general attitude toward the threat (e.g., AIDS). However, in the context of this message framework, both types of arguments are appropriate for the message.

4. This approach is adapted from Ajzen and Fishbein's (1980) instructions for constructing a questionnaire (Appendix A). Ajzen and Fishbein also discuss methods of determining modal salient beliefs of a population in detail (chap. 6).

REFERENCES

Ajzen, I., & Fishbein, M. (1980). *Understanding attitudes and predicting social behavior.* Englewood Cliffs, NJ: Prentice-Hall.

Amaro, H. (1988). Women in the Mexican-American community: Religion, culture, and reproductive attitudes and experiences. *Journal of Community Psychology, 16,* 6-20.

Becker, M. H., Haefner, D. P., Kasl, S. V., Kirscht, J. P., Maiman, L. A., & Rosenstock, I. M. (1977). Selected psychosocial models and correlates of individual health-related behaviors. *Medical Care, 15,* 27-46.

Boster, F. J., & Mongeau, P. (1984). Fear-arousing persuasive messages. In R. N. Bostrom & B. H. Westley (Eds.), *Communication yearbook 8* (pp. 330-375). Beverly Hills, CA: Sage.

Brooks-Gunn, J., Boyer, C. B., & Hein, K. (1988). Preventing HIV infection and AIDS in children and adolescents: Behavioral research and intervention strategies. *American Psychologist, 43,* 958-964.

Burgoon, M. (1989). Messages and persuasive effects. In J. J. Bradac (Ed.), *Message effects in communication science* (pp. 129-164). Newbury Park, CA: Sage.

Carrier, J. M. (1976). Cultural factors affecting urban Mexican male homosexual behavior. *Archives of Sexual Behavior, 5,* 103-124.

Carrier, J. M. (1989). Sexual behavior and the spread of AIDS in Mexico. *Medical Anthropologist, 10,* 129-142.

Coates, T. J. (1990). Strategies for modifying sexual behavior for primary and secondary prevention of HIV disease. *Journal of Consulting and Clinical Psychology, 58,* 57-69.

Fishbein, M., & Ajzen, I. (1975). *Belief, attitude, intention, and behavior: An introduction to theory and research.* Reading, MA: Addison-Wesley.

Fishbein, M., & Ajzen, I. (1981). Acceptance, yielding and impact: Cognitive processes in persuasion. In R. E. Petty, T. M. Ostrom, & T. C. Brock (Eds.), *Cognitive responses in persuasion* (pp. 339-359). Hillsdale, NJ: Lawrence Erlbaum.

Flora, J. A., & Thoresen, C. E. (1988). Reducing the risk of AIDS in adolescents. *American Psychologist, 43,* 965-970.

Gibbons, P., Busch, J., & Bradac, J. J. (1989, November). *Powerful versus powerless language: A peripheral cue, an "argument," or a distractor in persuasion?* Paper presented at the annual meeting of the Speech Communication Association, San Francisco.

Janis, I. L. (1967). Effects of fear arousal on attitude change: Recent developments in theory and experimental research. In L. Berkowitz (Ed.), *Advances in experimental social psychology* (Vol. 3). New York: Academic Press.

Job, R. F. S. (1988). Effective and ineffective use of fear in health promotion campaigns. *American Journal of Public Health, 78,* 163-167.

Johnson, B. T., & Eagly, A. H. (1989). Effects of involvement on persuasion. *Psychological Bulletin, 106,* 290-314.

Kleinot, M. C., & Rogers, R. W. (1982). Identifying effective components of alcohol misuse prevention programs. *Journal of Studies on Alcohol, 43,* 802-811.

Koop, C. E. (1986). *Surgeon General's report on Acquired Immune Deficiency Syndrome.* Washington, DC: U.S. Department of Health and Human Services.

Leventhal, H. (1970). Findings and theory in the study of fear communications. In L. Berkowitz (Ed.), *Advances in experimental social psychology* (Vol. 5; pp. 119-186). San Diego, CA: Academic Press.

Leventhal, H., Safer, M. A., & Panagis, D. M. (1983). The impact of communications on the self-regulation of health beliefs, decisions, and behavior. *Health Education Quarterly, 10,* 3-29.

Longshore, D. (1989). Reaching populations at higher risk for AIDS. *AIDS & Public Policy Journal, 4,* 101-105.

Maddux, J. E., & Rogers, R. W. (1983). Protection motivation and self-efficacy: A revised theory of fear appeals and attitude change. *Journal of Experimental Social Psychology, 19*, 469-479.

Marin, B. V., & Marin, G. (1987). Attitudes and expectancies regarding AIDS among Hispanics. In *Psychology and AIDS* (pp. 46-47). Washington, DC: American Psychological Association.

Marin, G. (1989). AIDS prevention among Hispanics: Needs, risk behaviors, and cultural values. *Public Health Reports, 104*, 411-415.

Mays, V. M. (1988). Education and prevention: Section introduction. *American Psychologist, 43*, 948.

Mays, V. M., & Cochran, S. D. (1988). Issues in the perception of AIDS risk and risk reduction activities by black and Hispanic/Latina women. *American Psychologist, 43*, 949-957.

McGuire, W. J. (1984). Public communication as a strategy for inducing health promoting behavioral change. *Preventive Medicine, 13*, 299-319.

McGuire, W. J. (1985). Attitudes and attitude change. In L. Gardner & E. Aronson (Eds.), *Handbook of social psychology: Volume 2* (3rd ed.; pp. 233-346). New York: Random House.

Mongeau, P., & Stiff, J. B. (1989, May). *The effects of message and source processing on attitude: Testing the elaboration likelihood model of persuasion.* Paper presented at the 56th annual meeting of the International Communication Association, San Francisco.

Navarro, M. (1989, December 29). AIDS in Hispanic community: Threat ignored. *New York Times*, pp. B1, B10.

Peterson, J. L., & Marin, G. (1988). Issues in the prevention of AIDS among black and Hispanic men. *American Psychologist, 43*, 871-877.

Petty, R. E., & Cacioppo, J. T. (1986). *Communication and persuasion: Central and peripheral routes to attitude change.* New York: Springer/Verlag.

Richwald, G. A., Schneider-Munoz, M., & Valdez, R. B. (1989). Are condom instructions in Spanish readable? Implications for AIDS prevention activities for Hispanics. *Hispanic Journal of Behavioral Sciences, 11*, 70-82.

Rogers, R. W. (1975). A protection motivation theory of fear appeals and attitude change. *Journal of Psychology, 91*, 93-114.

Rogers, R. W. (1983). Cognitive and physiological processes in fear appeals and attitude change: A revised theory of protection motivation. In J. T. Cacioppo & R. E. Petty (Eds.), *Social psychophysiology* (pp. 153-176). New York: Guilford.

Rogers, R. W., & Mewborn, C. R. (1976). Fear appeals and attitude change: Effects of a threat's noxiousness, probability of occurrence, and the efficacy of the coping responses. *Journal of Personality and Social Psychology, 34*, 54-61.

Shilts, R. (1989). AIDS reaches the eve of the 100,000th US case. *Los Angeles Times*, pt. I, p. 1f.

Stall, R. D., Coates, T. J., & Hoff, C. (1988). Behavioral risk reduction for HIV infection among gay and bisexual men. *American Psychologist, 43*, 878-885.

Stiff, J. B. (1986). Cognitive processing of persuasive message cues: A meta-analytic review of the effects of supporting information on attitudes. *Communication Monographs, 43*, 75-89.

Stiff, J. B., & Boster, F. J. (1987). Cognitive processing: Additional thoughts and a reply to Petty, Kasmer, Haugtvedt, and Cacioppo. *Communication Monographs, 54,* 250-256.

Stanley, M. A., & Maddux, J. E. (1986). Cognitive processes in health enhancement: Investigation of a combined protection motivation and self-efficacy model. *Basic and Applied Social Psychology, 7,* 101-113.

Thompson, L. (1987, August 11). AIDS and minorities. *Washington Post,* p. 7.

Wurtele, S. K., & Maddux, J. E. (1987). Relative contributions of protection motivation theory components in predicting exercise intentions and behavior. *Health Psychology, 6,* 453-466.

II

DATA AND RESEARCH APPROACHES

7

What Makes News

Western, Socialist, and Third-World Television Newscasts Compared in Eight Countries

JOSEPH D. STRAUBHAAR ● CARRIE HEETER ●
BRADLEY S. GREENBERG ● *Michigan State University*
LEONARDO FERREIRA ● *University of Miami, Coral Gables*
ROBERT H. WICKS ● *Indiana University*
TUEN-YU LAU ● *Purdue University*

One week of nightly national television news was videotaped in eight countries, segmented among Western industrialized, socialist, and developing nations. The news content was empirically analyzed for its domestic and international coverage of economic, political, military, scientific, and other news categories to identify the news agenda in each country; additionally, the news images portrayed of other countries in each host country was identified. Western nations concentrated more on disaster and crime, but the foremost topic in each country was its reporting of political events, followed by economic and/or military issues.

This chapter focuses on two issues. First, it examines the applicability of several normative theories to television news, centering on the four theories of the press (Siebert, 1956) and the concept of development journalism (McPhail, 1987; Ogan, 1982, 1984). Does the definition of what is news and the treatment and interpretation of news found in actual television newscasts from a country reflect what might be expected from its professed or ascribed news philosophy? Second, is there a connection between such philosophies, the definition of news for that country, and the manner in which images of other countries are portrayed, so that, for example, Western news media might tend to misrepresent Second- and Third-World countries (Boyd-Barrett, 1980). These

EDITOR'S NOTE: This chapter was written prior to the dissolution of the Soviet Union.

questions are examined through a content analysis of television news in eight countries.

These questions have become major issues particularly because of the New World Information and Communication Order debate (NWICO). Some NWICO positions hold that in the United States and other Western industrialized countries, news covers the wrong issues—that is, sensational failures, accidents, and disasters instead of social progress; conflict instead of stability; military affairs instead of economics; and so forth (McPhail, 1987; Ogan & Fair, 1984). Furthermore, some critics say this news ethic is detrimental to developing countries when adopted by their own journalists (McPhail, 1987). The Western countries have also been charged with either ignoring or distorting news of the Third World, frequently because of emphases such as those mentioned above. On the other hand, some Western countries charge that many Eastern European and Third-World countries censor criticism and stifle creativity in their efforts to present good news and support government development efforts (Mickiewicz, 1988).

An overview of prior research can aid in establishing definitions of some conflicting concepts. First, what is contained in the Western approach to news? In a pioneering study of what Swedish editors thought was newsworthy, Galtung and Rouge (1965) identified a set of criteria that reflect almost uncannily the set of complaints in the NWICO debate about the orientation of Western news values: News should be recent, intense, or splashy, unambiguous of interpretation, preferably set in a culture close to that of the audience, directly related to national interests, predictable (but slightly unexpected), involving elite persons or countries, individualized or personalized, and negative or conflictual. Other studies have found similar criteria used by American, British, and other Western or industrialized nation news reporters and editors (Boyd-Barrett, 1980; Edelstein, 1982; Ogan & Fair, 1984). Studies such as those pioneered by Schramm (1959) show that comparison by content analysis is useful.

In contrast, socialist or "Second-World" countries such as the USSR have long defined news as that which supports the Communist party in achieving national goals. Specifically, Paulu (1974) and Mickiewicz (1981) noted avoidance of conflict or criticism. Criticism was allowed under specific circumstances in party print media and on specific subjects that actually helped party efficiency, or against countries considered enemies. News emphasized positive role models (heroic workers, exemplary farms, etc.), workers, and work goals. Timeliness was much less important than in Western countries and there was a endency to delay reporting until a correct interpretation had been worked out. Despite avoiding domestic conflict news, there was coverage of and support for revolutions in other countries. These tendencies have changed, but this study looks at the pre-Glasnost period of June, 1984.

Yet another approach, "development journalism," has been proposed as a news ethic appropriate to the Third World (Ogan, 1982). In most formulations, it also stresses emphasis on work goals, success stories, and positive role models (Ogan, 1982). Most current proponents would add an emphasis on cooperating with government development goals and projects: Original proponents in India and the Philippines emphasized a more critical approach in which journalists assumed more responsibility for promoting development, including criticism of government programs when necessary (Ogan, 1982). A lively debate goes on about how much criticism of government is useful or appropriate (Aggarwala, 1979; Lent, 1977; Ogan, 1982; Ogan & Fair, 1984; Sussman, 1978). Third-World countries' approaches and policies vary considerably on most issues.

Internationally, controversy comes from the implications of these models for news coverage of international events and other countries. In studies of American television news, Larson (1979) found that American television network news covered the Third World less than other industrialized countries. When the Third World was covered, the stories tended to be on crises and sensational events. Schramm and Atwood (1984) found that Asian countries' news was almost as sensationalistic an approach as "Western" news, however.

Stevenson et al. (1984) found that most countries covered their neighbors more than distant countries but cast doubt on many other supposed differences in First-, Second-, and Third-World coverage. Nordenstreng (1984) noted a problem in that study: it covered countries and topics but not tone or treatment, where distortion and unequal coverage might still reside. The present content analysis will attempt to quantify some of the elusive tone and treatment qualities that have been absent from other studies.

RESEARCH QUESTIONS

Based on a review of the literature, the following general and specific research hypotheses were developed to test the issues introduced above.

1. Western or industrialized countries emphasize military topics, accidents, and crime over politics, economics, social issues, culture/

arts/religion, sports, and science more than newscasts from the USSR or Third-World countries.

2. Within Western political news stories, criticism of government and protests predominate over electoral or legislative processes and domestic and diplomatic meetings. Underlying themes in Western stories frequently depict a wrong or incapable government, which does not support human rights or contribute to social progress. In contrast, socialist news stories show little criticism or protest, emphasizes governments' acts and social contributions, and portray government as correct and capable. Third-World news stories have emphases similar to socialist news but, depending on the country, show more criticism of government.

3. Within economic stories, Western news themes reflect problems more often than solutions in population, health, and food issues, and tend to question whether the overall economy is strong or weak. In contrast, both socialist and Third-World news themes emphasize solutions and strength.

4. On social issues, socialist and Third-World countries emphasize development of social programs and show social issues as getting better. Western news show more problems.

After establishing a country's basic news agenda and its self-image, we will look at which other countries seem to be important enough to be covered in TV news:

5. Despite NWICO charges of Western/industrialized nation dominance in news and news dissemination, neighboring countries or those within the same region are covered more often. Countries at the same stage of development are covered more often. Western news primarily covers other industrialized countries before the USSR and the Third World. Similarly, socialist countries cover those with similar systems, but in the interest of "socialist internationalism," they also cover Third-World countries more than the Western countries do. Due to the political and economic importance of the industrialized Western countries to them, Third-World countries will report more on industrialized countries than others.

METHODS

Sample

By agreement between the United States Information Agency and the researchers, U.S. embassies in six countries were asked to videotape the major national evening newscast for one full week. The countries ncluded China, India, Italy, Japan, West Germany, and the Soviet Union. Videotapes of evening news also were collected from Colombia and the United States and added to the study. Six newscast were obtained from each site over the same nine-day period in June, 1984.

The newscasts vary in length, in the exact time of day they were broadcast (all were evening newscasts), in the number of news stories per broadcast, and in other factors. The chart below identifies newscast length, network or networks coded, average number of stories per newscast, and total stories coded for each country.

Country	Length (min.)	Network(s)	Avg. # Stories	All Stories
China	40	CCTV	27.7	166
Colombia	30	Various	19.7	118
India	20	AIR	14.5	87
Italy	40	RAI-TGI	13.8	83
Japan	35	NHK	9.2	55
West Germany	20	ARD	9.2	55
United States	30	ABC, NBC	10.0	60
USSR	30	VREYMA	18.5	111

The tapes arrived in three different formats, in seven languages, and in the television standard appropriate in each country. Multistandard 3/4 inch and VHS videocassette players were used to make audiocassette dubs of the newscasts for transcription and translation purposes. Paid, volunteer, and for-credit student translators reviewed the audio tapes and created transcripts of the newscasts. They then translated the newscast into English from the transcript, returning to the videotape to check details not immediately interpretable from the audio. Where possible, a native speaker of the language worked in conjunction with a native speaker of English who had studied the language. Locating qualified linguists to work for low wages took nearly nine months. Translation into English was deemed essential to provide intercoder agreement on application of the coding system. Systematic biases could have been introduced by having one research team with Japanese proficiency code all of the Japanese tapes, while a German team coded all German tapes. Certainly, some components of the original language will be lost in translation, but the topics, themes, people, and countries portrayed in the news should generally survive the translation process.

The Coding Process

A series of seminars discussing problems with and suggestions fo improving first-draft coding forms were held with coders who had initially coded a subset of 345 stories. From this process, streamlined coding forms and revised instructions were developed. A team of 1. coders was carefully trained and supervised. All news stories were completely recoded; reliability estimates are provided after the conten factors are defined below.

Content Variables

The major newscast elements coded were focus, topics, portrayal o home country, intercountry interactions, themes, and portrayals o foreign countries.

Focus

The domestic or international focus of each news story was coded Domestic stories dealt with the home country only, with no foreign country or person. Foreign stories involved both the home countr (country originating the newscast) and one or more other countries o foreign persons. International stories did not involve the home country but instead reported about some internal matter in one foreign country or relations between two or more other countries, excluding the hom country.

News Topics

Nine major topic areas and numerous subtopics were coded as presen or absent from a story. If present, they were identified as either a majo or minor topic in the story. The nine areas and subtopics were a follows:

- accidents (defined as disasters of nature, transportation accidents, propert damage, injury and death, nonmilitary/noncriminal explosions, etc.)
- politics (electoral/congressional processes; executive actions, appointment. policies, requests; domestic meetings/relations; international diplomacy meetings, and relations; demonstrations and protests; criticism of government
- economy (industry, manufacturing; agriculture; trade and commerce [sales banking, loans]; labor union activities/issues)

- social welfare (social services and programs, population, and nutrition; formal subtopics of education, health, and infrastructure [communication and transportation])
- culture (art, religion, music, dance, etc.)
- sports
- science and technology (inventions, space travel, new developments in various fields)
- judicial crime (interpretations by courts, civil suits, and laws not political or economic in character; criminal trials, reporting of acts of crime, arrests, punishments, jails, and prison conditions)
- military (defense, intelligence, war, nuclear arms, guerrilla activities, terrorism)

Coders were also asked to identify which of the nine topics was the primary topic in the story. When it was difficult to choose a single topic, the first guideline was which topic took up most of the story text. If two or more topics were fairly evenly reported, the topic covered first in the story was selected.

Portrayals of the Home Country

In domestic and foreign stories that portrayed the country originating the newscast, the presence of six themes related to the home country were coded: population, health, food supply, violence, peace, and human rights. If a theme was present, coders noted whether it was mentioned in the context of problems, solutions, both problems and solutions, or neither.

Based on the topics and themes, coders made judgments about the portrayal of the home country, specifically about how the home country, political party in power, home economy, social welfare, technology, and military were shown. Specifically, coders indicated (a) whether the party or leader in power was shown as capable/correct (supported overwhelmingly, effective, in control, praised) or incapable/wrong (threatened to be overthrown, lame duck, ineffective, criticized) or neither; (b) whether the home economy was shown as strong (favorable balance of trade, sufficient revenue for budget, investments are domestic, minimal foreign debt, agriculture shown as productive, low inflation) or weak (negative trade balance, unbalanced budget, considerable foreign debt, agriculture failing, high inflation, widespread unemployment) or neither; (c) whether technological development in the home country was shown as strong (expanding, improving, accomplishing, progressing) or weak (cutbacks, stagnation, failed launches, etc.) or neither; (d) whether the home country was shown as actively developing social programs, receiving assistance, or neither and whether the home country social issues were shown as good, bad, improving, or getting worse; (e) whether the science or technology being covered was domestic (made in the home country) or foreign (imported from or invented in another country); and (f) whether the home military was shown as strong (military forces in large number, praised, new capabilities, successful battle or maneuvers) or weak (forces depleted, criticized, losses) or neither.

When the home country was shown interacting in some way with another country, that interaction was analyzed for themes of dependency, cooperation, conflict, and competition. Dependency occurred as a theme if (a) the home country was depicted as under the control or influence of another country in an economic, political, or cultural sense or (b) the home country was shown as controlling or influencing another country. Cooperation between the home country and another was coded if (a) aid was provided to the home country, (b) aid was provided by the home country, (c) countries were shown negotiating, or (d) the home country was shown acting together in accord with another. Conflict occurred if (a) the home country initiated a situation where their interests or actions were at odds with another, (b) another country initiated a conflict with the home country, (c) there was conflict but no clear initiator, or (d) there was conflict but the home country was not involved. Competition occurred when the home country competed with another (e.g., in sports, military, or economy).

Portrayal of Foreign Countries

All foreign countries mentioned in a news story were identified. A count was made of how many foreign countries proximate to the home country (from the same continent or adjacent) and how many OECD (Organization for Economic Cooperation and Development)/industrial, developing, and Eastern countries (based on World Bank classifications) were mentioned. In addition, a separate "country analysis form" was filled out for each country mentioned in a news story.

Reliability

Intercoder reliability was calculated on the basis of 18 coding forms across 3 randomly selected coders among the 13 coders. Depending on the repetition of each type of variable throughout the coding form, the percentage of intercoder agreement is based on anywhere from 18 to 810 comparisons.

The identification of topics as absent or present, story focus, specific foreign countries mentioned by proximity, and stage of development all reached at least 90% intercoder reliability. Identification of the presence or absence of the various themes achieved 85% reliability. Coder selection of a single primary topic had 80% agreement. Within major topic areas, the identification of presence or absence of each subtopic showed 70% or better reliability. Identification of whether themes were absent, shown in terms of problems or solutions or both also achieved 70% agreement. Coding of intercountry interactions yielded 66% agreement on whether or not dependency, cooperation, conflict, and competition occurred; this demonstrated agreement between two of three coders.

A total of 735 news stories across six evening newscasts for eight countries were coded; there were 908 mentions of a foreign country in the coded news stories.

RESULTS

First, the news values of the Western industrialized nations in the sample (the United States, West Germany, Italy, and Japan) will be compared with the socialist country (the USSR) and the Third-World countries (China, Columbia, and India). These news values are inferred from the detailed content analysis of the topics and themes portrayed in each country's news. The general notion of sensationalism in choice of topics is examined first.

Sensationalism

Some of the anticipated Western versus socialist and Third-World differences in coverage of sensational topics were found. Table 7.1 reports coverage of the major topics across countries. At least 20% of American, Italian, and Japanese news stories featured disasters or crime as the primary topic; West Germany, the USSR, and China had the least coverage of these issues (2% to 3%). Although military topics are also considered sensationalistic by many, military coverage did not show the same pattern. Japan had the most military coverage, followed by India, and the United States had the least.

TABLE 7.1 News Topics Covered

Topics	United States	Japan	West Germany	Italy	India	Colombia	China	USSR
Accidents/	13	9	2	6	7	8	3	0
disasters	(13)	(9)	(2)	(6)	(7)	(8)	(3)	(0)
Politics	30	31	35	35	39	25	35	40
	(54)	(56)	(60)	(56)	(65)	(57)	(66)	(58)
Economics	8	15	27	11	16	11	19	24
	(22)	(36)	(42)	(32)	(26)	(33)	(45)	(35)
Social issues	15	11	4	6	5	11	7	11
	(22)	(26)	(18)	(22)	(21)	(23)	(20)	(26)
Culture/arts	5	0	15	7	5	6	4	2
	(15)	(4)	(22)	(14)	(12)	(13)	(10)	(7)
Sports	5	0	6	11	10	25	8	7
	(5)	(0)	(6)	(11)	(10)	(30)	(8)	(7)
Crime	8	11	0	16	0	4	0	2
	(11)	(15)	(4)	(16)	(6)	(10)	(0)	(2)
Science/	3	2	4	0	2	1	10	3
technology	(7)	(9)	(8)	(2)	(6)	(8)	(18)	(21)
Military/	12	22	9	8	16	9	13	12
security	(12)	(44)	(20)	(23)	(33)	(27)	(26)	(28)
Based on all stories (*n* =)	60	55	55	83	87	118	166	111

NOTE: The first number for each topic is the percentage of stories for which each topic was deemed the primary topic. The numbers in parentheses are the percentage of stories that in some way mention each topic, in either a major or minor emphasis.

The converse of sensationalism was less clear. There were no clear patterns among groups of countries in coverage of economics, social issues, and culture/arts, except that socialist countries (USSR and China) covered science and technology the most.

In general, politics was consistently the featured or primary topic among all countries (25% to 40% of stories). Economics was second in several countries but not all (8% to 27%), followed perhaps by military issues (8% to 22%) and social issues (4% to 15%). Sports was a major topic in Colombian national news, and less so elsewhere.

Political Coverage

Table 7.2 describes political coverage in detail. "Sensational" political topics—demonstrations, protests, and criticisms of government—

TABLE 7.2 Portrayal of Political Topics (in percentages)

	United States	Japan	West Germany	Italy	India	Colombia	China	USSR
Subtopics								
Elections	34	13	21	23	9	18	6	17
Executive actions	41	36	55	47	68	79	50	53
Domestic relations	19	26	24	19	36	22	16	27
Relations/ diplomacy	25	45	52	32	21	27	57	47
Demonstrations/ protests	25	3	15	17	13	18	12	16
Criticism of government	38	29	18	17	13	31	12	27
Political stories (n =)	(32)	(31)	(33)	(47)	(56)	(67)	(109)	(64)
Themes (in portrayal of home country)								
Praise for government								
Program	2	0	3	0	2	1	5	4
Person/group	6	5	11	13	13	4	14	11
Home government	4	0	6	5	2	7	5	2
Foreign government	0	0	3	0	0	2	6	2
(n =)	(52)	(38)	(36)	(63)	(67)	(90)	(112)	(83)
Party in power shown as								
Capable	12	5	30	13	13	30	16	19
Wrong	24	15	10	7	8	13	0	0
Neither	40	25	10	39	67	11	27	11
Both	4	10	0	3	0	7	0	0
Interactions with other countries								
Cooperation	32	52	65	37	15	34	47	44
Dependency	9	0	13	4	10	6	2	3
Competition	27	10	6	19	10	31	6	31
Conflict	27	10	24	11	20	13	3	18
(n =)	(22)	(21)	(17)	(27)	(20)	(32)	(66)	(39)

were more widely covered on American news than elsewhere, although there was little pattern after that among First-, Second-, and Third-World countries. All countries covered political topics more than anything else.

As the "development journalism" pattern might lead one to expect, among political stories, Colombia (79%), India (68%), China (50%), and the USSR (53%) gave more coverage to government actions than any country save West Germany (55%). Criticism of the home and other governments was most prominent in the United States (38% of political stories), Colombia (31%), Japan (29%), and the USSR (27%) and least prominent in China (12%) and India (13%). Comparing Colombia on the one hand with China and India on the other shows some of the expected differences within Third-World countries on the amount of criticism of government expected in "development journalism." Praise for government progress or praise in general for home of foreign governments was seldom found anywhere; individual politicians were more likely singled out and praised. China most often covered politics with praise for people or programs (about 30% of political stories); Japan did so less often (5%).

The party or government in power was most often shown as wrong or incapable in the United States (24% of stories where the home government was mentioned), followed by Japan (15%), Colombia (13%), and West Germany (10%). The government was never shown as wrong in China or the Soviet Union. Although a developing country, China resembles the USSR more in the way government was treated in overall themes.

Fewer systematic differences emerged for story themes showing a government as right or capable: Colombia and West Germany were highest (30%) and Japan lowest (5%).

Political Interactions with Other Countries

Patterns of political interaction between the home country of the newscast and foreign countries seemed to reflect cultural differences rather than developmental or political approaches. The United States and the USSR were most often reported engaging in the most competition with other countries (27% to 31%). Colombia also reported high levels of competition—but 30% of their news stories dealt with sports, which is a very specialized and ritualistic form of competition. China and Japan showed a strong tendency to portray themselves as cooperating with other countries and as not competing, in conflict, or involved in dependent relationships. West Germany and the USSR also had very high proportions of cooperation portrayals. Excluding Colombian sports, the developing countries tended not to show themselves being in conflict or competition with other countries; however, the USSR evidenced competition more often.

Although Third-World countries might be expected to show more themes of dependency on other countries, this is not evident. No country

TABLE 7.3 Portrayal of Economic Topics (in percentages)

	United States	Japan	West Germany	Italy	India	Colombia	China	USSR
Subtopics								
Industry/								
manufacture	39	10	39	12	41	28	40	54
Agriculture	8	10	4	4	32	31	30	31
Trade/commerce	62	55	30	39	36	33	34	23
Labor unions	23	30	52	35	0	26	12	41
Economic stories								
(*n* =)	(13)	(20)	(23)	(26)	(22)	(39)	(73)	(39)
Themes (in portrayal of home country)								
Economic								
Problem	8	8	25	13	3	9	1	1
Solution	0	3	14	0	3	0	11	25
Both	0	5	8	5	3	4	4	4
Neither	0	0	0	2	3	4	9	4
(*n* =)	(52)	(38)	(36)	(63)	(67)	(90)	(112)	(83)
Home economy shown as								
Strong	8	0	6	0	10	0	15	53
Weak	23	13	28	18	10	21	0	3
Neither	54	33	44	50	60	29	43	16
Both	8	0	0	0	0	11	2	3
(*n* =)	(13)	(15)	(18)	(22)	(10)	(28)	(53)	(32)

showed dependency in its news stories with much frequency. West Germany covered dependency most (13% of interactions), the United States next, and Japan least (none).

Economic Coverage

Within economic topics, notable differences emerge between the interests or agenda of industrialized countries, as Table 7.3 shows. Most coverage went to trade/commerce (United States, 62%; Japan, 55%; Italy, 39%) and labor (West Germany, 52%). The USSR (54%), India (41%), and China (40%) gave the most coverage to industry/manufacturing; India, China, the United States, and West Germany all were close (range = 39% to 41%). Agriculture was covered most in India (32%), Colombia (31%), the USSR (31%), and China (30%).

TABLE 7.4 Portrayal of Social Welfare Topics (in percentages)

	United States	Japan	West Germany	Italy	India	Colombia	China	USSR
Subtopics								
Education	15	36	10	18	17	40	31	11
Health	46	29	40	41	50	33	28	21
Infrastructure	39	50	40	35	28	63	47	57
Based on social stories (*n* =)	(13)	(14)	(10)	(17)	(18)	(27)	(32)	(28)
Themes								
Population	6	0	3	0	2	1	2	1
Health	10	3	9	4	10	7	5	3
Food supply	0	3	0	4	7	3	11	2
Human rights	8	9	6	3	4	3	0	0
(*n* =)	(52)	(38)	(36)	(63)	(67)	(90)	(112)	(83)
Social issues shown as								
Good/improving	31	0	33	21	25	17	60	57
Bad/declining	30	25	0	21	25	39	4	0
(*n* =)	(13)	(8)	(6)	(14)	(12)	(23)	(25)	(21)

As predicted, socialist states were much more likely to cover economic solutions (USSR, 25%; China, 11%) than problems (1% each). Development journalism precepts seem less applicable as India reported both equally (3%). Colombia and the four developed nations reported more problems (8% to 25%) than solutions (0.14%). All industrialized countries showed more problems than solutions by more than two to one, reflecting a critical, even negative approach.

Similarly, the industrialized countries and Colombia showed their economies as weak far more often than strong. India showed both equally, and China and the USSR showed their economies as strong much more often.

Social Issues Coverage

As noted above, coverage of social issues was infrequent but fairly consistent across countries. Colombia and China focused most on general problems of infrastructure, as did Japan and the USSR, whereas the United States, Italy, and India focused most on health issues, as reported in Table 7.4. Colombia, China, and Japan also covered educational issues more than the others.

Some social issues themes discriminated more so between groups of countries. Human rights was a theme primarily for Western industrialized countries, appearing most often in Japan, the United States, and West Germany, slightly less in India, Italy, and Colombia, and not at all in China and the USSR. Food supply themes reflected a concern of some developing countries; China and India gave more coverage to the issue than did the others. Population issues were not major themes anywhere. These social issues were uniformly reported as improving in China, Germany, and the USSR, deteriorating in Japan and Colombia, and balanced in the other three nations.

Military Coverage

Overall attention to military topics did not discriminate much between groups of counties, although a breakdown by subtopics does. Terrorism is most frequently covered in the developing countries of Colombia and India. In this case, China is again more like the USSR, with little terrorism coverage. The industrial countries fall between these two extremes. On the other hand, nuclear arms received greatest coverage in the USSR and the industrialized United States and Japan, and not as much in Italy and West Germany, both NATO countries where antinuclear arms movements are active. Table 7.5 contains these findings.

Although theoretically one could treat coverage of current wars as a type of sensationalism, war coverage does not follow the predicted pattern for sensationalism. War received the most coverage in the United States, China, Japan, Italy, and the USSR—a broad mixture of countries. However, the developing countries of India and Colombia covered war the least. Another related aspect of sensationalism, coverage of violence, was very frequent only in India, likely due to events at the Golden Temple, a major national event not likely to be termed *sensationalism.*

No predicted differences were found for the depiction of a country's military forces as strong or weak. Very few instances of either portrayal occurred.

Science and Technology Coverage

One pattern emerged in coverage of science and technology (see Table 7.6). Only China and the USSR had more than a handful of stories about science and technology. Both clearly showed it as improving and domestically based.

TABLE 7.5 Portrayal of Military Topics (in percentages)

	United States	Japan	West Germany	Italy	India	Colombia	China	USSR
Subtopics								
Defense	42	38	27	10	18	25	19	30
War	75	58	36	40	29	16	64	40
Nuclear arms	25	33	18	10	4	13	10	37
Terrorism	33	21	36	30	54	66	19	13
Based on military								
stories ($n =$)	(12)	(24)	(11)	(20)	(28)	(32)	(42)	(30)
Themes (in portrayal of home country)								
Peace	12	3	17	3	16	11	11	19
Violence	10	5	3	6	33	13	3	1
($n =$)	(52)	(38)	(36)	(63)	(67)	(90)	(112)	(83)
Military shown as								
Strong	50	25	33	0	8	0	13	11
Weak	17	0	0	20	0	20	0	0
Neither	33	0	0	20	67	60	33	11
($n =$)	(6)	(4)	(3)	(5)	(12)	(5)	(15)	(9)

Complexity of News Stories

Each story was also rated as having a single major topic or multiple major topics. Western news was expected to evidence more single topic stories for unambiguous interpretation. In the United States and Italy, more than 80% of all stories had a single topic. In contrast, Japan had the most complex news, with 45% of its stories having multiple main topics. The developing countries each had about 70% single topic stories; the USSR approached American levels.

Coverage of Foreign Countries

One basic difference expected between Western and other news approaches would be in coverage given domestic (home country only) versus foreign (the home country and other countries reported) versus international stories (involving only other countries). West Germany, Italy, China, and the USSR showed a fairly even split across these three locations, as found in Table 7.7. The United States, India, and Colombia were much more focused on domestic events. The United States also

TABLE 7.6 Portrayal of Science and Technology (in percentages)

	United States	Japan	West Germany	Italy	India	Colombia	China	USSR
Where home country science/technology shown, it is								
Improving	75	0	100	0	67	50	81	71
Declining	0	0	0	0	0	13	0	0
Neither	0	100	0	33	33	13	8	12
Where science/technology shown, it is								
Domestic	50	100	0	0	0	29	54	59
Adopted	0	0	0	33	0	29	15	6
Unclear	50	0	100	66	100	42	31	35
($n =$)	(4)	(1)	(1)	(3)	(3)	(8)	(26)	(17)

notably gave least coverage to international events in which it was not an actor (15%). There were no systematic differences between other Western, socialist, and Third-World countries.

In terms of focus on countries far or near, West Germany, Italy, and the USSR were most focused on countries from the same continent, as shown in Table 7.8. The United States and India had the least focus on countries on the same continent. Similarly, West Germany and the USSR also covered neighboring countries more often. Something quite similar to the expected results occurred in respect to which groups of countries were covered most. Except for India, all countries covered the industrialized or OECD countries more than any others. The United States devoted the largest proportion of its foreign coverage to OECD countries. India covered other developing countries most, with China, Japan, and the United States following. The most attention to socialist countries was paid by the United States, the USSR, and West Germany. In no instance (including the USSR) did socialist countries comprise more than one fourth of all countries in the news. The developing countries of India, Colombia, and China covered socialist countries minimally. Developing countries composed 28% to 52% of all countries in the news, with India and China covering developing countries the most (43% to 52%), lending support to the notion that developing countries cover other developing countries most. The United States was by far the most frequently covered foreign country, across both individual country newscasts and in overall coverage figures.

TABLE 7.7 News Story Focus (in percentages)

	United States	Japan	West Germany	Italy	India	Colombia	China	USSR
Domestic stories	53	29	35	39	59	48	29	33
Foreign stories	32	40	31	33	12	30	33	34
International	15	31	35	29	30	22	38	32
Based on all stories ($n =$)	(60)	(55)	(55)	(83)	(87)	(118)	(166)	(111)

DISCUSSION

Perhaps the strongest impression that arises from this study is that the concept of "what is news" was in fact fairly consistent across these eight countries, which differ widely along many dimensions. Certainly their concepts of "what is a newscast" shared some sweeping common elements. Each had a national evening newscast of quite similar format: nightly, 20 to 40 minutes long, anchors plus reporters, news unitized into discrete stories. These similarities lend credence to the concern that news formats at least have been somewhat homogenized on the "Western" model.

There were sweeping, although sometimes deceptive, similarities in topics between countries. The most prominent topics in virtually all countries were politics, economics, military, and social issues. In general, dependency, human rights, science, crime, accidents, culture, and sports were not national news. News was not parochial: at least 40% of all stories in all countries referred to one or more foreign countries. Developing countries were not ignored and they did make news. Between 28% and 52% of all foreign countries mentioned in each country's newscasts referred to developing countries. This reinforces some of the conclusions by the International Association for Mass Communication Research study (Stevenson, 1984) that Third-World countries were not as neglected in world news media as some critics had feared. Similarly, this study also found that nearby countries were also covered more heavily, whether First, Second, or Third World.

Prior content analyses used to compare news values across countries have focused primarily on major topics. This study attempted to go beyond categorization of topics in earlier studies (Stevenson, 1984) to characterize how topics and themes were portrayed. Some success was

TABLE 7.8 Portrayal of Other Countries (in percentages)

	United States	Japan	West Germany	Italy	India	Colombia	China	USSR
From same continent	10	18	62	44	12	18	26	50
Adjacent to home country	8	9	20	10	0	7	10	17
OECD	39	52	47	55	44	65	51	43
Third World	36	38	28	28	52	31	43	31
Socialist	27	13	25	19	4	4	7	26
Based on number of newscasts mentioning one or more foreign countries ($n =$)	(28)	(36)	(35)	(50)	(34)	(58)	(117)	(72)

achieved in ascertaining treatments or directions, such as positive versus negative, successful versus failed, weak versus strong, or correct versus wrong (or contested).

Many findings are not surprising but are still worthwhile in what they verified. For instance, although an overall objective was to discriminate distinct approaches to news coverage by Western industrial, socialist, and Third-World countries, the clearest portrait was for the news approach of the two socialist countries. The Soviet and Chinese newscasts almost never criticized or portrayed their governments, militaries, or economies as weak and often praised their government and individuals for social contributions. In more novel but consistent findings, the Soviet and Chinese newscasts covered science and technology (in a positive light), whereas other countries did not. Economic solutions (not problems) were most commonly portrayed in the USSR and China. Strong patterns like these with their face validity supported the idea that the coding developed here has external validity in addition to the internal validity evidenced by intercoder reliabilities. Clearly the nature of Soviet coverage has changed after glasnost under Gorbachev (Mickiewicz, 1988) and may have changed in China. Still, for the period studied here, 1984, there was some consistency between predictions made on the basis of political philosophy and the actual content of television newscasts in the USSR and China.

Despite a relatively powerful coding scheme, only some of the expected consistencies in news coverage in Western industrial and Third-World countries emerged. The Third-World countries did show less conflict and competition than either the Western countries or the USSR. (In this regard, as in some others, China groups together with the Third-World countries more than the USSR.) Specific predictable interests emerged that unify Third-World countries, such as an emphasis on agriculture versus trade and commerce, with an additional tendency, at least in India and China, to also cover industry heavily. Food supply themes also are more prominent, although not so with some other themes expected from some written commentaries on the Third World, such population, dependency, and so forth. Although they cover the industrial countries quite heavily, Third-World countries do seem to cover each other as well. What they do not seem to cover extensively are the socialist countries. These are similar to results found by Stevenson and Shaw (1984).

What separates Third World India and Colombia from Third World China most is the tendency in China to avoid "negative" news and criticism, and to stress certain "positive" topics like science. Although widely attributed to "development journalism," the tendency to avoid negatives and criticism—and to stress the positive—seems in fact to characterize socialist news approaches more aptly. The differences between India and Colombia, on the one hand, and China, on the other, may also reveal a split among those within the Third World on their espousal of "development journalism," especially on the issue of government criticism, as the literature reviewed earlier suggests (Ogan & Fair, 1984).

The Western countries do in fact reveal somewhat more "sensationalism" in their choice of news topics, if the definition of what is sensational is limited to accidents, disasters, and crime. Although infrequently covered, human rights as a theme appears most in Western industrial countries, as expected from Western political values. Western economies and governments are more often criticized by their own newscasts, reflecting the watchdog role claimed by Western media. Western newscasts also tend to cover more of certain common economic interests in trade/commerce and industry and common security interests in their fairly extensive coverage of the USSR. Nevertheless, there are almost as many divergences among the four "Western" countries as commonalities. Major differences exist in patterns of political, economic, social, military, and cultural coverage, as well as in the pattern of covering foreign countries. Perhaps the differences within blocs of nations are as important for subsequent study as are the similarities with blocs, or the differences between blocs.

REFERENCES

Aggarwala, K. (1979, Spring). What is development news? *Journal of Communication, 29*(2), 181-182.

Atwood, L. E. (Ed.). (1982). *International perspectives on news.* Urbana: University of Illinois Press.

Boyd-Barrett, O. (1980). *The international news agencies.* Beverly Hills, CA: Sage.

Edelstein, S. (1982). *Comparative communication research.* Beverly Hills, CA: Sage.

Galtung, J., & Ruge, M. H. (1965, Spring). The structure of foreign news. *Journal of Peace Research, 2,* 64-69.

Hachten, W. (1981). *The world news prism: Changing media, changing ideologies.* Ames: Iowa State University Press.

Katz, E., & Wedell, G. (1977). *Broadcasting in the Third World.* Cambridge, MA: Harvard University Press.

Larson, J. F. (1979). International affairs coverage on U.S. network television. *Journal of Communication, 29*(2), 136-147.

Lent, A. (1977, September/October). A Third World news deal? Part one: The guiding light. *PS Index on Censorship, 6*(5), 17-26.

MacBride, S., and collegues. (1980). *Many voices, one world.* New York: UNESCO/UNIPUB.

Martin, L. (1983). *Comparative mass media systems.* New York: Longman.

McPhail, T. (1987). *Electronic colonialism: The future of international broadcasting and communication.* Newbury Park, CA: Sage.

Merrill, J. (1983). *Global journalism: A survey of the world's mass media.* New York: Longman.

Mickiewicz, E. (1981). *Media and the Russian public.* New York: Praeger.

Mickiewicz, E. (1988). *Split signals: Television and politics in the Soviet Union.* New York: Oxford University Press.

Nordenstreng, K. (1984, Winter). Bitter lessons: The world of the news study. *Journal of Communication, 34,* 138-142.

Ogan, C. (1982). Development journalism/communication: The status of the concept. *Gazette, 29,* 3-13.

Ogan, C., & Fair, J. (1984). A little good news: The treatment of development news in selected Third World newspapers. *Gazette, 33,* 173-191.

Paulu, B. (1974). *Radio and television broadcasting in Eastern Europe.* Minneapolis: University of Minnesota Press.

Schramm, W. (1959). *One day in the world's press.* Stanford, CA: Stanford University Press.

Schramm, W., & Atwood, E. (1981). *Circulation of news in the Third World: A study of Asia.* Hong Kong: Chinese University of Hong Kong Press.

Siebert, F., Peterson, T., & Schramm, W. (1956). *Four theories of the press.* Urbana: University of Illinois Press.

Stevenson, R. L., & Shaw, D. L. (1984). *Foreign news and the new world information order.* Ames: Iowa State University Press.

Sussman, L. (1977). *Mass news media and the Third World challenge.* Beverly Hills, CA: Sage.

UNESCO. (1985). *Foreign news in the media: International reporting in 29 countries* (Reports and Papers on Mass Communication). New York: Author.

8

Comprehension of Transitional Editing Conventions by African Tribal Villagers

RENÉE HOBBS ● RICHARD FROST ● *Babson College*

In a naturalistic field experiment, 40 subjects from the Pokot tribe of western Kenya participated in a study to determine the comprehensibility of two film and television editing conventions. Information about how to dip cattle to kill parasites was presented in four ways: (1) in narrative format wiht live storyteller and forward chronology; (2) in narrative format with live storyteller in reverse, flashback chronology; (3) in video format in forward chronology; and (4) in video format in reverse, flashback chronology. The substantive content was identical in all four treatment conditions. Subjects in all four treatment groups were equally skilled in understanding the basic elements of the narrative, including the ability to comprehend information that was presented nonsequentially.

Many people have heard anecdotes about what happens when people who have never seen film or television encounter it for the first time. Forsdale and Forsdale (1966) recount the experience of John Wilson, a British filmmaker who made a film about malaria to be shown to people who had never experienced film before. Although the film focused on the efforts of a sanitation worker to remove standing water from local areas to reduce the breeding areas for mosquitoes, the viewers claimed that the only thing they had seen in the film was a chicken. The authors suggest that perhaps the chicken in the corner of the screen was the only familiar object for the viewers.

In another familiar anecdote, the filmmaker John Humphrey found that "if you showed a fly . . . in close-up, and it filled the screen . . . [the

AUTHORS' NOTE: The authors would like to express grateful acknowledgment to Dr. John Stauffer and Arthur Davis who provided valuable field-work assistance. The authors also acknowledge the Babson College Board of Research, which provided financial support for this research. Address inquiries to Professor Hobbs, 213 Kriebel Hall, Babson College, Wellesley, Massachusetts 02157, (617) 239-4975.

audience would comment] 'We don't have flies that big' " (Forsdale & Forsdale, 1966, p. 612).

Although these anecdotes are provocative and amusing, they provide little insight on how people with no prior experience with the media of film or television make sense of what they have seen. If broadcasting is to be used to communicate about nutrition, health care, sanitation, and development, systematic efforts to examine the comprehension skills of television-naive viewers are essential.

Aggarwala (1978) explains why broadcast development news can be so useful in bridging the enormous gulf between the First World and the Third World: at the very least, such information serves as an agent of change by motivating individuals to seek out additional information. As a tool of technological modernization, broadcasting brings its own agenda, with its specific techniques of editing, particularly in the way narrative is structured, the manipulation of time and space, and the use of image-sound relationships to develop associations between ideas. The information provided by television has its own particular form and structure, and the extent to which this structure presents barriers to access is examined here.

Viewers process television images and sounds with the same cognitive apparatus they use in making sense of the rest of the world. Although traditional theorists of "media literacy" have noted that the skill of decoding film and television messages is a sophisticated one, most recognize that mental processing of these messages does not require formal training (Pearl, Bouthilet, & Lazar, 1982). Research with young children has suggested that some combination of developmental age and experience with the medium is necessary to successfully decode the complex array of cuts, zooms, pans, music, and other techniques commonly used in film and television editing (Abelman, 1990; Anderson, Lorch, Field, & Sanders, 1981; Lesser, 1974; Salomon, 1979).

The impact of such characteristics of the media of film and television, however, has been subject to much speculation (with considerably less empirical evidence), from the early psychologists at the turn of the century (Munsterberg, 1970) to communication theorist Marshall McLuhan (1964) to cognitive psychologist and communication scholars of the present day (Messaris, 1987; Salomon, 1979; Worth & Adair, 1972). The theoretical justification for the systematic empirical study of editing conventions and other formal characteristics of the media is its potential, over time, for shaping the cognitive and perceptual skills of the users (Salomon, 1979).

Recent research has attempted to examine the comprehensibility of different editing conventions by examining the reactions of adults who have never seen it before (Hobbs, Frost, Davis, & Stauffer, 1988). Previously, empirical studies of the comprehension of editing conventions or "formal features" of film and television have relied on the use of young children as subjects (Rice, Huston, & Wright, 1982; Salomon, 1979). Not surprisingly, young children fail to understand many common editing conventions, but researchers attribute the lack of skill in decoding both to the combination of children's developmental level and their lack of experience with the medium.

The use of adult subjects new to the experience of watching film or television allows researchers to separate the variables of developmental age from experience with the medium, a problem not possible to examine directly in the United States, where young children are routinely exposed to large amounts of viewing at a young age. Television-naive adults are a rare and rapidly diminishing group of people in a world where the rapid modernization of telecommunications technology brings video images to people in remote areas of the world. Such information could be useful in the design of televised messages for particular populations, including young children and people from Third-World nations who are receiving televised information for the first time. In addition, a better understanding of the natural strategies for processing audiovisual information could provide a valuable arena for further systematic exploration of visual-cognitive skills in general. Such evidence may help explain the communicative and persuasive power of the medium of television as it compares with other communication tools.

This chapter reports on a naturalistic field experiment conducted with a small sample of Pokot villagers in northwest Kenya with no experience with film or television. We compare the comprehension of a development message, presented within a familiar context, in both video and live storyteller formats. Because of the unique nature of the population (from a remote section of western Kenya) and the small sample size, this research is an exploratory examination of the comprehensibility of different presentational formats commonly used to edit television programming.

COMPREHENDING THE STRUCTURE
OF FILM AND TELEVISION

What types of intellectual activities are involved when viewers process audiovisual messages? There are at least three critical processes to the task of decoding televised messages. In examining the comprehension skills of people who have never before seen film or television, we must consider the intellectual demands involved in processing such information, which may pose challenges for the naive viewer. First, the visual and auditory information must be recognized as representations of actual objects and events. When we consider this skill from the point of view of traditional people of Africa, the people and events which appear as two-dimensional images on the face of a small rectangular box must be interpreted as representations of actual living persons and physical objects. Developmental evidence with children shows that American babies as young as 9 months will watch television in a way that suggests they recognize the people and events displayed (see Lesser, 1974, for review).

However, people from cultures that do not engage in two-dimensional representation (painting, photographs, representational drawing) frequently lack skills of pictorial representation as measured by conventional psychological tests (Deregowski, 1968a, 1968b). Although this skill is not universal, the recognition of two-dimensional images as representations of actual events that appear on a black-and-white television screen does not appear to be an obstacle to the Pokot villagers from the region under study, even though this cultural group does not engage in pictorial representation (Hobbs et al., 1988).

Film and television require a second level of processing that involves the decoding of symbols displayed on television that are non media-specific, symbols that are commonly understood by members of the culture, like language and gestures. The use of language, in particular, is a non media-specific code that must be decoded by viewers in order to understand the televised message (Rice et al., 1982). But when an off-camera narrator is used, where the viewer hears the voice of an authority without seeing the individual who is speaking, the skill of decoding and interpretation may become potentially more challenging. Other commonly used codes are non media-specific, particularly pictographic and gestural codes. Gestural codes are especially important on television due to the importance of physical action in many televised messages.

Some of these non media-specific codes have been found to dramatically influence children's attention and comprehension, with action, physical activity, changes in characters, and unusual sounds and music being the types of non media-specific codes that rank high in perceptual salience among young children, and even among adults (Anderson, 1981; Rice et al., 1982).

Research with adults with no experience with television has not yet determined whether the nonmedia specific codes used in televised messages are effectively comprehended, and whether or how nonmedia specific elements of the visual display are used as cues. However, in a study of the comprehensibility of point-of-view editing techniques it was found that most of the message was comprehensible to naive viewers (Hobbs et al., 1988). This may be a result of the relative ease in decoding the non media-specific codes, which included gestures, facial expressions, language, and action.

The third crucial process involves the ability to decode the symbols that are unique to film and television editing, the media-specific symbolic codes that are used to manipulate point-of-view, location in space, temporal sequence and order, pacing and rhythm, and specific visual effects including fades, dissolves, and wipes. These complex codes, which form the basic aesthetic building blocks of the media of film and television, are practically invisible to habitual viewers and have fascinated film and communication scholars for years (see Andrew, 1976, for review).

In examining the range of media-specific film and television editing conventions, it is valuable to identify a number of significant techniques, including point-of-view editing conventions, transitional editing conventions, and analogical editing. Point-of-view editing conventions are used to display different images within a single scene; shifts in camera position are used to bring the viewer into the scene by simulating the act of moving to a new position (Hobbs et al., 1988). For example, many film and television formats show in rapid succession a long shot, a medium shot, a close-up, a reaction shot, and other types of shots that manipulate perspective.

Transitional editing conventions are used for more complex manipulations of space and time, sometimes within a scene, but more frequently to make a transition from one scene to another (Messaris, 1982). For example, transitional editing can be used to show an inferred action, where the beginning and end of an action are shown visually, but some intervening action is edited out to compress time. A transitional edit can also be used to shift location, or to shift time (either forward or backward). Today, viewers of typical Western film and television programs are expected to infer from the message content whether a simple cut merely changes the physical location of the action, the time in which the action takes place, or both time and space.

Turim (1989) has examined the transitional film convention of the flashback and reviewed the extensive psychological and historical explorations of this technique in European, Japanese, and American filmmakers. Although the subject of discussion by film scholars, it is unclear whether such transitional editing conventions need to be "learned" by viewers or if they are immediately comprehensible by individuals who have never seen film or television. The research reported here attempts to address this issue.

Neilsen and Messaris (1989) have explored the comprehensibility of non-narrative editing conventions commonly found in television advertising. They found that American viewers were not particularly skilled in interpreting "analogical" editing techniques, editing that juxtaposes a product with an image where an analogy is implied between the product and the image. Viewers with television production backgrounds were more skilled in verbally describing the implied visual analogy, suggesting perhaps that some combination of experience and education is necessary to explicitly recognize the communicative meaning of analogical editing techniques.

Bellman and Jules-Rosette (1977) used informant-made video and film as a tool to examine cross-cultural differences in the production of mediated messages. As a contribution to image-based ethnography, their work found particular differences in how people in African tribal communities organized and structured their own video messages, their use of framing and composition, and their manipulation of time and space.

Bellman and Jules-Rosette found so many important differences in how Africans structured their own video messages compared with Western Hollywood production styles, they recommended that "if videotapes or films are to be used, a presentational format can be developed that has communication effectiveness for the particular cultural group" (p. 25).

COMPREHENSION AND PERCEPTUAL EXPERIENCE

Scholars have hypothesized that the comprehensibility of specific audiovisual techniques may be explained by examining their relationship to naturally occurring perceptual skills (Hobbs et al., 1988; Messaris, 1982, 1987; Munsterberg, 1970). Those editing conventions that bear an analogous relationship to normal perceptual processes may be easier to comprehend than those that are arbitrary conventions. "The extent to which the interpretation of any particular kind of editing requires a special set of skills . . . must depend on how much that kind of editin departs from everyday visual experience" (Messaris, 1982).

Visual inspection of the most common types of point-of-view editin techniques suggests that they appear to be similar to normal perceptua skills. The brain is well used to integrating multiple fragments of visua information to form a coherent scene; this is the essential work of visua information processing (National Conference on Visual Informatio Processing, 1974). The comprehension of point-of-view editing tech niques may mirror the natural process of perceptual experience, so tha viewers with no experience with audiovisual media are able to decod televised messages that fragment and manipulate point-of-view.

Previous research has found that naive television viewers were abl to decode a video treatment using point-of-view editing as easily as control group who viewed an unedited version with identical conten (Hobbs et al., 1988). This finding may be due to the analogous relation ship that exists between point-of-view editing techniques and naturall occurring perceptual skills. Point-of-view editing conventions simpl provide multiple perspectives of a visual scene; when the camera shift perspective, the visual effect resembles the act of physical movemer to gain a different view. When the camera shifts to enlarge an image (a in a close-up), the visual effect resembles the process of paying atten tion, a naturally occurring perceptual skill.

But not all film and television editing conventions may be analogue of perceptual experience. Unlike point-of-view editing, transitiona editing techniques may not be linked to basic perceptual skills, becaus the manipulation of time and space involves a rather complex array o inferences, which are highly dependent on the viewer's ability to inter pret the message content and context. Transitional editing convention frequently compress time, so that some events are not directly portraye in front of the camera, forcing the viewer to make an inference from th visual information provided about actions or events that took place i the interim. Transitional editing conventions may also compress tim in reverse by presenting the order of temporal sequence as in a flash back, using a visual representation of "memory" to show events in reverse chronological order.

The value of examining the comprehension of transitional editin conventions by viewers who have never seen film or television may b examined as we consider the relationship between particular editin conventions and perceptual processes. Communication scholars hav long noted that some film editing conventions appear to be similar t perceptual processes, visually resembling some natural, visual cognitive skills (Munsterberg, 1970; Salomon, 1977, 1979). Other editing conventions seem like arbitrary symbols, without any resemblance to perceptual experience. Arbitrary editing conventions, then, would demand that viewers learn the appropriate interpretation of the code through repeated experience with the medium.

If transitional editing techniques are arbitrary conventions then, as a result, they will not be easily comprehended by naive viewers, because they would need to be learned. We hypothesize that the transitional editing technique of sequential time manipulation may be more easily understood than the technique of reverse (flashback) chronology, because the former requires only the single cognitive skill of inference making, and the latter requires two decoding skills—that of inference making and the skill of reordering the visual information into a chronological sequence. It is important to examine the unique problems of conducting cross-cultural research to investigate such theoretical issues of the comprehensibility of film and television editing conventions.

CULTURAL ISSUES IN NATURALISTIC FIELD EXPERIMENTS

Because of the ubiquitous nature of film and television in the lives of most people from Western cultures, cross-cultural studies of the comprehensibility of film and television are necessary to examine the role of experience in our comprehension of the medium. It would be virtually impossible to obtain a sample of Western people who had never been exposed to film or television messages in order to examine their ability to decode commonly used editing conventions. As a result, cross-cultural methodology, despite its unique strengths and limitations as a research tool, is the only viable approach to permit the examination of the role of experience with the media as it relates to the skills of effective comprehension of the symbol systems of film and television.

Cross-cultural studies of communication skills, particularly in the field of print literacy, have been conducted to explore the complex relationships between culture and cognition (Bellman & Jules-Rosette, 1977; Scribner & Cole, 1981). As with the 100-year history of experimental psychology, of course, one of the most important difficulties in the design of such research has been in the construction of appropriate measures of intellectual functioning. Scribner and Cole point out some of the inherent weaknesses in using experimental methods with people from non-Western cultures, particularly the use of standardized test and questionnaires, because problems of validity are magnified when the research is conducted in a culture that is alien to the investigators

Anthropological research methods are occasionally employed in order to minimize the difficulties of measurement, by using less structure and directed measures, adapted to the individual, frequently employing open-ended questions. These methods are useful in overcoming the cultural differences that might be evident with more structured testing but such methods may be faulted for the difficulty in generalizing beyond the specific case. Scribner and Cole recommend that some combination of both methods of measuring performance provides check and balance on the individual deficiencies of each.

In the present study, we attempted to use more structured measure of comprehension and learning, because open-ended measures of performance had previously been successfully used to measure comprehension for a smaller sample of African tribal villagers (Hobbs et al 1988) and we expected that more structured measures of performance would yield even better data quality.

THE SAMPLE

Subjects were drawn from the Pokot of northwest Kenya. They were selected for study because they have been particularly isolated from any Western cultural influence. The nomadic, pastoral Pokot herd goats and sheep and are nonliterate. Only a small number of individuals have ever seen film or television, and they have no experience with formal education.

The Pokot use storytelling as an important form of cultural expression. Nearly everyone participates in the art, either as a storyteller or listener. Older children tell younger children stories that often involve animals. Sitting around the campfire at night, elders and warriors tell hunting tales of great bravery and daring. The Pokot have an intense rivalry with the Turkana tribe, who often invade Pokot territory to steal their cattle. Children listen with glee to hear of Turkana raids and the inevitable retaliation by the Pokot.

The Pokot do not use representational drawing in their decorations preferring instead geometrical shapes and lines for body decoration and jewelry.

OVERVIEW OF RESEARCH METHODOLOGY

Experimental research in the field is a daunting task, both for the complexity of the administration, the challenging physical conditions in a remote field setting, and the design and measurement problems that are unique to the setting and population. Conditions at the testing site were dry, dusty, and hot. The experiment was carried out during Kenya's dry season and temperatures during the middle of the day reached 90 degrees or more. The testing apparatus, including a color television monitor, generated by power from portable batteries, was set up in the shade of some trees near a watering hole where the Pokot brought their cattle.

Subjects were recruited near the watering hole after our field contact consulted with the elders in the community and offered them money and supplies. A translator worked with our field contact, translating from Pokot to English. Details of the construction of the treatment materials and the administration of measures are described below.

We examined two treatment variables and two medium variables to create a 2 × 2 factorial design for the experiment, which involved the presentation of a development message about the usefulness of using a cattle dip as a means to prevent the spread of disease and to ensure the health of the animals. We examined the impact of medium by using the conditions of videotape and live storytelling as the methods of presentation; we examined the presentational format by using either a sequential or reverse chronological (flashback) approach to presenting the story.

In each treatment condition, subjects were exposed to the stimulus in small groups of ten. Each group was composed of equal numbers of men and women. Specifically, in the live sequential condition, ten subjects listened to a storyteller present to them a story about a man who had problems with cattle and successfully used a cattle dip to improve the health of his herd. In the live flashback condition, ten subjects listened to the storyteller present the identical story, in reverse chronological order, beginning with the healthy herd and moving backward in time to learn of how the cows and herdsman came to such good fortune.

In both the video sequential and video flashback conditions, videotapes of the story of how cattle are dipped were created at the testing site using the Pokot people themselves for actors. Both videotaped versions used a combination of medium shots, close-ups, and long-shots to compress time and space. In the flashback version, fade-outs to black were used to suggest recall of events in the past. Dialogue was in the Pokot language and both videotapes were about four minutes in length and identical in verbal content to both storytelling (live) conditions.

It is worthwhile to note some of the technical difficulties of preparing such video materials in a remote field setting such as in Pokot country, hundreds of miles away from electricity, running water, or roads. Only a 1/2-inch VHS video camera and a 19-inch color monitor could be brought to the site, powered by a portable generator. As a result, both video presentations were created using in-camera editing, a procedure that is necessary when video editing equipment is unavailable. In-camera editing demands that each shot of the presentation is created in the order of the final sequence. For example, the first image to appear is shot first, then the next. This method is extremely time consuming and laborious, but it results in a videotape that appears to have been edited in a studio. Sixteen hours with camera, actors, sound testing, translators, and researchers resulted in two 3-minute videotapes, which served as two of the four treatment conditions.

RESEARCH PROCEDURE AND MEASURES

Forty subjects from among the 220,000 nomadic Pokot tribe were asked to participate in the study, the subjects evenly divided between genders. Subjects were asked some questions about their exposure to media and other demographic information, and completed Part A of the Raven Colored Progressive Matrices. We used this general nonverbal measure of intelligence to determine whether variations in intellectual ability were related to first-time comprehension of television. Part A of Raven's Matrices consists of 12 colored, multiple choice items. Each item consists of a pattern from which a piece is missing. Below the pattern are six choices, only one of which belongs in the pattern. This nonverbal test of intelligence is specifically designed to reduce dependence on acquired knowledge and keep cultural content to a minimum while calling upon reasoning skills. According to Jensen (1980), the Raven test is

> generally regarded as one of the most "culture-reduced" tests, being wholly nonverbal and expressly designed to reduce item dependence on acquired knowledge and cultural and scholastic content while getting at basic processes of intellectual ability. (p. 570)

Subjects assigned to the two live storyteller treatments simply listened to the storyteller in small groups. Subjects assigned to the two video treatments viewed the video presentations on a 12-inch television monitor.

After exposure to one of the four treatments, each subject was questioned individually to determine comprehension by responding to a series of seven questions involving the comprehension of the story elements, facts which were related to the action, dialogue, and narrative. For example, these questions inquired about subjects' ability to describe people and animals portrayed visually, to determine the chronological order of events, and to restate the verbally presented information about ticks, disease, and the cattle-dipping procedure. A question about the chronological order of events was used to determine whether subjects in the flashback conditions could appreciate the reversed presentation structure of the information. Specifically, three of the comprehension questions concerned information that was presented only verbally; three additional questions concerned information that was presented verbally with accompanying matched visual presentation of the message content (in the two video conditions); and one question required the identification and reordering of temporal sequence. Comprehension questions were designed so that it would be equally possible to answer them in all four treatment groups but required careful attention to elements of narrative structure, plot, characterization, and actions. Performance on these questions was used as the measure of comprehension.

Villagers were asked to report information about themselves, including their age and social status. Pokot men are differentiated into three status groups (elders, warriors, and headmen) that reflect their roles within the social group. Pokot women are differentiated by their marital status only. In addition, information about their exposure to elements of Western culture was also gathered, including their experience with radio, newspapers, photographs, and film.

To compensate the villagers for their participation in the study, the community was provided with the chemical liquid needed to create a cattle dip. In addition, small amounts of money were paid to those who participated in the experiment, including the elders, the participating subjects, the storyteller, and the actors who performed for the videotape presentation. But because this research was concerned primarily with examining the comprehensibility of editing conventions, no systematic measures of the value of the development message were undertaken.

TABLE 8.1 Mean Comprehension Scores by Medium and Treatment Conditions

Medium and Treatment	Comprehension	N
Storyteller sequential	6.6	10
Storyteller flashback	6.8	10
Video sequential	6.7	10
Video flashback	6.5	10
Treatment effect	$F(1,34) = 0.06$, $p = .80$ NS	
Medium effect	$F(1,34) = 0.21$, $p = .65$ NS	
Interaction medium and treatment	$F(1,34) = 1.16$, $p = .29$ NS	

RESEARCH RESULTS

When we examined the comprehension scores from the four treatment groups, we found no significant differences across the four treatment groups. As shown in Table 8.1, comprehension for all treatment groups was high, with no significant differences between those exposed to video treatments compared with those exposed to live storytellers. In addition, there were no significant differences between those who were presented information in a sequential order compared with those who were presented information in flashback temporal order.

Neither age, intelligence, nor social status was significantly related to scores on the learning and comprehension tests. We found that some of the variation in the learning and comprehension scores could be explained by differences in social status. Multiple regression analysis was used to determine the contribution of status to the learning and comprehension variables. Approximately 20% of the variance in the learning scores was explained by differences in status among the villagers (multiple $r = .44$, $r^2 = .194$). Similarly, about 16% of the variance in the comprehension scores is explained by differences in status (multiple $r = .39$, $r^2 = .152$).

In addition, differences in social status also explained some of the variance in the intelligence scores. About 19% of the variance in the intelligence quotient scores was explained by social status (multiple $r = .43$, $r^2 = .185$). Elders clearly outperformed warriors, headmen, and married and unmarried women in both learning, comprehension, and intelligence.

We found that the recency of exposure to radio and film was correlated with lower comprehension scores. Only 35% of the sample had any exposure to film, and in all cases, this was a single experience with a development film made by the Kenyan government and shown to a group in a nearby village. In contrast, 80% of the subjects had exposure to radio (also run by the government), with most claiming that on at least one occasion in their lifetime they had heard news programming, even though this programming is not spoken in the Pokot language. Correlations between exposure to radio and performance measures show that Pokot villagers who had more recent exposure to radio tended to have lower comprehension scores ($r = -.24$) $P > .10$. Subjects with more recent exposure to film tended to have lower comprehension scores ($r = -.34$) $P < .05$. This evidence suggests that the novelty of viewing television may have caused those subjects with less experience with the new medium to be more diligent and motivated than those who had seen a film or had heard radio recently.

DISCUSSION

In this study, we sought to examine the comprehension and learning skills of a small sample of African tribal people who had no prior exposure to the medium of television. In particular, we were interested in viewers' ability to decode messages presented through two different transitional editing conventions as compared with their ability to decode messages presented in two different traditional oral narrative forms.

The Pokot villagers showed high levels of ability in comprehending the basic elements of the televised narrative, including recall of information presented through verbal channels only, and information presented both verbally and visually. Most important, they demonstrated the ability to reconstruct the temporal order of a sequence of events that was presented in reverse chronological (flashback) order. We comment on both methodological and theoretical issues relevant to this study below.

Methodological Issues

The use of structured instead of open-ended measures of comprehension permitted us to compare subjects in four different treatment groups but may not have captured subtleties in the knowledge that the Pokot villagers possessed. Both structured and open-ended measures should be included in future research investigations of comprehension in cross-cultural settings. Because of the need to translate from Pokot to English, structured questions serve a valuable purpose by simplifying the work of the translator and minimizing interpretations based on translated data. With open-ended questions the translator has the challenging job of repeating back exactly what the subject speaks, but in structured questions, the translator and the researcher are aware that the only relevant issue is whether the subject's response was correct or incorrect. This expectation may increase generalizability of the accuracy of the data but may cause both the translator and researcher to overlook subtle elements of a subject's response that illuminate the quality of comprehension. Although relying on translation is a built-in weakness of this type of cross-cultural research, and although responses to open-ended comprehension questions suffer from lack of generalizability, it seems preferable to collect the closest representation of the subjects' responses by coding their direct responses to open-ended questions.

Design of the message to be communicated needs to include the Pokot elders themselves in a far more intimate fashion to ensure that the message is relevant and truly informative. We had expected that the message content of cattle dipping would be more intellectually challenging than a non-development message. Our field contact suggested the message content would be new information to the Pokot. Yet the Pokot proved to be familiar with the process of cattle dipping, even though none had actually observed the procedure.

We heed the advice of anthropologists on the practical difficulties of experimental fieldwork in Africa, as Scribner and Cole (1981) note the myriad of difficulties, from lack of roads, to lack of cooperation from the subjects, to lack of privacy in administering surveys—always unanticipated and unexpected problems that profoundly affect the research project. Beyond these practical problems, however, the most difficult to remove is the problem of the Western researcher's expectations and bias. Only a sustained length of time in the field, living with the population under study, can alter that critical obstacle.

Finally, there is a need to ensure that the measurement of intellectual functioning be more directly relevant to the skills and environment that are found within the culture. In particular, we found that the use of Raven's Progressive Matrices did not provide a useful measure of intelligence for the Pokot villagers in our sample. When observing the villagers' response to our questions, it was apparent through their nonverbal behavior that they felt quite competent in answering comprehension questions about the content of the televised message; in contrast, they seemed tentative and anxious in responding to the Raven's

Matrices. Cross-cultural psychologists have long suspected that the actual physical materials of commonly used Western measures of psychological functioning might bias the performance of non-Western peoples. For example, when Price-Williams (1962) used photographs of familiar animals for his study of the sorting and classification skills of children in Africa, he found higher levels of functioning for this task than when children were asked to sort abstract shapes like triangles, squares, and circles. Development of performance measures that integrate the basic elements of Pokot life will be an important goal for our future research.

Theoretical Issues

Despite the obstacles in conducting cross-cultural communication research, it is clear that even the rather complex structure of transitional editing conventions, with its reverse chronological order, presented no major difficulty to the comprehension skills of naive viewers. Subjects in all four treatment conditions were able to comprehend the basic elements of plot and action to gain information with a high level of competence, even though almost 70% of the subjects had never before seen film or television.

As we continue to see that naive viewers are able to decode editing conventions without any prior experience with the media of film or television, we have found that even with no experience, the existing cognitive and perceptual skills of the adult viewer are adequate for the task of extracting information from television programming that relies on transitional editing conventions to structure changes in time and space.

One future goal will be to determine which, if any, editing conventions are not easily comprehended by naive viewers, including the use of the blurry lens to convey dream states or the use of the subjective camera to suggest internal mental states, as when a shaky camera represents the perspective of a man with a hangover. In addition, there are a range of sound editing techniques that need to be explored for their comprehensibility to naive viewers, including the use of music to convey the mood states of characters and differences between the voice over of the unseen narrator as compared with on-screen authorities.

Based on the research conducted thus far, we believe that the content of the message serves as an aid to comprehension of different editing conventions. Perhaps viewers are able to use the familiarity of the message content as an aid to "leapfrog" past the more complex task of interpreting the editing conventions. For example, viewers may use the familiar sounds and images in the decoding process to interpret the meaning of a particular cut that alters the time and space of the setting. Future research should vary the familiarity of the message content presented to naive viewers. What happens to comprehension and learning skills when the images that appear on the screen are not familiar representations of events and activities in their normal environment? It may be useful to explore the impact of the familiarity of message content as it affects the ability to extract information from televised messages.

Using a cognitive information-processing model of comprehension, we can speculate on the role of villagers' experience with information presented in narrative story formats. Because storytelling is such a vital part of their culture, it is likely that the Pokot possess strong mental schema for the comprehension of narrative. Neilsen and Messaris (1989) found that the comprehension of non-narrative editing techniques was more challenging, therefore it is important to assess the extent to which familiarity with the narrative format interacts with the comprehension of different editing techniques.

CONCLUSION

Although the concept of media "literacy" has been a long-standing theme in the field of media studies, this research suggests that the process of decoding the audiovisual information that flickers across the screen bears little resemblance to the process of learning to read a printed text. Indeed, the very power of film and television to communicate to mass audiences comes from the fact that these media call upon ordinary and pre-existing perceptual and cognitive skills. Unlike print, viewers do not need to learn how to decode the messages. No experience with the medium is required.

Communication scholars might productively examine the non-Western editing conventions of film and television that are invented or discovered when Third-World people use film and video cameras for the first time, following in Worth's (1981) path to uncover the relationship between editing techniques, perceptual skills, and cultural values.

Hugo Munsterberg (1970), one of the first experimental psychologists at Harvard, posed a provocative question more than 75 years ago when he saw the new medium of film become such a central part of American culture in the first decade of the 20th century. Why do film images hold us and engross us in their world of imagination? Why do they seem so real? Could the study of film enlighten us about human perceptual processes? Munsterberg never states explicitly that film editing techniques like the close-up or the use of transitional editing are conventions that were created by a creative artist upon reflective examination of his own thought processes. But we marvel at the communicative power of the "language" of editing conventions, invented by Western filmmakers nearly 100 years ago, which are easily comprehensible by people halfway around the world who have never before apprehended the technology of communication. It is no wonder that McLuhan (1964) suggested that television would create a "global village," through the use of a communication tool that demands no special skills or knowledge to comprehend.

REFERENCES

Abelman, R. (1990, June 26). *You can't get there from here: Developmental differences in children's understanding of time-leaps on television.* Paper presented at the International Communication Association Conference, Dublin, Ireland.

Aggarwala, N. K. (1978, May-June). A Third World perspective on the news. *Freedom at Issue.*

Anderson, D. R., Lorch, E. P., Field, D. E., & Sanders, J. (1981). The effects of TV program comprehensibility on preschool children's visual attention to television. *Child Development, 52,* 151-157.

Andrew, D. (1976). *Major film theories.* New York: Oxford University Press.

Bellman, B. L., & Jules-Rossette, B. (1977). *A paradigm for looking: Cross-cultural research with visual media.* Norwood, NJ: Ablex.

Berry, J. W. (1969). Ecology and socialization as factors in figural assimilation and the resolution of binocular rivalry. *International Journal of Psychology, 4,* 271-280.

Cole, M., & Bruner, J. (1971). Cultural differences and inferences about psychological processes. *American Psychologist, 26,* 867-876.

Cole, M., Gay, J., & Glick, J. (1969, March). *Communication skills among the Kpelle of Liberia.* Paper presented at the Society for Research in Child Development, Santa Monica, CA.

Cole, M., & Scribner, S. (1974). *Culture and thought.* New York: John Wiley.

Deregowski, J. B. (1968a). Difficulties in pictorial depth perception in Africa. *British Journal of Psychology, 59,* 195-204.

Deregowski, J. B. (1968b). Pictorial recognition in subjects from a relatively pictureless environment. *African Social Research, 5,* 356-364.

Forsdale, J. R., & Forsdale, L. (1966). Film literacy. *Teacher's College Record, 67,* 608-617.

Foster, G. (1974). *Traditional societies and technological change* (2nd ed.). New York: Harper & Row.

Herskovits, M. (1965). Foreword. In F. Boas (Ed.), *The mind of primitive man* (rev. ed.). New York: Free Press.

Hobbs, R., & Frost, R. (1989, October 6). *Comprehending transitional editing conventions: No experience necessary?* Paper presented at the seventh International Conference on Culture and Communication, Philadelphia, PA.

Hobbs, R., Frost, R., Davis, A., & Stauffer, J. (1988). How first-time viewers comprehend editing conventions. *Journal of Communication, 38,* 50-60.

Hudson, W. (1962). Cultural problems in pictorial perception. *South African Journal of Science, 58,* 189-195.

Hudson, W. (1967). The study of the problem of pictorial perception among un-acculturated groups. *International Journal of Psychology, 2,* 89-107.

Jensen, A. (1980). *Bias in mental testing.* New York: Free Press.

Lesser, G. (1974). *Children and television.* New York: Viking.

McLuhan, M. (1964). *Understanding media: The extensions of man.* New York: McGraw-Hill.

Messaris, P. (1982). To what extent does one have to learn to interpret movies? In S. Thomas (Ed.), *Film/culture.* Metuchen, NJ: Scarecrow Press.

Messaris, P. (1987, November). *The role of "visual literacy" in film communication.* Paper presented to the Speech Communication Association Annual Meeting, Boston, MA.

Munsterberg, H. (1970). *The film: A psychological study.* New York: Dover. (Originally published as *The photoplay: A psychological study.* New York: Appleton, 1916.)

National Conference on Visual Information Processing. (1974). [Report to the National Institute of Education]. Washington, DC: Author.

Neilsen, K. O., & Messaris, P. (1989, October 6). *Viewers' interpretations of analogical editing.* Paper presented at the seventh International Conference on Culture and Communication, Philadelphia, PA.

Pearl, D., Bouthilet, L., & Lazar, J. (Eds.). (1982). *Television and behavior.* Washington, DC: U.S. Department of Health and Human Services.

Price-Williams, D. (1962). Abstract and concrete modes of classification in a primitive society. *British Journal of Educational Psychology, 32,* 50-61.

Rice, M., Huston, A., & Wright, J. (1982). The forms of television: Effects on children's attention, comprehension and social behavior. In D. Pearl, L. Bouthilet, & J. Lazar (Eds.), *Television and behavior. Vol. 2: Technical reviews.* Washington, DC: U.S. Department of Health and Human Services.

Riley, M. (1989). *Indigenous resources in Africa: Unexplored communication potential.* Paper presented to the International Communication Association, San Francisco, CA.

Rivers, W. (1901). Introduction and vision. In A. Haddon (Ed.), *Reports of the Cambridge Anthropological Expedition to the Torres Straits* (Vol. 2). Cambridge, England: University Press.

Rogers, E. (Ed.). (1976). *Communication and development: Critical perspectives.* Beverly Hills, CA: Sage.

Salomon, G. (1977). *The language of media and the cultivation of mental skills* (report of the Spencer Foundation). Chicago: Spencer Foundation.

Salomon, G. (1979). *The interaction of media, cognition and learning.* San Francisco: Jossey-Bass.

Schramm, W. (1964). *Mass media and national development.* Stanford, CA: Stanford University Press.

Scribner, S., & Cole, M. (1981). *The psychology of literacy.* Cambridge, MA: Harvard University Press.

Segall, M., Campbell, D., & Herskovits, M. (1966). *The influence of culture on visual perception.* Chicago: Merrill.

Turim, M. (1989). *Flashbacks in film: Memory and history.* New York: Routledge.

Witkin, H. (1967). A cognitive-style approach to cross-cultural research. *International Journal of Psychology, 2,* 233-250.

Wober, M. (1969). Distinguishing centri-cultural from cross-cultural tests and research. *Perceptual and Motor Skills, 28,* 488.

Wober, M. (1975). *Psychology in Africa.* London: International African Institute.

Worth, S. (1981). *Studying visual communication.* Philadelphia: University of Pennsylvania Press.

Worth, S., & Adiar, J. (1972). Navajo filmmakers. *American Anthropologist, 74,* 9-34.

9

Video and Cultural Identity
The Inuit Broadcasting
Corporation Experience

KATE MADDEN ● State University of New York, Geneseo

This chapter analyzes Inuit Broadcasting Corporation (IBC) attempts to create a culturally specific video network to strengthen the social, linguistic, and cultural fabric of Inuit life. IBC efforts to help sustain Inuit culture represent part of a larger Inuit political struggle to create a homeland from what is now Canada's Northwest Territories and to establish stronger bonds with the Inuit worldwide to create an Inuit voice in Arctic affairs. This geopolitical situation on Inuit-Canadian life provides the context to understand problems and possibilities inherent in IBC's communication efforts. This chapter focuses on a message analysis of selected videotaped texts produced from 1983 to 1985 to determine (a) cultural values portrayed in the texts, (b) their relationship to traditional Inuit values, and (c) the possibility of encoding an accurate representation of those values in the texts for creating and reinforcing cultural and political reflexivity to help advance the Inuit's struggle for survival as a distinct cultural identity. The study concludes that IBC has the potential for creating culturally specific video texts and affecting degrees of cultural and political reflexivity and may provide a model for other such efforts in the Third World and Third-World subcultures within the First World.

On January 11, 1982, the Inuit Broadcasting Corporation (IBC) began broadcasting regularly scheduled television programs designed to use video to help preserve the culture of the Inuit population spread across Canada's far north. It marked the first institutionalized step in an Inuit dream of developing a comprehensive communications system, linking their people through media that reflected distinctly Inuit values and provided an alternative vision to the ideology presented by Canadian

AUTHOR'S NOTE: Research for this chapter was supported in part by a Canadian Graduate Studies Programme Fellowship, which helped underwrite the author's dissertation, from which this chapter is derived. An earlier version of this chapter was presented at the International Communication Association conference in Dublin, June, 1990.

and American broadcast signals distributed throughout the Arctic by satellite. IBC's attempt to realize its dreams has potential ramifications for social policy issues that turn on questions of media imperialism and for aesthetic issues regarding the language of video.

IBC's creation from the 3-year Inukshuk experiment occurred in an era of acrimonious debate between First- and Third-World countries over economic development and information distribution framed in arguments about a New World Economic Order and a New World Information and Communication Order (NWICO). Its success or failure can be particularly instructive because it represented one of the first efforts to prove an underlying assumption of many of the NWICO's arguments—that unshackled by media imperialism, Third-World peoples could create culturally specific media.

The Background

The Inuit share cultural characteristics and historical circumstances with much of the Third World, as discussions of Inuit history make clear, implicitly or explicitly (Brody, 1983; Creery, n.d.; Crowe, 1974; Paine, 1977; Raine, 1980; Valentine & Vallee, 1968). Indeed, the Inuit represent a Third-World cultural component within the First-World setting of Canada. The Inuit and the Third World suffered colonialization for many of the same reasons—trade, resources, and establishing territorial dominance to safeguard their economic interests and insure national sovereignty.

When many Third-World countries achieved political independence in the late 1940s, 1950s, and 1960s, they embarked on major development efforts to transform their societies. They emulated the West's progress. With its help, many Third-World governments implemented what Everett Rogers (1976) came to call the dominant paradigm of development. That paradigm emphasized industrialization, capital intensive technology, and economic growth as the bootstraps by which the masses of underdeveloped populations would pull themselves up from what were essentially oral cultures into the electronic, postindustrial era (Lerner, 1958; Rogers, 1969, 1976).

During roughly the same period, the Canadian government initiated major development efforts in the North that paralleled those introduced to developing countries in many ways. Those efforts, too, were driven by concerns about resource development, national security, and ultimately, Inuit welfare (Crowe, 1974). Canadians moved Inuit wholesale from their hunting camps to newly created villages in an Arctic version of urbanization. The Ottawa government instituted a variety of medical and welfare programs. It initiated industrial projects. It stepped up efforts to educate Inuit, to move them into the modern era through literacy. That meant taking children to centralized schools in the Arctic where they were admonished against speaking or writing their language (Creery, n.d.).

By the late 1960s and early 1970s, Third-World nations and the Inuit felt the development efforts they had endured following the dominant paradigm had brought minimal benefits and substantial problems, among them cultural devastation. They sought redress from this perceived cultural and political economic devastation. Through what Rogers (1976) referred to as alternative paradigms of development, these new development efforts focused on self-reliance and greater equity in the distribution of wealth. They became integrated with the New World Economic Order and NWICO, concepts designed to provide greater economic and communication equity (Hedebro, 1982; UNESCO, 1981).

The Inuit, too, initiated action designed to meet those goals. The creation of the Inuit Broadcasting Corporation followed a 12-year period during which Inuit increasingly began to assert themselves in political and communication spheres. In quick succession in 1970, 1971, and 1972, Inuit founded the Committee of Original Peoples Entitlements (COPE), the Inuit Tapirisat of Canada (ITC) and the Northern Quebec Inuit Association (NQIA) to try to establish control over their own lives in the North. Inuit hoped to regain that control in part through creation of Nunavut ("the people's land"), a political entity carved from the Northwest Territories and governed primarily by Inuit.

But Inuit and many Third-World forces also realized that they could not obtain the cultural autonomy they wanted without controlling their own communications systems, because "communication is the symbolic process whereby reality is produced, maintained, repaired, and transformed" (Carey, 1989, p. 23).

Unlike some segments of the Third World, Inuit had had no control over their electronic communication. Television was introduced in the North the same way, for the same reasons, with the same amount of access, as radio had been in the 1920s—without any consultation with the Inuit (indeed, against their wishes), for white transients in the North, and with minimal access for Inuit (Marquand, 1983; Mayes, 1972). Television was introduced first in videotaped packages designed for the white transient populations who were mining mineral resources in 1967

(Cowan, 1970). Television signals spread throughout the North by the early 1970s via satellite distribution designed to improve communications in the South. Their proliferation was the final blow in what Inuit saw as the encroaching devastation of their culture, this time through media imperialism (Inuit Broadcasting Corporation, 1982, 1984; Inuit Tapirisat of Canada, 1975, 1976, 1980; Lauritzen, 1983; Northern Quebec Inuit Association, 1974; Valaskakis, 1983).

INUIT CULTURAL VALUES

The culture Inuit wanted to preserve is fundamentally different from Southern Canadian culture in significant ways (Briggs, 1970; Brody, 1983; Carpenter, 1973; Lange, 1978; Mick Mallon, personal interview, 1985; John McDonald [Head, Cultural and Linguistics Section, Department of Indian and Northern Affairs, Canada], personal interview, August, 1984; Paine, 1977; Raine, 1980). Part of its distinctiveness has to do with the different environmental factors that frame Inuit lives. The struggle for survival has always been a key to Inuit culture. To survive, Inuit needed to live with nature. They could not control it. That fact molded Inuit values.

But as Harold Innis (1977, 1986), Walter J. Ong (1980), Clifford Geertz (1973), and others would argue, another major part of that difference comes from the relative positions Southern Canadians and Inuit occupy on a continuum defining dominant communication technologies from oral to scribal, print, industrial, electronic, and postindustrial. Into the 1950s, and significantly today, Inuit culture is defined in large measure by its relative closeness to the oral tradition, Southern Canadian culture by its absorption of print, electronic, and postindustrial cultures.

A synthesis of the work of Ong (1980) and Carpenter (1973) illuminates the differences that can exist between Inuit and Southern Canadian culture. The Southern Canadian absorption of the values of print culture brings with it a stress on linearity, on cause and effect, and an emphasis on the future. Inuit closeness to orality fosters looking at things from multiple perspectives, an emphasis on creation as the revelation of natural form in life rather than the imposition of will onto something, a concern with tradition. Southern Canadians tend to see things as a series of separate actions; Inuit view them as a continuum of activities or impressions. Southern Canadians separate the functional and artistic; Inuit see them as one.

Southern Canadians are steeped in the democratic tradition of arriving at decisions through battles of conflicting ideas; Inuit value non-confrontational behavior and consensus building. Southern Canadians form coalitions that appoint leaders to speak for them as a group; the Inuit stress on personal autonomy fosters decentralized leadership, precluding any individual from claiming the right of decision-making power for anyone other than himself or herself.

This central concern Inuit have with personal autonomy means that no aspect of interpersonal relationships can be "taken for granted" and that any action "which would restrict an individual's sense of autonomy" is absolutely rejected (Lange, 1978, pp. 110, 107). Such an intense emphasis on respect for the individual necessitates a heightened sensitivity toward others that encourages reflexivity (Briggs, 1970, p. 67; Carpenter, 1973, p. 64). That respect and responsiveness is demonstrated in a reticence often present in Inuit interpersonal dealings and in a patience to wait for someone to express himself, in his time. Inuit "have an extremely strong sense of privacy with regard to their thoughts, their feelings and motivations" and "do not like to be asked questions" that they consider "boorish and silly" (Briggs, 1970, pp. 21, 3). Questions infringe on personal autonomy. "When you ask questions," an Alaskan Inuk told folklorist Margaret Yocum (1984), "you are the ones telling the stories."

The sensitivity, the reticence, the patience, and a certain comfort with silence contribute to "characteristic" Inuit indirection because "the meticulous honesty of Eskimos does not extend to the public expression of one's motivations, and it is common practice to phrase one's own wishes in terms of concern for others" (Briggs, 1970, p. 103; Mallon, 1985). But Inuit are not particularly solicitous of each other either and, lest it seem an insult, seldom adapt "their activities to the presence of a visitor" (Briggs, 1970, p. 26). If Inuit valued individuality and developed traits to secure it, they also have understood that it is impossible to survive alone. They have found a way to maintain their individuality within a framework that emphasizes cooperation and nonconfrontational behavior (Briggs, 1970; Lange, 1978).

Inuktitut, the Inuit language, incorporates and reinforces these values (Carpenter, 1973; Farrell, 1983; Gagne, 1968). It mitigates against the imposition of will on a person or object and thus bears a symbiotic relationship to the Inuit emphasis on personal autonomy and a reluctance to impose their will on each other and nature. It establishes/reinforces the Inuit emphasis on consensus and cooperation through a structure that stresses process and revelation of form rather than the imposition of will. Its ingredients and the nature of their use reflect a strong connection to the oral tradition in its emphasis on the simultaneity of the senses involved in message sending and reception, its predilection for concreteness, metaphor and repetition, and its interrelationship of times past and present (Ong, 1982).

Clearly Inuit and Southern Canadians have some fundamentally different approaches to life. And what Inuit saw on their television sets in the 1970s were Southern Canadian faces and values, not their own. They felt the need to rectify that, to try to use television "to strengthen the social, cultural, and linguistic fabric of Inuit life" (Inuit Broadcasting Corporation, 1982, p. ii).

Ultimately they were able to do that because of two factors. Canadians are particularly sensitive to concerns about retaining cultural identity, and Canada's media policy has reflected that (Babe, 1979). That policy has developed in reaction to what Canadians have felt to be a threat to their own cultural autonomy from American media that sweep across their southern border. Any argument against allowing Inuit an opportunity to use media to try to preserve their culture would be an ironic contradiction to its own philosophy. Additionally, the Canadian Broadcasting Corporation (CBC) Northern Service admitted that "We are largely a gross cultural intrusion on the people who were, in fact, the founding races of this country" (cited in Inuit Broadcasting Corporation, 1982, p. 10). CBC and the Canadian government regularly expressed its concern with the effect of southern television in the North (Canadian Broadcasting Corporation, 1982; Canadian Department of Indian Affairs and Northern Development, 1979; Canadian Minister of Communications, 1983).

Because of these factors, the Inuit were able to pressure the Canadian government for funds to develop their own broadcasting system. They honed their skills in an experimental project called *Inukshuk*. Success there led to IBC's founding. Introducing culturally specific media will not itself preserve Inuit culture, as IBC's Terry Rudden pointed out (personal communication, April, 1984). IBC productions could become nothing more than an audiovideo history of the last days of a dying people. If they are to be more than that, they need to help Inuit become aware of and utilize their ability to grab control of their own lives as individuals and a culture. IBC programs need to encourage reflexivity among the Inuit (Dahlgren, 1981; Myerhoff & Ruby, 1982), in the filmic (symbolic/media centered) sense that calls attention to the process of video making and the manipulation of reality it entails (Benson, 1984; Michaels, 1982), in the cultural sense of signaling and emphasizing the uniqueness of the culture, and in the political sense of helping Inuit understand and formulate alternatives to the dominant ideology in video produced by Southern Canadian and American culture distributed in the Arctic (Chaney, 1981; Dahlgren, 1981).

The film work that Sol Worth and John Adair did in 1966 with the Navajo demonstrated the possibility of producing specific filmic visions and being culturally reflexive (Worth & Adair, 1968). The National Film Board of Canada's Challenge for Change program, also in the 1960s, showed film could be put in the hands of people to be used for social change and be politically reflexive (Gwynn, 1983). But Worth and Adair and Challenge for Change operated without the structure imposed by the necessity of producing specific quantities of programs to air at a specific time. IBC is attempting to institutionalize the production of this culturally specific media.

WESTERN NEWS FORMS

What Peter Dahlgren (1981) argues about network news can be said of American and Canadian television generally; it "is a form of social knowledge, a way of defining and making sense of the world" (p. 101). That knowledge is conveyed through the interplay of what Barton and Gregg call conventional and organic story elements (1984). Conventional elements are predetermined forms and structures imposed on content; they are generally accepted ways of doing things. Organic aspects evolve naturally from the story's content.

News, the adage says, is history written on the wing, objectively reported and presented through neutral channels of communication. Its focus is predominantly on conflict (because conflict is deemed to be out of the ordinary in Western society). News is also timely. It is about events that have a geographical or psychological proximity to their audience, events that affect large numbers of people, events that occur to important or prominent people, or events that contain some element of human interest.

News is something the public has a right to know about—information that helps them lead their daily lives. Reporters, acting in the public's stead, try to ferret out that information by asking the time-honored journalistic questions of who, what, when, where, why, and how—repeatedly and specifically. The public's right to know supersedes privacy rights and any expectations of comity between reporters and news subjects because it allows/forces reporters to delve into personal lives. It forces camera people to hunt for "bang bang" shots and the extreme close-ups that create a sense of intimacy. It encourages an editing style that not only juxtaposes stories but often intercuts the viewpoints people express to create a sense of conflict (or at least disagreement).

These and other conventional aspects of news, Barton and Gregg (1984) suggest, create programs with a "dramatistic format, the personalizing of issues and the juxtaposition of news stories" (p. 134). Reporters, and particularly anchors, are established as necessary guides through this morass. News anchors serve as viewers' "point of access to the outside reality" (Nichols, 1981, p. 175). They are the ones who have direct eye contact with the viewers, who introduce stories briefly then turn to reporters to substantiate what they have said. Reporters, for their part, are shown to be on the spot with firsthand information, demonstrated by their visual appearance in front of an identifying place marker (such as the White House). Reporters, who are allowed some direct eye contact with viewers, summarize key points and extend the story by their own reporting, by interviewing witnesses and participants and/or by voice-overs on video serving as "images of illustration" (almost like graphic charts) for the story (p. 177). The actual participants in events, particularly those not being interviewed, often appear as the least important part of the story.

Building on these factors, Barton and Gregg (1984) suggest that the actual arrangement of spoken and visual text serves to develop a pattern of reporter/anchor predictions of news events that are then born out and reestablished through continuing newscasts. Given that, it should not be surprising to find that some critics argue that the interaction of these conventional and organic elements subordinates the reality of the world and the importance of the actors in it to the authority of television anchors and news organizations and that television news' "mediating levels" create a nonreflexive consciousness where individuals feel they need not—perhaps cannot—shape their world and so should subordinate themselves to official institutions (Barton & Gregg, 1984; Chaney, 1981; Dahlgren, 1981; Nichols, 1981).

That is not the message Inuit see as their vision of the world, as expressed by the values they hold important. Indeed, there is a fairly clear distinction between Western journalistic concepts and Inuit values. Adopting Western news traditions for its own shows would simply subvert basic values of Inuit culture. So how then have Inuit coped with this contradiction in values, particularly when they have learned much of their television and news techniques from Southern Canadians? Have they been able to create video that reflects Inuit values in content and style? And can IBC programs in espousing those values invite Inuit audiences to a reflexive posture vis-à-vis the larger Canadian society?

THE METHOD

The search for answers to those questions involved viewing more than 50 productions created between 1983 and 1985 in IBC's five program categories: news/current events, cultural programs—including the land series, information/public service, children's programs, and entertainment. Of these productions, 38 were examined in depth and on a shot-by-shot basis. One third were fully translated; others were translated in summary form; some needed no translation. Several programs were viewed in the presence of and/or discussed with the translator. Elements of the analysis were discussed with the program translator and various IBC administrative and production personnel.

The focus here is on two specific program types that represent seeming polarities of IBC style and that together accounted for approximately 58% of IBC's output during that period. *Qagik* is IBC's current events/news program. The land series consists of productions documenting life on the land. Looking at programs along a print/oral or Western/Inuit continuum, *Qagik* would fall at the print/Western end, the land series the oral/Inuit end.

This chapter is, at its heart, a rhetorical textual analysis. IBC was created out of a rhetorical exigency; it exists to affirm the efficacy of Inuit culture and to help strengthen it. This analysis takes place on three levels, extratextual, textual, and intertextual. The extratextual analysis is grounded in an extensive exploration of Inuit culture in the literature of Inuit, anthropologists, social scientists, communication scholars, and journalists, which was coupled with, and crosschecked through, personal communication with academics, government experts, IBC personnel (in Ottawa, Montreal, and in IBC's production headquarters in Iqaluit, the Northwest Territories), all designed to develop an understanding of Inuit values, IBC's purpose, and its approach to news and to video production generally. Salient aspects of that work have been reported here.

The extratextual work provided the context for a thorough textual analysis of IBC programs to identify the relationship between values espoused in IBC programs and Inuit values as articulated by Inuit and experts on them. For the textual analysis of these programs, the Inuit values discussed earlier were collected under three overarching Inuit cultural concerns: (a) the way authority is claimed, given, and assumed, which incorporates the central Inuit value of personal autonomy and concomitant concerns with patience, indirection, reticence in interpersonal relationships, and decentralized leadership; (b) the nature of the Inuit decision-making process, which subsumes the value Inuit place on consensus, process, and interconnectedness; and (c) the interwoven support for cooperation and concomitant rejection of confrontational behavior, which includes sharing and emotional control. IBC productions were then examined focusing on three separate but interrelated elements to determine whether they contained Inuit cultural values and, if the values were there, how they were presented: (a) the social interactions among Inuit and between Inuit and whites depicted within the programs and the settings within which they occurred (and the extent to which they reflected Inuit cultural characteristics); (b) the relationship of IBC reporters/interviewers to their Inuit subjects on camera (and the extent to which they modeled American/Southern Canadian information-gathering characteristics or deviated from them and adopted approaches consonant with Inuit cultural characteristics); and (c) the separate and interactive nature of the organic and conventional elements present in a programs' audiovideo mix (and the extent to which they reflected American/Southern Canadian presentational style or more Inuit-centered styles).

Examination of the intertextual level determined the existence of values and stylistic traits that extended across program categories.

THE ANALYSIS

Qagik: *The News/Public Affairs Program*

In the fall of 1984, *Qagik* ran Tuesdays and Fridays at 10 p.m. It reached approximately 70% of its Inuit audience (Valaskakis & Wilson, 1984, p. 58). New *Qagik* shows ran from October to May. During the summer, IBC produced one new show a week. Ten *Qagik* were examined in depth. The shows aired Oct. 20, 1983, and April 26, May 21, May 24, Nov. 19, Nov. 23, Nov. 26, Nov. 30, Dec. 3, and Dec. 7, 1984.

On the surface, *Qagik* bears similarities to Southern newscasts. It use
anchors, chromakeyed window inserts and keys. *Qagik* may, then, loc
Western. It even adheres to several characteristics applied to Souther
news—on its own terms. Programs focus on items of geographic c
psychological proximity to its audience (the Inuit and issues important t
them). Timeliness is a concern (but that can mean something that happe
within weeks, not minutes and hours). Significance plays a major role i
story selection (but what is significant can be the rescue of a snowy owl a
well as the Nunavut Constitutional Forum, alcoholism, or environmenta
issues. Visuals are important (but the style differs).

The differences between *Qagik* and standard CBC or CBS fare sta
with the translation of the world itself. *Qagik* means "coming togethe
in Inuiktitut. Its goal is to let Inuit share information about issue
important to them. *Qagik's* very title and purpose, then, encompas
Inuit values of personal autonomy, cooperation, consensus buildin;
and noncombative behavior. And they proscribe certain convention
Qagik will respect a person's autonomy by not doing a story about the
without their permission, and reporters work with interviewees in tel
ing the story. Personal autonomy takes precedence over the public
right to know. Reporters and subjects are not put in adversarial relatio
ships with each other.

Qagik will not cover stories dealing with trauma (something th.
could cause a family pain and invade their privacy) or direct confro
tation in the form of typical police blotter stories because they are see
as an intrusion on the individuals and families involved. Several yea
ago CBC radio in Labrador reported a family feud in which one membe
was killed. The reporting caused anguish and consternation within th
Inuit community, which felt CBC had intruded on them. IBC would n
run that type of story. Additionally, Rosemarie Kuptana, IBC's pres
dent in 1984-85, explained that IBC would not run a story showir
someone who has died for at least a year after the death because it coul
upset the person's family and community. (Traditionally, the name c
an Inuk who died was not spoken until it was passed on to a newbor
child.) Moreover, *Qagik* avoids stories that would embarrass someon
If its staff wants to deal with a controversial subject or a problem lik
alcohol abuse, they will hire people to act drunk rather than filmin
drunks. To do otherwise, an IBC official implied, would be unethica
There is almost no public "right to know" that overrides individu
privacy. Stories *Qagik* covers are about issues or events more tha
individual people; people in them may or may not be identified.

Inuit values also dictate specific roles for IBC anchors and reporters that are at variance with those in the Western/Southern Canadian tradition. Anchors and reporters are certainly present in news and current affairs programs like *Qagik*. But they are much less visible than in American/Southern Canadian productions, and their manner and presentation do not contain the conventions that pinpoint them as the focus of authority. *Qagik* "anchors," are more introducers/welcomers than anchors controlling the flow of a program. They do not summon and excuse reporters. They seldom use the 45-degree angle introduction or wrap to reporters and stories. They do also serve as reporters, suggesting a horizontal relationship with fellow workers. Their dress, introductory comments, and closing requests for viewer comments suggest an egalitarian relationship.

Reporters themselves are not singled out as authorities or interrogators. They are simply people asking people about a specific topic. They seldom use stand-ups in front of a site to establish their authority. They are often not visible parts of stories; when they are, their presence is less intrusive. They seldom have more camera eye contact than interviewees, which is minimal in both cases, possibly because direct eye contact might seem to assert authority over viewers.

The questions they ask are few in number (often one or two in a 10- to 20-minute period) and they express their viewpoints with minimal interruption. This is augmented by the lack of intercutting between people of opposing viewpoints or between anchors and interviewees. This lets the interviewee say what he wants in the way he wants to say it. It gives him as much control over the story as the reporter. It also allows viewers more autonomy to decide how to interpret what they see and hear.

It is, of course, this emphasis on personal autonomy that allows, even forces, the Inuit to operate by group consensus. A bridge from personal autonomy to group consensus is the lack of emphasis on establishing leaders in the Western sense. Personal autonomy cannot be preserved, consensus cannot be performed, if some one person is constantly being singled out as a leader and/or if that person tries to force his opinions on others.

People interviewed may certainly be official authority figures. Just as often they are "regular" Inuit considered knowledgeable—based on experience, not just titles. Even experts present themselves as regular Inuit, as one of the group sharing information and concern, not directing events. An Inuit Member of Parliament explains that "Since I am a member of Parliament, I'll try to help as much as I can, because I want

to have Nunavut [the quasi-independent Inuit province], too" (*Qagi*
Feb. 10, 1983).

Sharing suggests an exchange among two equal parties. To gi\
information or material goods or to profess to lead suggests a hierarch\
cal structure that violates personal autonomy and can constitute me\
dling (the giver may be providing something the recipient may n\
want—like the South providing television for the North; Briggs, 1970
Sharing invites cooperation.

Qagik itself shares information about itself and how its programs a\
made. One 20-second segment that opened many *Qagiks* in 1983-\
visually demonstrated how the program was created and transmitte
showing the process from a satellite in the night sky through the stud\
to Inuit being interviewed, combining the value of sharing with the Inu\
experiential learning tradition.

Qagik also shares autonomy with the audience and seeks their coo\
eration by actively recruiting Inuit opinions on a continuing and con\
munity-wide basis. Viewers regularly suggest story ideas to IBC pe\
sonnel in the field. *Qagik* ends with an invitation to its audience \
suggest story ideas, comment on stories seen, and raise any questio\
they would like answered. Developing consensus can also occur throug
monthly phone-in programs that allow callers to share information wi\
each other and panelists assembled to discuss important issues.

Moreover, by presenting program content and programming styl\
that respect personal autonomy and Inuit notions of leadership, IB\
creates the climate for consensus. Consensus building appears subtly \
Qagik in the audiovideo mix and in the program selection and dialogu
Virtually any *Qagik* that deals with a community issue, a meeting \
discuss Nunavut or housing in Baker Lake, or a festival event spen\
as much time providing a more inclusive visual rendering of communi\
activity at meetings and events as it does focusing on any individu\
"experts" who might be present and presenting information. There is \
consistent pattern of including large numbers of people in video\
showing young and old, interested and bored, men and women, aud\
ence as well as participants.

In addition, explicit controversy and conflict (in Southern term\
simply do not appear in *Qagik*. That does not mean that Inuit never ha\
conflict or that they do not reveal it. But they show it with subtlet\
indirection, and an eye toward consensus building. A non-Inuit has \
listen closely to even know there is disagreement over an issue. Th\
absence of confrontation, including intercutting of people with differe\

viewpoints, works to project an air of cohesion around issues. The absence of controversy and conflict, coupled with *Qagik's* reporters' nondirective, nonconfrontational approach (which lets interviewees express themselves fairly fully and viewers make their own assessments of what they have heard) establishes an atmosphere of conciliation that helps create consensus.

In all these respects then, *Qagik* demonstrates that IBC has managed to put together a news/current events show that espouses Inuit values. Its definition, organization, and structure promote the Inuit value of personal autonomy through sharing information in cooperative, non-combative, consensus-building ways. It does not copy American/Southern Canadian conventions. If anything, it sets those conventions on their ear, in the sense that the convention in *Qagik* seems to be allowing the organic to develop. *Qagik* then, is no clone of American/Southern Canadian productions. Indeed, *Qagik* might provide a cautionary tale to those quick to surmise that a program that looks Western on the surface necessarily espouses Western values or demonstrates the imprint of cultural imperialism.

The Land Series

If *Qagik* is the most "Western" of IBC programs, the land series programs are clearly Inuit-centered. They are perhaps the most self-consciously Inuit of IBC efforts. These programs were filmed over several years and in different locales. Yet they exhibit certain consistent characteristics of subject matter and style that suggest they constitute an IBC program genre. Those characteristics coalesce around subject matter, storytelling style, and the treatment of individuals and the environment in the four programs translated and discussed here.

The subject of the land series programs is Inuit life on the land—away from the village, the permanent settlement. The titles of translated programs evoke images of the life most traditional to the Inuit: "Clyde River Hunting Trip" (the quarry is seal), "Spring Fishing and Camping" (traveling to and from and activities at the campsite), "Kazan Summer" (fishing and caribou hunting), and "Floe Edge" (hunting and traveling). The themes are the naturalness of Inuit life on the land, the unity of Inuit with the land, and respect for the personal, physical, and animal environment. Two events appear to be important ingredients of this genre: the journey and skinning and butchering the harvested animal. Both serve important informational roles for the audience, providing experiential learning about living on the land. Both help delineate this form of Inuit video from Southern programs.

The land series programs all share a consistent storytelling style that displays characteristics consistent both with Inuit cultural values and distinctive features of oral culture. The story is told almost totally through visual elements shot in combinations of subjective and objective camera perspective, predominantly through primary movement. The land series pieces reveal the presence of a reporter/videographer only peripherally/organically. The reportorial perspective is simply not used. None of the pieces has narration. Dialogue is minimal (and what there is is often inaudible). Synchronous natural sound predominates. Music is used briefly in two pieces. Editing techniques vary somewhat between continuity and analytical sequential or sectional complexity editing. Violations of the 3:1 cutting ratio, which helps establish subject continuity, and of vector rules occur relatively frequently. The violations, however, serve to provide multiple perspectives on an object or scene, and that may explain their occurrence and the Inuit audience's apparent acceptance of them. The pace of the programs is slow by American and Southern Canadian standards. The average cut is around 27 seconds, but a 60-second cut is not infrequent.

Respect for personal autonomy in the land series surfaces in the relative lack of staging and interference with the people being filmed. In the land series, people go about their business as if the cameras were not there. They are not introduced, not named, not interrupted. People are allowed to keep their individuality intact, not forced to be actors for a story.

Individuals in the land series are often seen in relative isolation. They are frequently alone, or at most in small groups. Hunters, fishermen, and campers are generally working as individuals. They come together to harvest animals. They laugh and talk—but only minimally by Southern standards. They generally display little emotion or affection of the sort Southerners might expect, although it is there in the more reserved Inuit sense.

"Clyde River Hunting Trip," for instance, concentrates on the activities of one man seal hunting. "Spring Fishing and Camping" depicts less solitary activity. A number of residents of Igloolik are seen fishing and camping. But although more people are involved, they are still portrayed as relatively independent from each other. Large groups do not congregate except when ferried across water from one land strip to another. People walk in ones, twos, or threes. They gather around four ski-doos, help pack or move a boat; a family encircles a man cutting fish.

But often the shots, particularly close-ups, are of singular things—a man walking across the horizon, a boy running, a child licking her lips while reaching toward the camera, a child in back of mother's parka, a child picking berries. Animals and the environment are portrayed in much the same way; a singular dog rolls in the snow; a bird rests in the water.

In the land series, individuals appear in these videos almost as part of the environment. They are there like everything else—no less important, but no more important either. Inuit are seldom shot in close-up, although their hands may be. They are often shot from the side or behind; and it is often difficult to distinguish who is whom. Moreover, a video may follow several different people doing the same activity and present them as essentially a composite character. In these and other instances, the Inuit themselves receive no more (sometimes less) visual attention in terms of identifying visual close-ups than part of the environment—caribou or seal remains, birds, bird's eggs, fish.

The land series pieces are visibly egalitarian. The focus on cooperation in interpersonal relations is visually explicit, and the proscription against confrontational behavior implied, in the land series. Everyone shares equally in the activities. Cooperative behavior is routinely displayed—people helping each other harvest animals, move boats or three-wheelers or ski-doos, share food, and the like—they contain no visible conflict among the individuals portrayed in the land series. Moreover, a variety of people are featured, so the focus is seldom on one individual. Even when it is, it is the activity, not the person, that is the center of attention.

The elements that help retain the autonomy of the land series subjects do the same for audience members. They can insert themselves into a program and derive their own meaning from it rather than being told what to feel.

The land series videos work implicitly to create a consensus about what it means to be an Inuk and to reinforce traditional values. They do that by the production of programs with a consistent vision of how to live on the land and the pleasures of such a life. These programs create their implicit consensus by the repetition of themes and activities, within individual programs and across programs. The repetition reinforces the value of the activity. The absence of conflicting visions feeds into the creation of consensus by suggesting that they do not exist. These programs make their points almost totally through the visuals, natural sound, and asynchronous music. Dialogue and narration are nonexistent.

Moreover, there is no sense of conflict with the land. There is no need to overcome it, simply to live with it. "Spring Camping and Fishing" shows people working together to ferry people across water, a family eating fish together. "Kazan Summer" shows people helping with sledges, three young men kill and clean caribou, two older people kill and butcher caribou, eat around the fire, play cards. In "Clyde River Hunting Trip" the hunter throws a piece of seal back to the gulls in the water in what is a traditional sharing of the hunt with the animals.

In all of this, the land series invites viewers to experience life on the land and the values that sustain that life. Its existence speaks not only of contemporary Inuit relationship to the land. It also serves as a connecting link to the Inuit traditions and of the past, reinforcing them and demonstrating their relevance today. The land series demonstrates even more clearly than in *Qagik*, that organic form is an IBC convention in keeping with Inuit values and with the symbiotic relationship between those values and Inuktitut.

DISCUSSION

Qagik and the land series demonstrate that the IBC possesses the potential to create a culturally sensitive television broadcasting service that can help Inuit preserve their culture by helping promote cultural and political reflexivity. The content and style of IBC programs, even at seemingly opposite ends of a Western/Inuit or print/oral spectrum, clearly display basic Inuit values. A distinction between ends of such a continuum, then, is between programs more or less Inuit, not programs that are Inuit and those that are not.

Saying that IBC has the potential to help preserve Inuit culture by helping to create cultural and political reflexivity is not, however, saying that that potential will always be realized (audiences do not receive messages in uniform ways). Nor is it underestimating the very real obstacles IBC faces. IBC's culturally specific media will always be an alternative media. Southern Canadians in the North and the Inuit population generally have grown accustomed to television programming from the South. Inuit like portions of it as entertainment. They see CBC as a teacher of the aspects of Southern Canadian culture that they feel a need to understand—adapting aspects of the culture they feel useful, rejecting those they feel detrimental, finding an accommodation between both cultures' needs that will allow the Inuit to survive (Inuit

Tapirisat of Canada, 1980; *The Northerners,* 1974). Moreover, the cost of providing television services to the North is simply too high to be born by the Inuit population, even if, as the Canadian government suggests, IBC can develop and distribute programs there more cheaply than the CBC. Consequently, Inuit, will have to rely on the largess of the majority culture for support—political and financial. That can create difficulties even in a country that sees itself as a cultural mosaic and as particularly sensitive to concerns about cultural identity.

But IBC's ability "to strengthen the social, cultural and linguistic fabric of Inuit life . . . to teach, to entertain, and to inform with the images and languages of the North" (Inuit Broadcasting Corporation, 1982, p. ii) can help encourage cultural reflexivity, which helps sustain political reflexivity. Life for the Inuit, as for all cultures, is, of course, changing. The trick is for Inuit to be able to control and direct that change in a way that insures their survival on their terms. Rosemarie Kuptana, IBC president in 1984, is optimistic that can be done. "The Inuit people have always been surviving," Kuptana says (personal interviews, April 1984-April 1985). "The methodology for survival may have changed, but it's always there." Now that methodology includes television.

REFERENCES

Babe, R. E. (1979). *Canadian television broadcasting structure, performance and regulation.* Hull, Quebec: Canadian Government Publishing Center.

Barton, R. L., & Gregg, R. B. (1984). Middle East conflict as a TV news scenario: A formal analysis. In M. Medhurst & T. Benson (Eds.), *Rhetorical dimensions in media: A critical casebook* (pp. 33-46). Dubuque, IA: Kendall/Hunt.

Benson, T., & Anderson, C. (1984). Good! Great! Beautiful . . . and a little bitchier: The cultural world of Fred Wiseman's *Model.* Paper presented to the American Culture Association, Toronto.

Briggs, J. L. (1970). *Never in anger.* Cambridge, MA: Harvard University Press.

Brody, H. (1983). *The people's land* (rev. ed.). New York: Penguin.

Canadian Broadcasting Corporation. (1982). *Television in the Baffin region of Canada's Northwest Territories: A survey of viewing behavior and audience preferences among the Inuit of Cape Dorset and Pond Inlet.* Ottawa: Author.

Canadian Broadcasting Corporation. (1983). *The strategy of the CBC.* Ottawa: Author.

Canadian Department of Communications. (1983). *Toward a national broadcasting policy.* Ottawa: Author.

Canadian Department of Indian Affairs and Northern Development. (1979). *Ongoing and recently completed research studies concerned with the social implication of the development of communications systems in Northern Canada.* Ottawa: Author.

Canadian Minister of Communications, Minister of Indian and Northern Affairs, Secretary of State. (1983). *Northern broadcasting discussion paper.* Ottawa: Author.

Carey, J. (1989). A cultural approach to communication. In J. W. Carey (Ed.), *Communication as culture* (pp. 13-36). Winchester, MA: Unwin Hyman.

Carpenter, E. S. (1973). *Eskimo realities.* New York: Holt, Rinehart & Winston.

Chaney, D. (1981). Public opinion and social change: The social rhetoric of documentary and the concept of news. In E. Katz & T. Szecsko (Eds.), *Mass media and social change* (pp. 115-134). Beverly Hills, CA: Sage.

Creery, I. (n. d.). *The Inuit of Canada* (Report No. 60). London: Minority Rights Group.

Crowe, K. J. (1974). *A history of original peoples of Northern Canada.* Kingston, Ontario: Arctic Institute of North America.

Dahlgren, P. (1981). TV news and the suppression of reflexivity. In E. Katz & T. Szeckso (Eds.), *Mass media and social change* (pp. 101-114). Beverly Hills, CA: Sage.

Farrell, S. (1983). Literacy and the Canadian Inuit. In G. Valaskakis (Ed.), *Communication and the Canadian North* (pp. 1-21). Montreal: Department of Communication Studies, Concordia University.

Geertz, C. (1973). *The interpretation of cultures.* New York: Basic Books.

Gwynn, S. (1983). Citizens' communication in Canada. In B. Singer (Ed.), *Communications in Canadian society* (pp. 313-327). Don Mills, Ontario: Addison-Wesley.

Hedebro, G. (1982). *Communication and social change in developing nations.* Ames: Iowa State University Press.

Innis, H. A. (1977). *The bias of communication* (rev. ed.). Toronto: University of Toronto Press.

Inuit Broadcasting Corporation. (1982, Aug.). *Position on northern broadcasting.* Ottawa: Author.

Inuit Broadcasting Corporation. (1984, Nov.). *A research and development proposal for Inuit Children's Television.* Ottawa: Author.

Inuit Tapirisat of Canada. (1975). *Inuit today, 4,* 9.

Inuit Tapirisat of Canada. (1976). *Inuit today, 5,* 7. Special Communications Report. Ottowa: Author.

Inuit Tapirisat of Canada. (1980). *The Inukshuk project.* Ottawa: Author.

Lange, P. (1978). Some qualities of Inuit social interaction. In V. Valentine & F. Vallee (Eds.), *The White Arctic* (pp. 107-128). Toronto: McClelland & Stewart.

Lauritzen, P. (1979). *Oil and amulets.* Ottawa: Breakwater Books.

Lerner, D. (1958). *The passing of traditional society.* New York: Free Press.

Marquand, J. (1983). Inuit use of radio and television in Arctic Quebec. In G. Valaskakis (Ed.), *Communication and the Canadian North* (pp. 99-119). Montreal: Department of Communication, Concordia University.

Mayes, R. G. (1972). *Mass communication and Eskimo adaptation in the Canadian Arctic.* Unpublished master's thesis, McGill University, Montreal.

Michaels, E. (1982). How to look at us looking at the Yanomami look at us. In J. Ruby (Ed.), *A crack in the mirror* (pp. 133-148). Philadelphia: University of Pennsylvania Press.

Myerhoff, B., & Ruby, J. (1982). Introduction. In J. Ruby (Ed.), *A crack in the mirror* (pp. 1-38). Philadelphia: University of Pennsylvania Press.

Nichols, B. (1981). *Ideology and the image.* Bloomington: Indiana University Press.

Northern Quebec Inuit Association. (1974). *The Northerners.* Fort Chimo, Quebec: Manitou Community College.

Ong, W. J. (1982). *Orality and literacy*. New York: Metheun.

Paine, R. (Ed.). (1977). *The White Arctic: Anthropological essays on tutelage and ethnicity* (pp. 3-6, 7-28, 77-106). Toronto: University of Toronto Press.

Raine, D. F. (1980). *Pitseolak: A Canadian tragedy*. Edmonton, Alberta: Hurtig.

Rogers E. M. (1969). *Modernization among the peasants: The impact of communication*. New York: Holt, Rinehart & Winston.

Rogers, E. M. (Ed.). (1976). *Communication and development: Critical perspectives*. Beverly Hills, CA: Sage.

UNESCO (1981). *Many voices, one world*. London: Kogan Page.

Valaskakis, G. (1983). Communication and participatory development in the North: Inuit interactive experiments. In G. Valaskakis (Ed.), *Communication and the Canadian North*. Montreal: Department of Communication Studies, Concordia University.

Valaskakis, G., & Wilson, T. (1984). *The Inuit Broadcasting Corporation: A survey of viewing behavior and audience preferences among the Inuit of ten communities in the Baffin and Keewatin regions of the Northwest Territories*. Ottawa: Inuit Broadcasting Corporation.

Valentine, V. F., & Vallee, F. G. (Eds.). (1968). *Eskimo of the Canadian Arctic*. Toronto: McClelland & Stewart.

Vallee, F. G. (1978). The emerging northern mosaic. In D. Dlenday, H. Guindon, & A. Turowetz (Eds.), *Modernization and the Canadian state* (pp. 317-333). Toronto: MacMillan of Canada.

Ward, D. (1978). *CBC Northern Service oral submission to the CRTC hearings on CBC network licenses*. Ottawa: CRTC.

Worth, S., & Adair, J. (1972). *Through Navajo eyes*. Bloomington: Indian University Press.

Yocum, M. R. (1984, November). *Iluganag Katukgurak: The village-based Eskimo heritage program of Nome, Alaska*. Paper presented at Etudes Inuit Studies Conference, Montreal.

10

Parental Mediation of Children's Mass Media Behaviors in China, Japan, Korea, Taiwan, and the United States

BRADLEY S. GREENBERG ● LINLIN KU ●
HAIRONG LI ● *Michigan State University*

This study examines ways in which parents are reported to monitor, discuss, or mediate some of their children's mass media behaviors, for television, movies, and books. Original data were collected from more than 2,000 young people in Beijing, Tokyo, Seoul, and Taipei and compared with a parallel American sample. Cross-cultural results are offered within the context of prior parental mediation and parent-child interaction research. Alternative forms of mediation are examined, including coviewing, discussion, knowledge of the children's activities, and rule making. In addition to differences among the five countries, within-country differences are examined by gender, age of the youngster, and socioeconomic characteristics. Finally, mediation practices are predicted from a series of model testings, which include both media access and media usage factors and demographics.

Key among the findings are the consistent differences among countries with regard to parental mediation of television, movies and books. Within-country differences are notable for gender and for age, with females and younger offspring more likely the objects of parental involvement with their media experiences. The models tested show the preeminence of demographic characteristics in predicting mediation practices.

This study examines ways in which parents are reported to monitor, discuss, or otherwise mediate some of their children's mass media behaviors, principally for television, movies, and books. From original data collected from sixth and tenth graders in Beijing, Tokyo, Seoul, and Taipei, and compared with parallel American information, cross-cultural results are offered within the context of parental mediation and parent-child interaction practices.

Parental Mediation Practices

Thirty years ago, research showed that interaction rarely occurred in British families during television viewing (Himmelweit, Oppenheim, & Vince, 1958). Similar results were found in American television households, with no more than 20% of the parents mediating their children's viewing (Schramm, Lyle, & Parker, 1961). Much mediation takes the nonrestrictive form of coviewing and discussion (Abel, 1976; Brown & Linne, 1976), and actual viewing prohibitions are seldom practiced (Mohr, 1979). In a recent Taiwan study (Wu, 1985), only 15% of a sample of third through sixth graders said they often discussed what they saw on television with their parents. Studies have shown that parent-child coviewing facilitates the child's cognitive processing of television content (Atkin & Greenberg, 1977) and parental interpretation of television content enhances the child's learning processes (Desmond, Singer, Singer, Calam, & Colimore, 1985; Mohr, 1979).

Most evidence from Asia does not contradict this pattern. In Taiwan, Feng (1976) reported that one fourth of his third through sixth grade sample had no rules in their homes about television watching; one third said there were rules about how much time they could watch, and one third said their parents selected shows for them. Wu (1985) also interviewed third through sixth graders in Taiwan, and 60% said there were no specific rules in their homes about which children's shows could be watched. In a sample of sixth graders in Korea (Han, 1986), one half of a rural sample and two thirds of an urban sample indicated they could usually watch whatever they wanted on television; one fourth of the rural youngsters said their parents paid no attention to their television watching. In China, however, three fourths of a large high school sample said there were rules at home about how long they could watch television (Research Group on Adolescence and Television, 1984). In Japan, three fourths of an elementary school sample said they were told not to watch television until late at night, with two thirds indicating there were a few rules about television watching in their homes; in this sample, amount of viewing decreased as the number of rules increased (Mitsuya, 1988).

Parental involvement in monitoring or mediating their children's television viewing also declines with age. Several studies (Greenberg & Dominick, 1969; Lyle & Hoffman, 1972; McLeod, Atkin, & Chaffee, 1972) note that parental control over children's viewing behavior declines from early (12 to 13 years) to middle (15 to 16 years) adolescence. Mohr

(1979) found that parents of elementary-school-age children indicated more positive guidance (recommendations and use of media as reward) and negative guidance (disrecommendations and withholding media as punishment) than parents of seventh through ninth graders. Data from Taiwan (Feng, 1976) show that in the narrow area of show selection by parents, there was more reported by fifth and sixth graders than by third and fourth graders, an unexpected reversal of the age guidance pattern.

Parents also are more likely to make rules for girls than for boys (Gross & Walsh, 1980); Feng (1976) reports this same finding in Taiwan, and in Korea, boys were more likely than girls to say that their television viewing was not monitored by their parents (Han, 1986).

The level of perceived mediation may differ for various groups of parents and children. Parents have typically reported more viewing rules than their children (Greenberg, Ericson, & Vlahos, 1972), suggesting that parents typically face normative pressures to appear in control, whereas children often seek to be independent of such oversight. One study reported greater mediation by higher socioeconomic status families (Himmelweit & Swift, 1976), whereas another failed to show such differences (Gross & Walsh, 1980). The latter study also found that larger families are not as restrictive regarding controls over television viewing; having more children likely poses greater difficulties in supervising viewing among the siblings. In Taiwan, Wu (1985) found that fathers of higher education more often specified the time period their children in third through sixth grades could watch television and that these same fathers more likely had specific rules about which shows could be watched. Finally, family structure plays a role in media behavior; in the United States, Stanley (1986) and in Korea, Ko (1983) report that television viewing time is longer in one-parent than in two-parent families.

New video (e.g., cable and VCR) homes are more likely to have multiple television sets, including one personally controlled by a child viewer; this contributes to longer television viewing time (Brown, Bauman, Lentz, & Koch, 1987), which in turn is negatively related to parental supervision of viewing (Brown et al., 1987; Gross & Walsh, 1980). Small but consistent differences in mediation of viewing across VCR and non-VCR homes have been identified (Greenberg & Heeter, 1987; Kim, Baran, & Massey, 1988). Viewing of videotapes is no more likely to be used as a reward for VCR users than over-the-air viewing by children with access only to broadcast television (Kim et al., 1988). In their study of parental mediation and rulemaking among children with a home VCR, Lin and Atkin (1989) found that the two were highly correlated, and that both decreased as the child grew older.

From these studies, the common forms of mediation practices used by parents included talking about the medium's content with their offspring, being aware of what was being done with the medium, jointly sharing the media experience, guiding their children to certain content, guiding them away from other content, making rules about when and how often the medium could be used, and offering (or denying) access to the media as either reward or punishment. Here, we wish to determine how these forms may differ among countries. Mediation practices also varied by which medium was the object of interest, with television the primary target of study and little attention given to films or to books. When studied concurrently, we anticipate variation across media, as well as across countries.

It is expected further that mediation behaviors by parents are related to certain background characteristics of the child and the family; these include, but are not limited to, the child's gender and age, and the family's education and finance levels, as well as family size and family structure—all variables identified from this review of domestic and international findings.

Parent-Child Interaction Patterns

The more general phenomenon of parent-child interaction is related to the parent's mediation of the child's television behavior. A child's internalization of moral values is strongly influenced by parental practices and interactions. Studies show a relationship between parental disciplinary practices and internalized control of their children's social behavior (Hoffman & Saltzstein, 1967). Aronfreed (1961) and Hoffman (1975) identified two primary types of parent-child interaction related to social behavior—induction and sensitization. *Induction* refers to the use of reasoning to provide the cognitive structure within which the child can categorize their social experiences so that their behavior can be independent of external contingencies. *Sensitization* involves parental use of actual or implied power; the child refrains from doing certain things because of anticipation of external demands. Parents can use both induction and sensitization to influence the child's internalization of moral components (Hoffman & Saltzstein, 1967). In terms of children's television viewing behavior, parents using induction techniques are more likely to use nonrestrictive types of mediation (e.g., discussion), whereas sensitization techniques require the use of television viewing as a reward or punishment and a set of strict rules.

Parent-child interaction patterns in the Asian sites included in the present study are little discussed in English-language literature on the subject. In most prewar Japanese families, children under 7 years were raised with the least amount of discipline. From age 7, however, discipline suddenly became strict; occupational training was begun by requiring the child's help in work. Adolescents were trained to be hardworking and rank conscious; they would be physically punished for undesired behavior. According to a 1980s opinion poll, 69% of Japanese argued that strict discipline of children was necessary (Long, 1987). Contrary to the prewar period, many mothers have become solely responsible for childrearing and fathers less available as role models. In a study of the morality gap between the prewar and postwar generation in Japan, Lebra (1974) suggests that young people may resist traditional morality, although they are not alienated from moral values in general.

Here, parent-child interaction patterns are assumed to be reflected in the parents' interactions with their children about media use and are not otherwise assessed. A greater presence of strict rules than of talking about media content, for example, would identify stronger use of modes of sensitization than of induction. Again, the extent to which this occurs in different Asian sites, by comparison with the United States, provides the focus of these analyses.

METHODS

Data were collected in 1988 by researchers in China, Japan, Korea, Taiwan, and the United States.[1] Questionnaires were administered in classroom settings; usable questionnaires were available from 2,484 students. Among them, 554 were from China, 488 from Japan, 478 from Korea, 488 from Taiwan, and 476 from the United States.

Sample Characteristics

The total sample consisted of 53% males and 47% females. Half the respondents were in grade 6 and half were in grade 10. Their ages ranged from 10 to 18 years, concentrated at 11 (18%), 12 (23%), 15 (17%), and 16 (22%).

Respondents were asked which parents lived with them: 76% reported living with their original parents (mother and father); 7% said they lived with an original parent and a stepparent; 13% reported living with their mother only; 3% reported living with their father only. The following people also lived with the respondents: 62% cited brothers; 56% sisters; 23% grandparents; 12% cousins; 13% aunts; 12% uncles; 7% nephews; 5% nieces; and 14% reported living with others.

Respondents were asked about their parents' education. Among those who knew, 41% reported their father had a college degree; 22% said their mother had a college degree; 21% reported both their mother and father had college degrees. Those whose fathers and mothers both had jobs counted for 60% of the sample. Those whose fathers only had jobs constituted 32% and those whose mothers only had jobs accounted for 3%.

Dependent Variables

Parental mediation practices of children's media usage were measured with three sets of questions: (a) parental mediation of children's media usage, (b) family rules about media usage, and (c) access to media as reward or punishment.

Parental mediation of children's media usage was measured for four different media. Six questions that focused on television, movies, and VCR usage all had the same format: How often they watched television (saw a movie or watched videotapes) with a parent; talked about the shows (movies, videotapes) they had watched with a parent; a parent knew what they were watching (what they went to see); a parent recommended some show (movie, videotape) for them to watch; and a parent told them not to watch some show (movie, videotape); a parent told them that they watched too much television (went to too many movies, spent too time watching videotapes). Five questions were about book usage: How often a parent knew what books they read; they talked with a parent about a book they read; a parent recommended a book to them; a parent told them not to read some book; and a parent told them that they read nonschool books too much. Response categories for all mediation items were *never, sometimes, often,* and *very often.*

The subset of mediation items for each medium was averaged into a cumulative index. A second set of mediation indices was created by averaging the same form of parental mediation across television, movies, and books (e.g., averaging the three items that asked about talking about media content, averaging the three items that asked about parental knowledge of their media activity, and so on). Thus, there were indices for six forms of mediation: co-viewing (excluding books), discussion, knowledge of activity, recommendations, disrecommendations, and excessive use. Parental involvement in mediating VCR usage was not included in the by-form indices because the VCR respondents were only 56% of the sample.

Family rules about media usage were measured by asking if there were rules at their home about: How many hours and how late they could watch television on school days; how late they could watch television on weekends; what kinds of shows they could watch on television; how often they could go to movies each week; what kind of movies they could go to; what kind of videotapes they could watch; how often they could watch videotapes in a week; and how late they could watch videotapes on school nights. For these questions, the response categories were *yes, sometimes,* or *no.*

Two rules indices were created: the first averaged the four television and two movie rules items regarding amount of use of television and movies; the second averaged the two items that dealt with rules about the content of television and movies. The index for VCR rules was created by averaging the three VCR rule items.

Access to media as reward or punishment was assessed by determining if in the last 4 weeks, a parent had let them watch television as a reward, or forbidden them to watch television as a punishment; if a parent had let them go to movies as a reward, or forbidden them to go out to movies as a punishment; and if a parent had let them watch videotapes as a reward, or forbidden them to watch videotapes as a punishment. The response categories for these questions were *yes* or *no.* The reward and punishment indices were created by summing the comparable mediation items across television and movies. VCR reward and punishment were handled separately for the subset of VCR homes.

Independent Variables

Independent variables encompassed six media-related areas: access to media, media usage, media credibility, media dependency, media gratifications, and demographic variables.

Access to media was measured by asking the respondents if they had their own personal television (yes or no), and how many color and black and white television sets were at their home (0 to 6+). The total number of sets was cumulated.

Media usage was measured by asking how many hours yesterday they watched television for three parts of the day—in the morning before school, after school but before supper, and after supper until they went to sleep (0 to 3+ hours). These were summed into an index and standardized within each country.[2] They also were asked how many times they went out to the movies in the last four weeks (0 to 6+ times) and how many hours yesterday they spent reading books for fun (0 to 3+ hours).

Media credibility was based on eight questions: How much they believed the news they found in television, radio, newspapers, or magazines (very little, little, much, very much). The respondents were also asked how much they believed the advertising they found in newspapers, magazines, television and radio (very little, little, much, very much). Answers to the eight questions were averaged to provide an overall index of media credibility.

Media dependency was measured by asking which news source they depended on most for news about what's happening in the world—television, radio, newspaper or magazine, and if they received different information from the newspaper, television, radio, or a magazine, which one they believed the most. These were then recorded as television or not television and summed into an index.

Gratifications with various media were measured by asking which among television, movies, and books was the best when they wanted to relax, to pass time, to learn about life, to forget about problems, to learn about themselves, to get away from what they're doing, to feel less lonely, to calm down, and to learn how to handle their problems, and which was best for company, today's news, excitement, entertainment, something to do, some thrills, and some fun. Indices were formed for each medium—the number of times television, movies and books were chosen as the single best source of gratification.

Demography included gender, age (grade in school), self-estimates of their school grades, father's education, family size, family structure, and socioeconomic status.

Schoolwork was measured by asking the respondents to judge their school grades as above average, average, or below average.

Father's education was categorized at three levels: low (eighth grade or lower), medium (part or all of high school), and high (part or all of college).

Family size was categorized as small family (two or fewer family members), medium family (three to four), and large family (five or more).

Family structure was categorized as two-parent family and single-parent family. Respondents living with no parent were very few and were not included in the analyses.

Socioeconomic status was based on different measurements in different countries. Questions about number of bedrooms, bathrooms, and cars were asked in Korea, Japan, Taiwan, and the United States. Questions about how many rooms and if the respondents had washing machines and refrigerators at their home were asked in China. All responses were standardized for each question within each country and then summed to create the socioeconomic status measure. The index was divided into thirds to create high, medium, and low status clusters.

RESULTS

This examination of parental mediation practices in five countries will present the following analyses: (a) a cross-country comparison by medium for television, movies, books, and VCR mediation, and by form of mediation; (b) within-country differences in mediation by gender, age, education of father, family size, family structure, socioeconomic status, and the quality of the child's schoolwork; and (c) the testing of multivariate models predicting the different mediation practices.

Cross-Country Comparisons

Table 10.1 examines mediation among the five countries. By medium, the most active mediation occurs with television in all countries. The absolute level of mediation for television, however, is not high; the typical response from the young people for the index of television mediation (parents knowing what they're doing, talking about it, doing it with them, etc.) yielded an average response between "sometimes" and "often." For all the remaining indices by medium, the average response was between "sometimes" and "never." In most instances, the mediation of movie behaviors and the existence of movie rules provided the lowest levels of mediation.

The highest levels of television mediation were found in Korea and Taiwan, and the lowest was reported by the Japanese youngsters. The highest frequency of television rules was reported from China and the lowest from Japan. The mediation of moviegoing, by contrast, was highest within the American sample and lowest in Japan. Rules about going to the movies was highest in China as was the mediation of book reading; for both of these, it was consistently Japan where the least parental oversight was reported. Thus, it was Japan where, for all three

TABLE 10.1 Comparisons of Mediation Practices Across Countries[1]

	China (N = 543)	Japan (N = 494)	Korea (N = 495)	Taiwan (N = 473)	U.S. (N = 477)
By medium					
TV mediation[2]	2.18[a]	2.04[d]	2.30[bc]	2.33[c]	2.21[ab]
TV rules[4]	2.07[c]	1.40[b]	1.87[d]	1.71[a]	1.67[a]
Movie mediation[2]	1.78[a]	1.53[c]	1.65[d]	1.75[a]	1.90[b]
Movie rules[4]	1.84[c]	1.31[b]	1.68[a]	1.55[a]	1.62[a]
Book mediation[2]	2.03[c]	1.64[a]	1.89[b]	1.82[b]	1.66[a]
By form of mediation[2]					
Co-view	2.24[b]	2.13[a]	2.01[d]	2.21[ab]	2.38[c]
Discuss	1.96[d]	1.56[a]	1.84[c]	1.70[b]	2.10[e]
Knowledge	2.69[c]	2.44[a]	2.48[ab]	2.53[ab]	2.60[bc]
Recommend	1.90[b]	1.55[c]	1.89[ab]	1.78[a]	1.77[a]
Disrecommend	1.73[b]	1.43[a]	1.80[b]	1.95[c]	1.51[a]
Excessive use	1.54[b]	1.48[ab]	1.69[c]	1.75[c]	1.41[a]
Reward[3]	.10[a]	.17[b]	.30[c]	.10[a]	.19[b]
Punishment[3]	.09[ab]	.06[a]	.28[d]	.15[c]	.12[bc]
Rules/use[4]	2.04[c]	1.41[b]	1.72[a]	1.66[a]	1.64[a]
Rules/content[4]	1.89[b]	1.30[c]	1.97[b]	1.64[a]	1.67[a]
VCR	(N = 97)	(N = 375)	(N = 195)	(N = 332)	(N = 387)
VCR mediation[2]	1.92[bc]	1.67[a]	1.77[ab]	2.03[cd]	2.12[d]
VCR reward[3]	.05[a]	.20[bc]	.17[abc]	.12[ab]	.24[c]
VCR punishment[3]	.03[ac]	.04[a]	.16[ab]	.10[bcd]	.06[d]
VCR rules[4]	2.13[c]	1.25[b]	1.70[a]	1.73[a]	1.73[a]

NOTES: 1. Means with the same superscripts are not significantly different from each other. All row comparisons (across countries) are $p < .01$.
2. The index scale is 1 = never, 2 = sometimes, 3 = often, 4 = very often.
3. The index scale is 0 = no, 1 = yes.
4. The index scale is 1 = no, 2 = sometimes, 3 = yes.

media, the lowest levels of parent involvement were reported for all indices. The highest levels varied among countries by medium.

By form of mediation, the most common activity reported in all countries was knowledge of what the young person was doing with the medium, averaging 2.5 on the 4-point scale used. Co-viewing also was reported with considerable regularity. Occurring most infrequently were admonishments of excessive media use and recommendations against specific content choices.

Knowledge or awareness occurred similarly across the countries, but somewhat more often in China. And the Chinese surpassed all others in making content recommendations. Co-viewing and discussion of media content were reported most often in the American sample and least often in Japan. Japanese parents also made positive and negative recommendations least often, matched by the American in the latter; the Taiwan sample was particularly strong in reporting that their parents recommended against specific content choices. The Taiwan and Korean youngsters most often indicated that their parents warned them about excessive media use.

Access to media as reward or punishment was rarely found, except in Korea. In no other country was it reported by as much as one fifth of the sample, but in Korea, 30% said they were rewarded and 28% said they were punished in this manner.

In China, there were the most rules about media use, and in China and Korea, the most rules about media content; for both rules indices, the Japanese reported fewest rules.

Parent involvement in VCR behaviors is also reported in Table 10.1, among the subsamples possessing video recorders in their homes. The index of VCR mediation shows the most activity in American and Taiwan homes, and the most VCR rules in Chinese homes; for both, the Japanese parents are reported as least active. Access to the VCR as a reward mechanism most often occurs in American and Japanese homes; VCR punishment is very rare.

Demographic Comparisons

Analyses paralleling those presented in Table 10.1 were completed within each country, looking for differences in mediation practices by gender, age, education of father, family size, family structure, socioeconomic status, and the quality of the child's schoolwork. Space does not permit presenting each of the seven tables that resulted from these analyses; Table 10.2 is an example, and the remainder are available from the senior author.

Age

Grade in school was used as a surrogate of age, and Table 10.2 presents the mediation practices reported by sixth and tenth graders in each of the five countries studied. By medium, without exception, each index of mediation indicates significantly greater parent activity among the younger group than the older, and this is the finding in each country. By form of mediation, there is more co-viewing, more discussion and

	China		Japan		Korea		Taiwan		United States	
	6 (269)	10 (274)	6 (235)	10 (245)	6 (247)	10 (245)	6 (230)	10 (242)	6 (240)	10 (218)
By medium										
TV mediation	2.23	2.13*	2.11	1.97*	2.38	2.21*	2.44	2.22*	2.35	2.06*
TV rules	2.22	1.92*	1.60	1.20*	1.95	1.79*	1.96	1.47*	1.91	1.40*
Movie mediation	1.87	1.70*	1.63	1.41*	1.67	1.63*	1.91	1.60*	2.06	1.74*
Movie rules	2.11	1.59*	1.53	1.11*	1.82	1.55*	1.81	1.30*	1.85	1.35*
Book mediation	2.17	1.90*	1.77	1.51*	2.03	1.74*	2.00	1.64*	1.75	1.57*
By form of mediation										
Co-view	2.31	2.17*	2.30	1.95*	2.14	1.89*	2.34	2.10*	2.63	2.13*
Discuss	2.05	1.86*	1.67	1.43*	1.99	1.69*	1.79	1.62*	2.15	2.06*
Knowledge	2.84	2.55*	2.57	2.31*	2.53	2.42*	2.60	2.47*	2.70	2.51*
Recommend	2.10	1.70*	1.67	1.42*	2.05	1.72*	2.04	1.52*	1.87	1.67*
Disrecommend	1.83	1.63*	1.47	1.39*	1.82	1.78*	2.18	1.73*	1.73	1.28*
Excessive Use	1.44	1.63*	1.51	1.44	1.69	1.71	1.86	1.65*	1.54	1.28*
Reward	.14	.06*	.22	.12*	.35	.18*	.13	.07*	.24	.12*
Punishment	.12	.06*	.09	.02*	.25	.22*	.19	.11*	.13	.10
Rules/use	2.17	1.91*	1.62	1.20*	1.78	1.66*	1.89	1.44*	1.86	1.40*
Rules/content	2.21	1.59*	1.50	1.10*	2.14	1.80*	1.94	1.36*	1.95	1.36*
VCR	(35)	(59)	(149)	(184)	(62)	(121)	(166)	(158)	(190)	(177)
VCR mediation	2.05	1.87	1.74	1.56*	1.87	1.74*	2.16	1.90*	2.21	2.02*
VCR reward	.09	.03	.20	.18	.37	.07*	.19	.05*	.34	.13*
VCR punishment	.09	.00*	.03	.03	.25	.10*	.14	.06*	.05	.04
VCR rules	2.39	1.96*	1.36	1.12*	1.96	1.60*	1.89	1.57*	1.98	1.48*

NOTE: *Within-country mean difference is significant at .05 level.

more frequent recommendations as to media content choices for the sixth graders. For four of the countries, there is more knowledge and more negative recommendations about content choices for the younger respondents. The same pattern obtains for use of media as reward and punishment and for both indices regarding rules in the home environment. Parental mediation of VCR practices also shows the same pattern, with more reported oversight of the younger children.

Gender

Gender differences were infrequent in China and most frequent in Japan. In China, the boys were more often told they made excessive use of the media and were more often punished by withholding media access; the girls more often co-viewed with their parents. In Japan, there was more mediation of all four media activities for the girls, as well as more co-viewing, discussion, knowledge, and recommendations about what to watch and read. In Korea, there was greater mediation of television, movies and the VCR, but not books, there was more discussion of media content, and there were more frequent recommendations and disrecommendations for the girls. In Taiwan, there was greater mediation only of television and books, in addition to more knowledge of what was being used and recommendations as to content among the girls; the girls also more often were punished by withholding media access. In the United States, the girls reported more mediation of all four media studied, plus more discussion with parents and that their parents were more aware of what they were doing than reported by the boys.

Father's Education

Father's education made for few differences in China, and when it did, it was not in any linear fashion. In Japan, this variable accounted for differences consistently with the several measures assessing the presence of rules in the household; those with the highest level of education were more likely to create rules for each of the media. The opposite pattern emerged in Korea; the fewest television rules, rules regarding use, and rules regarding content were primarily found among the children whose fathers had the most education; these same families reported the least frequent use of media as reward or punishment mechanisms.

Father's education as a factor related to mediation was more prominent in the Taiwan sample than in any other country. For all measures of mediation by medium and by form, and for rules regarding both content and use, those with the lowest level of education showed the lowest parental involvement. For 15 of 19 measures, this pattern was statistically significant. In the United States, the better educated fathers were more likely to discuss, to make recommendations, to create rules about use, to use the media for reward, and to admonish for excessive use.

Family Size

Groupings were made into small (1-2), medium (3-4), and large (5+) families. Only in the American sample did this factor account for consistent and linear differences. The largest American families reported more parental activity in television mediation, more television, VCR, and movie rules, and more rules about use and about content.

Family Structure

Here, respondents were grouped in terms of having a single parent or both parents in the household. This family structure variable was unrelated to mediation practices in China, Japan, and Korea. In Taiwan, having both parents led to more mediation of television and books, and to more frequent coviewing, discussion, knowledge, and negative recommendations about content. In the United States, having both parents led to the presence of more rules for all media and more knowledge of what the child was doing with the media.

Socioeconomic Status

Only for the Taiwan sample did socioeconomic status affect mediation activities. High-status Taiwan youngsters reported that their parents imposed more television and movie rules, discussed their media activities more often, and more often made program recommendations. In each comparison, the result was linear from high to low status.

Quality of Schoolwork

This factor did not differentiate with any consistency in China, Japan, or the United States, as assessed by the respondents' self-reports of their schoolwork as below average, average, or above average. However, in both Korea and Taiwan, the above-average students most often said there was less mediation by their parents—for television and for books, as well as less co-viewing, awareness, discussion, and recommendations.

Mediation Models

The analyses reported in the previous section examine the relation ship between a single independent variable and the set of mediation practices studied in the several countries. The final analyses took the set of independent variables in combination with each other and in combination with a specified set of media experiences to predict the mediation practices for television, films, and books. The media exper ences examined included access to media, media usage, credibility dependency, and gratifications as operationalized in the methods sec tion. For each mediation practice, the model tested used those variable most relevant to the practice; for example, amount of television viewin was used in testing the television mediation practices model, amount of moviegoing was used in testing the movie mediation practices. The models were tested by multiple regression. In all, 15 models were teste for television, film, and book mediation activities; no models wer created for VCR mediation practices, given the amount of variance i VCR access among the five countries. Models tested here were acros the five countries, and not within individual countries.

Each of the 15 models was statistically significant at $p < .001$, rangin from a multiple R of .187 for cautions about excessive use of media t .455 for parental activity in mediating book reading. So, at best, th variables introduced into the model accounted for 20% of the varianc in predicting mediation practices and at worst, accounted for 4%; th average multiple R accounted for 12% of the variance. Rather tha present each model in detail, given space limitations, the purpose o these analyses was to determine which covariates were most prominer across mediation practices, and which contributed uniquely to some o the regression solutions. Table 10.3 provides a summary of the result

For each of the mediation practices examined, the age (grade i school) of the youngster was a significant covariate. In all cases bu one, it was the strongest predictor and in all cases but one, it was th younger respondents (sixth grade) who received more mediation. Olde respondents (tenth grade) were more often told that they engaged i excessive media use. With several of these mediation indices, only th age of the respondent yielded significant covariance.

Females were more often the object of parental mediation than male for each of the mediation forms—co-viewing, discussion, and so on— and for each medium index which encompassed these forms, except fc the excessive use index; there was no gender relationship with th

TABLE 10.3 Multiple Regression Results Testing Models of Mediation Practices
Among Five Countries

Mediation practice by medium	R	Significant predictors[a]
TV mediation[b]	.320	Grade, Family structure, Gender (−), TV use, Personal TV set (−), Schoolwork (−), Education
TV rules	.416	Grade, Family structure, TV sets (−), TV use (−)
Movie mediation	.365	Grade, Gender (−), Moviegoing, Education, Schoolwork (−)
Movie rules	.354	Grade
Book mediation	.455	Grade, Family structure, Reading time, Schoolwork (−), Education, Gender (−), TV sets (−)
By form		
Co-viewing	.336	Grade, Gender (−)
Discussion	.382	Grade, Personal TV set, Gender (−), Schoolwork (−)
Knowledge	.314	Gender (−), Grade, Family structure, Schoolwork (−), Education
Recommendations	.401	Grade, Gender (−), Education, Schoolwork (−)
Disrecommendations	.220	Grade, Family structure, Personal TV set (−), Gender (−)
Excessive use	.187	Grade (−), Personal TV set (−)
Media as reward	.303	Grade
Media as punishment	.265	Grade
Rules on use of media	.341	Grade, Gender (−), TV use (−)
Rules on content of media	.438	Grade

NOTES: a. Predictor variables listed here are those whose standardized beta coefficients exceed .20 and which are statistically significant contributors to the overall model. They are listed in order from largest to lowest coefficient. The minus signs indicate negative relationships; gender (−) indicates that the mediation practiced was found more often for females.
b. This index summed the individual items that asked about TV co-viewing, discussion, knowledge, recommendations, disrecommendations, and excessive use. The movie and book mediation indices were constructed in a parallel fashion.

television and movie rules measures. Family structure also appeared consistently in these analyses, with the young people from two-parent homes indicating more mediation than those living with a single parent.

Two other demographic correlates were found repeatedly. Young people who perceived that they were doing better in school were less likely to have their media behaviors monitored; those whose fathers had higher levels of education reflected more parental mediation.

The media experience variables were significant correlates infrequently. Having a personal television set was the primary one; this was related to less mediation—in mediating television use, in discussing television shows, in indicating excessive use, and in recommending against certain television shows. In addition, the more television was viewed, the fewer television rules were reported overall, specifically with regard to television use but not content, and the more likely there was parental oversight, but not of any single form. Finally, the more television sets in the home, the less likelihood of finding television rules. Media credibility, media dependency, and media gratification did not emerge as significant predictors of any parental activity.

DISCUSSION

In the traditional Chinese society, human relations are characterized by authority: Subjects obey the emperor; wives obey husbands; students obey teachers; children obey parents. Children, especially boys, are considered the parents' property because they can help work on the farm. Parents have almost absolute control over their children, who are not treated as individuals; a child expressing his or her own opinion may be punished severely. These traditions of course pervaded other Asian societies who had moved earlier into the mainstream of development, and concurrent influence from the Western harbingers of development.

Since the mainland China open-door policy began in 1978, economic growth has fostered substantial social change, particularly in large cities. In a society that has become more diversified, the parent-child relationship also has been affected greatly. Western technologies and products are being imported and adopted by the public, who will inevitably be influenced by the Western culture that accompanies those technologies and products. Young people seek more freedom; they want to be treated as individuals, to make their own decisions. They are less willing to follow parental rules. In turn, parents sense that they now have less control over their children and many have softened their autocratic approach to parenting. Furthermore, the children are no longer as tied to their parents as they were a decade ago. Economic growth means that young people have more pocket money, which gives them more things to do and more places to go. Spending more time with their peers reduces at-home time. In this still dynamic context, communication patterns between parents and their children are changing; communication is less frequent and less authoritative.

In the Taiwan society, the influence of Western culture has had a longer and more intense impact on parenting practices, again primarily in the large urban centers. Young people are home even less because of the greater proliferation of alternative sites for socializing and recreation. In recent years youngsters can spend hours in a facility that features music videos, but their parents also are at home less often. Two-income families have become an important and pervasive trend, and parental efforts to make more money come at the expense of giving less attention to their children. Parents give gifts, even expensive ones, as a substitute for sharing time with their children. Taiwan experts have expressed concern about these changes in the parent-child relationship, and they now recommend more communication between parents and their children. This has a very recognizable symmetry to Western-style parent-child relationships and their subsequent difficulties.

Parental mediation of their children's media experiences in these countries is influenced by several factors. In the changing parent-child relationships in China and in Taiwan, parents monitor and oversee less of the media use of their children; they either do not make as many rules about media use or will not enforce the rules they have made. Furthermore, to the Chinese, advanced education for their offspring is extremely important. Competition for placements in schools is intense and the entrance examination is the most crucial test. There are very heavy time commitments to the school day and then to studying at home, which severely reduce available media time. Many youngsters refrain from spending much time with media (e.g., television viewing) so they can have more time for studying. To the extent this characterizes a given child, there is probably little need for parental mediation or rule making over television, movies, and so forth to occur. In China, competition for entering college continues to intensify and remains no less difficult. In Taiwan, a new policy permitting studying abroad at the age of 18 is too recent to estimate its impact on young people's media use patterns, or their parents' mediation of those activities. There is strong reason to argue that social changes in Korea parallel those in China, that the original and traditional parent-child relationships are weakening, and moving in the directions we have just described.

As for Japan, these patterns would seem to be even more prevalent— that the Westernization of the Japanese family with regard to parenting practices and to media activities, among others, has been active for a longer era than for China, Korea, or Taiwan. Further, the dramatically more successful Japanese economy has accelerated many changes in the social structure of Japan and intensified its contact with Western societies, particularly the United States. And in the United States, the erosion of parental control is well documented; its virtual absence with regard to the oversight of adolescents' media activities is of little surprise. Within this cultural framework, the present findings are discussed.

In all these countries, parental mediation is slight or moderate at best, as perceived by the recipients of that mediation. It occurs more so with television than for movies or books. The most persistent form of parental oversight is that which may be easiest to do—being aware of what the child is doing—although even that may slacken as personal television sets become more common in the Asian sites.

Parent types that reflected stricter approaches (more "sensitization") to controlling television and movie behaviors were found in Korea and in China. There, more rules about use and about content as applied to each medium were most evident, and in China, this also applied to VCR rules. In Korea, access to media as reward and punishment also prevailed in this more stringent parenting style. One would anticipate that in these two countries, a more traditional family prevails, in which the children function under sets of rules for various activities, including those of television viewing and moviegoing. By contrast, the style of parenting that is based more so on social exchange (induction) is better reflected in the mediation practices that were more prominent in the American findings—the co-viewing, discussion, and awareness of the child's activities. These activities in the United States, however, were greater for television and for movies than for books; American parents appear to exercise less oversight for book reading, and are probably pleased if the child is reading anything.

The Japanese results indicate basically a hands-off posture toward mediating any of these media, in any of the forms examined, according to the Japanese youth sample. Regardless of the medium or of the form of mediation, the most minimum mediation activity was in Japan. A possible answer lies in the changing nature of the Japanese family and the trend toward greater secularism, at least in Tokyo, where these data originated. Popular press reports indicate that the traditional Japanese family is weakening in the hold of parents over their offspring, that the youth want what they perceive as a more Western mode of family interaction, including greater independence in making personal decisions. Certainly, given the trends in Japan to Western fashions, Western music, let alone control of Western economics, any battleground over media behaviors becomes a relatively small and apparently easy arena in which to gain personal control.

The cross-country continuum of mediation typically places the Taiwan results in midstream. Their tendency to be neither the most nor the least restrictive, nor the most nor the least active in other forms of parental mediation may reflect a more gradual, less dramatic shift in family-child interactions about media, if not other activities as well. In Taiwan, father's education covaried with mediation most persistently— matched in no other location—and this may be an indication of Western-induced aspirations for the new generation of Taiwan youngsters. Taiwan does not have the new wealth of Japan to contend with, but its social, educational, and business contacts with the West have been important and more intense for a longer period than for Korea or China.

Clearly, mediation of these experiences is related to the age of the child and its gender. Age is dominant as a correlate of all kinds of mediation for all media; that it would be so prominent between these two age periods (for sixth and tenth graders) supports the original rationale that four years' difference in age at this particular period can make for dramatic differences in orientations to the mass media. The period in which one moves from preteen status to teenager involves substantial changes in parent relations as well as in physiology and social development; in fact, these changes may well be part of the social development shifts away from dependence to interdependence.

In four countries, gender differences were major sources of variation, with China the lone exception. In China, the longstanding social norm of gender equity has apparently been equally well extended to the media environment. The countries with the strongest gender differences were the two most developed nations, Japan, and the United States, a paradox that cannot be explained here. Although not reported in this chapter, similar gender differences existed in these same four countries for computer access and use; there was a computer in the males' homes two to three times as often as one was located in the girls' homes, and when access at home was controlled, the boys used the computers far more often than the girls.

Three other background characteristics showed consistent relationships with mediation, more so even in the multiple correlation analysis than in the univariate tests. These were family structure, father's education, and the respondent's assessment of the quality of their schoolwork. Having both parents at home provides a context of greater mediation, in part because such homes will likely generate more oversight of media activities during the day as well as at night; even if both are employed, there will be more opportunity for mediation from one of the parents if the other is unavailable. The contemporary notion of "latchkey" children and the implications of not having a parent at home after school should be examined separately from that of one- and two-parent families; the expectation would be that children with two working parents would have alternative mediation experiences from those with a single working parent.

The educational level of the father works to provide a mediation context that was primarily rules-based in Japan and Korea, but in opposite directions. In the former, more rules came from fathers with more education; in the latter, more rules came from fathers with less education. The father's role in the American findings was located more in the shared mediation activities (e.g., discussing and recommending media content). And in Taiwan, it was in all forms of mediation examined. This is perhaps the most complex finding reported here and one that cannot be explained further from these data. Perhaps its significance for subsequent research is that important conceptual distinctions have been made among types of mediation that should be maintained; that is, not all forms of mediation are alike, they are implemented differently in different countries.

The third factor, the students' self-report of their schoolwork acumen, shows that good students do not believe they are mediated as much; this applies to all mediation indices other than rules, for which in-school ability was not a predictor. So, the better the student, the less oversight for what they do with the media. More likely, it seems, is the logic that weaker students are perceived to need more monitoring of their media activities. Or, perhaps, the weaker student is prone to want to spend more time with media in part to avoid the punitive outcome of less satisfactory school experiences, and their parents respond to that with more strictures.

Subsequent research should more closely examine the expected fit between general parenting styles of the kinds discussed in this chapter's introduction and the forms and types of mediation extended by parents toward the mass media in their homes. It is probable that alternative communication and mediation styles can be subsumed conceptually under general parenting patterns.

Results from different countries reflect cultural, social, political, and economic differences. No single study can make all the necessary connections among those background characteristics. Here, we have begun to examine how similarly and differently the media are handled in the homes of two age groups of young people, and what some factors are that account for these mediation behaviors. The set of independent variables accounts for a significant, but not large, amount of the variance associated with these behaviors. A more comprehensive understanding would evolve from the opportunity to study young people and their parents concurrently. First, there is need to determine the commonality between the youngsters' and their parents' perceptions of what mediation activities exist, what need there is for them, and what outcome they have. Second, given evidence elsewhere that a strong predictor of young persons' media behaviors is their parents' media behaviors (with joint influence a more likely explanation than unidirectional influence), it is difficult to understand mediation practices without knowledge of the media behaviors that occur among both the child and parent. This would be an enriching way to extend what this project has begun; to do so in cross-cultural settings would be even more provocative.

NOTES

1. Collaborating researchers were Hiroshi Tokinoya of Tokai University, Jiangang Wang of the People's University of China, Hee Joung Yoon of EWHA Woman's University in Seoul, and Kuo-jen Tsang at National Chenchi University in Taiwan.

2. In Taiwan, there was no television in the early morning, so that was not asked; in Korea, the question about "after school" television was inadvertently omitted. For these reasons, the cumulative measures in each country were standardized before completing the analyses.

REFERENCES

Abel, J. D. (1976). The family and child television viewing. *Journal of Marriage and the Family, 38,* 331-335.

Aronfreed, J. (1969). The concept of internalization. In D. A. Goslin (Ed.), *Handbook of socialization theory and research.* Chicago: Rand McNally.

Atkin, C. K., & Greenberg, B. S. (1977). *Parental mediation of children's social learning from television* (CASTLE report No. 4). East Lansing: Department of Telecommunication, Michigan State University.

Brown, J. D., Bauman, K. E., Lentz, G. M., & Koch, G. G. (1987). *Young adolescents' use of radio and television in the 1980s.* Paper presented at the International Communication Association Convention, Montreal.

Brown, J. R., & Linne, O. (1976). The family as a mediator of television's effects. In R. Brown (Ed.), *Children and television* (pp. 184-198). Beverly Hills, CA: Sage.

Desmond, R. J., Singer, J., Singer, D., Calam, R., & Colimore, K. (1985). Family mediation patterns and television viewing. *Human Communication Research, 11*(4), 461-481.

Feng, J. (1976). *The effects of television on children's behaviors.* Taipei, Taiwan: Wenchin.

Greenberg, B. S., & Dominick, J. R. (1969). Race and social class differences in teenagers' use of television. *Journal of Broadcasting, 13,* 1331-1334.

Greenberg, B. S., Ericson, P. M., & Vlahos, M. (1972). A comparison of parental mediation behaviors for mothers and their children. *Journal of Broadcasting, 16,* 565-572.

Greenberg, B. S., & Heeter, C. (1987). VCRs and young people. *American Behavioral Scientist, 30,* 509-521.

Gross, L. S., & Walsh, R. P. (1976). Factors affecting parental control over children's television viewing: A pilot study. *Journal of Broadcasting, 24,* 411-419.

Han, R. H. (1986). *A comparative study of television watching behavior between rural and urban school children.* Unpublished master's thesis, Kangwon University, Wonju.

Himmelweit, H., Oppenheim, A., & Vince, P. (1958). *Television and the child.* London: Oxford University Press.

Himmelweit, H., & Swift, B. (1976). Continuities and discontinuities in media usage and taste: A longitudinal study. *Journal of Social Issues, 32*(4), 133-156.

Hoffman, M. S. (1975). Moral internalization, parental power, and the nature of parent-child interaction. *Developmental Psychology, 11*(2), 228-239.

Hoffman, M. S., & Saltzstein, H. D. (1967). Parent discipline and the child's moral development. *Journal of Personality and Social Psychology, 5*(1), 45-57.

Kim, W. Y., Baran, S., & Massey, K. K. (1988). Impact of the VCR on control of television viewing. *Journal of Broadcasting & Electronic Media, 32,* 351-358.

Ko, K. J. (1983). *Television viewing behavior of adolescents focused on relationship between TV viewing patterns and family disorganization.* Unpublished master's thesis, Hanyang University, Seoul.

Lebra, T. S. (1974). Intergenerational continuity and discontinuity in moral values among Japanese: A preliminary report. In W. P. Lebra (Ed.), *Youth, socialization, and mental health.* Honolulu: University of Hawaii Press.

Lin, C. A., & Atkin, D. J. (1989). Parental mediation and rulemaking for adolescent use of television and VCRs. *Journal of Broadcasting & Electronic Media, 33*(1), 53-67.

Long, S. O. (1987). *Family change and the life course in Japan.* Ithaca, NY: East Asia Program, Cornell University.

Lyle, J., & Hoffman, H. R. (1972). Children's use of television and other media. In E. A. Rubinstein, G. A. Comstock, & J. P. Murray (Eds.), *Television and social behavior: Vol. IV. Television in day-to-day life* (pp. 129-256). Washington, DC: Government Printing Office.

McLeod, J. M., Atkin, C. K., & Chaffee, S. H. (1972). Adolescent self-support measures from Maryland and Wisconsin samples. In G. A. Comstock (Ed.), *Television and social behavior: Vol. III. Television and adolescent aggressiveness* (pp. 173-238). Washington, DC: Government Printing Office.

Mitsuya, K. (1988, December). What is television for elementary school students? *NHK Monthly Report on Broadcast Research,* 26-45.

Mohr, P. J. (1979). Parental influence of children's viewing of evening television programs. *Journal of Broadcasting, 23*(2), 213-228.

Research Group on Adolescence and Television. (1984). High school students and television. *China News Yearbook,* 296-300.

Schramm, W., Lyle, J., & Parker, E. (1961). *Television in the lives of our children.* Stanford, CA: Stanford University Press.

Stanley, C. (1986). *Family structure and its relationship to adolescent television viewing.* Unpublished master's thesis, Michigan State University, East Lansing.

Wu, J. S. (1985). Viewing of children's shows on television by elementary school students. *Journal of Teacher's College of Taiwan, 1*(8), 289-338.

11

Comparative Cultivation Analysis
Television and Adolescents in Argentina and Taiwan

MICHAEL MORGAN   ●   *University of Massachusetts*
JAMES SHANAHAN   ●   *Boston University*

This study attempts to advance the literature on cross-cultural media effects, using cultivation theory and methodology to study adolescents in Argentina and Taiwan. U.S. cultivation hypotheses were more predictive of the correlates of television viewing among Argentine adolescents than in Taiwan. This may be explained by the fact that, compared to Taiwan, Argentine television presents more entertainment programming, and also because Argentine students spend much more time watching television. Gender-role stereotypes and authoritarian beliefs were strongly related to amount of viewing in Argentina. Although heavier viewing was associated with interpersonal mistrust in Taiwan, most relationships (overall and within subgroups) were much weaker than in Argentina. Exposure to programming imported from the United States was largely unrelated to the dependent variables in either country. The results suggest that complex interactions of media institutions, messages, political structures, and cultural practices need to be taken into account in studying comparative media effects.

Over the past few decades, television has transformed the sociocultural landscape of most countries around the world. In almost every corner of the globe, it has become an integral part of daily life for young and old, rich and poor, male and female, and urban and rural populations.

Quantitatively, the United States probably leads the world in the production, distribution, and consumption of media content. Also, more media research may be carried out in the United States than anywhere else, particularly on the social uses and impacts of mass communication. This may lead to an unintentional but implicitly ethnocentric view

AUTHORS' NOTE: We would like to thank Yi-Kuo Wu for making the Taiwan data available to us, and also wish to acknowledge Juan Carlos Gorlier and Alfredo Vivoni for their instrumental roles in the design and administration of the Argentine survey.

of media effects among many U.S. researchers, who often pay too little attention to the particular national, social, cultural, and historical contexts that frame and limit their data, especially about media "effects." Research findings too often are assumed to reflect fixed characteristics and universal consequences of television, per se, rather than the unique interactions of the technology and its messages with specific institutional systems, social patterns, and cultural practices.

This chapter attempts to advance the literature on cross-cultural, comparative media effects, using the concepts and methods of cultivation analysis, which studies the contributions of television viewing to audiences' conceptions of social reality (Gerbner & Gross, 1976; Gerbner, Gross, Morgan, & Signorielli, 1986; Signorielli & Morgan, 1990). Although the theory was developed in the United States, cultivation analysis raises questions that are ideally suited to cross-cultural comparative research (Gerbner, 1977). Do the patterns of associations between amount of television viewing and conceptions found in the United States also emerge in other countries? Do these relationships vary according to diverse policies, structures, cultures, and audiences? And how do the correlates and consequences of imported (usually from the United States) and local programming vary from culture to culture?

We explore some of these questions with data from two samples of adolescents, one Asian (from Taiwan) and one Latin U.S. (from Argentina). Both countries are media-rich with highly industrialized urban centers (Taipei and Buenos Aires). Both import a substantial amount of television programming and films from the United States but also produce much themselves. Yet, culturally, historically, and politically, they are extremely different both from the United States and from each other, thereby providing a useful context for comparative media effects analysis.

Cultivation

Over the past two decades, many cultivation analyses have been conducted on associations between amount of television viewing and audience conceptions of violence, interpersonal mistrust, gender-roles, aging, health, science, minorities, politics, and many other issues (for overviews, see Hawkins & Pingree, 1982; Signorielli & Morgan, 1990). The cultivation perspective assumes that the symbolic environment of any culture helps perpetuate the basic assumptions and cultural ideologies of the institutions and societies that produce them. Mass-produced and widely shared messages and images provide hidden but pervasive boundary conditions for social discourse and practices (Gerbner, 1958, 1969).

"Cultivation" is the process within which interaction through mediated messages shapes and sustains the terms on which the messages are premised (Gerbner et al., 1986; Morgan, 1989a). The task of cultivation analysis is to determine the extent to which a dominant message system—especially television entertainment—makes an independent contribution to conceptions of social reality that are congruent with the most stable and recurrent values and images expressed in those messages.

This becomes particularly complex outside the United States, however, simply because most countries tend to import a good deal of their television programming. U.S. media industries export more of their "product" and to more places than does any other country (Varis, 1984). This means that, in contrast to the United States, television message systems in other countries are less likely to provide relatively stable, consistent, and homogeneous images and portrayals (see Tamborini & Choi, 1990). Thus, a primary assumption of cultivation theory may not always be met.

In structure, policies, and programming, no two television systems are alike; each country's system reflects the unique historical, political social, economic, and cultural contexts within which it has developed. Consequently, cultivation may be highly culture specific. If a particular message system (and culture) contains a great deal of (for example) violence, then the media system of that society should cultivate corresponding conceptions; if it does not, then it should not.

Because most countries import so much U.S. programming, comparative cultivation analysis will inevitably touch on debates concerning cultural imperialism. The values and representations in U.S. programs may be congruent with, irrelevant to, or sharply in conflict with various aspects of the importing culture and its own programming. Thus we will pay special attention to the distinct and interactive correlates of U.S. versus local viewing in our analyses.

Previous International Cultivation Research

There were many attempts to replicate U.S. cultivation findings in other countries in the early 1980s, mostly in Western Europe, Canada, and Australia (e.g., Bonfadelli, 1982; Bouwman, 1984; Doob & Macdonald, 1979; Hedinsson & Windahl, 1984; Melischek, Rosengren, & Stappers,

1984; Pingree & Hawkins, 1981; Wober, 1984). Much less has been done in countries with cultural, political, and historical contexts far more different from the United States, such as Asia and Latin America (Morgan, 1990).

In Australia, Pingree and Hawkins (1981) found that exposure to U.S. programs (especially crime and adventure) was significantly related to students' scores on "Mean World" and "Violence in Society" indices concerning conceptions of Australia, but not of the United States. Viewing Australian programs was unrelated to conceptions, but those who watched more U.S. programs were more likely to see Australia as dangerous and mean. On the other hand, Weimann's (1984) study of 461 high school and college students in Israel found that heavy viewers had an idealized, "rosier" image of life in the United States, in terms of wealth, standard of living, and material possessions.

In England, Wober (1978) found little support for cultivation in terms of images of violence. But there was little violence in British programming, and U.S. programs only made up about 15% of British screen time. (See also Gunter, 1987; Wober, 1984, 1990; Wober & Gunter, 1988.) More recently, Piepe, Charlton, and Morey (1990) found evidence of political homogenization ("mainstreaming") in Britain that was highly congruent with U.S. findings (Gerbner, Gross, Morgan, & Signorielli, 1982).

In the Netherlands, Bouwman (1984) reported "very weak" support for cultivation, but his findings reveal the importance of cultural context in comparative cultivation research. Although content analyses showed a good deal of similarity between U.S. and Dutch television along standard violence measures (Bouwman & Stappers, 1984; Bouwman & Signorielli, 1985), it was found that both light and heavy Dutch viewers see about equal amounts of fictional entertainment, but heavy viewers see more "informational" programs. (See also Stappers, 1984; Bouwman, Nelissen, & Meier, 1987.) Complex patterns have also been found in Sweden (Hedinsson & Windahl, 1984; Reimer & Rosengren, 1990).

More recent studies have begun to deal with non-Western cultures. In the Philippines, where 60% of programs come from the United States, Tan, Tan, and Tan (1987) examined how amount of viewing related to values expressed in the Rokeach value survey among high school seniors. Heavy viewers of U.S. television were more likely to rate "pleasure" (allegedly frequently appearing on U.S. television) as an important value, and to deemphasize "salvation" and "wisdom." (For studies of Taiwan, Mexico, and Thailand, see Tan, Li, & Simpson, 1986, and Tan & Suarchavarat, 1988).

Kang and Morgan (1988) analyzed the contribution of U.S. programs to the attitudes of college students in Korea. (For a comparison of college students in Korea and Taiwan, see Daddario, Kang, Morgan, & Wu, 1988.) In general, exposure to U.S. television was associated with more "liberal" perspectives about gender-roles and family values among females. In contrast, greater viewing of U.S. television among Korean male students went with more hostility toward the United States and greater protectiveness toward Korean culture. This suggests that U.S. television may sometimes have a "backlash" effect, engendering opposition to an imported culture and raising nationalistic cultural consciousness, at least among some politicized college students.

The lesson of international cultivation research so far is that results typically obtained in the United States will not always hold for other cultures. It is also clear that "hypodermic" models of cultural imperialism are not supported by these studies. Just as U.S. research shows systematic variations in susceptibility to cultivation in different demographic subgroups, so too are cultivation patterns highly varied both across and within different countries. For the present study, this implies a need to approach the data in an exploratory fashion. We sought to uncover patterns of relationships between viewing and attitudes in Argentina and Taiwan, rather than to prove that cultivation "exists" in those countries. The data we explore can be used as a first step toward establishing a greater knowledge of the relationship between cultural, social, and structural factors and the effects of media.

This study also goes beyond most previous international cultivation studies, which have focused largely on violence, because looking at attitudes toward violence alone is not enough to provide a broad-based cross-cultural comparison. Thus, in addition to Mean World measures, this chapter also examines attitudes toward gender-roles and authoritarianism among adolescents in Argentina and Taiwan.

TELEVISION IN ARGENTINA

Television is the dominant medium in Argentina, in a socioeconomic and cultural sense (Schement & Rogers, 1984). Commercial television broadcasting in Argentina took off in 1960, and the medium spread very quickly. Today, 94% of the households in the federal capital of Buenos

Aires and its surrounding 41 towns have television sets; even in the interior, penetration is 84% (Ford, 1987).

The Argentine broadcasting system is highly centralized and dependent upon programs and decisions made in Buenos Aires. There are no formal networks, but programs from the main Buenos Aires channels are distributed throughout the country. New technologies such as cable and VCRs are beginning to develop, but are currently at an early stage of diffusion.

The three major U.S. television networks had extensive interests in the early Argentine television system, supplying large amounts of technology, programming, and money (Straubhaar & King, 1987). U.S. investments decreased in the late 1960s due to fears of expropriation by the state and a demand for local programming, especially the tremendously popular *telenovelas* (a Latin U.S. soap opera genre). But unlike most other Latin U.S. countries, broadcasting time in Argentina has been increasingly devoted to imported programming, from 20% in 1972 to 40% in 1982 (Antola & Rogers, 1984); the most recent figures place imported program hours at about 45% (Horvath, 1987). The vast majority of imports, and most all dramatic entertainment, come from the United States.

Five broadcast channels serve the greater Buenos Aires area (four of which are in the capital itself). Formal ownership of these channels has shifted back and forth several times between private and governmental hands, although military governments have exercised strong control even over privately owned channels. All channels have been essentially commercial despite large subsidies given to some by some governments of the day.

The last military dictatorship (during which color television was introduced in 1978) gave broadcasting licenses to people with close links to the junta. From 1976 to 1982 many journalists were murdered and others "disappeared," were jailed, or were exiled; newspapers were closed; blacklisting and censorship of local entertainment figures were common. However, the flow of U.S. programs continued unabated. The communications infrastructure stagnated, and the democratic government of President Raul Alfonsin of the Radical Party came into power in 1983 inheriting a television system that had become a hideously labyrinthine and convoluted bureaucratic mess (Landi, 1987).

The Radical Party's government found itself owning three of the capital's four channels, and spent several years trying to decide what to do with them, but nothing was done. It was not until the Peronist government of President Carlos Menem took over in 1989 that two of the three state channels were privatized (with considerable public debate and acrimony in the television industry). Throughout most of the 1980s, the ratings of the single privately owned channel usually dwarfed the others.

Despite the tumultuous and tragic events of the last few decades in Argentina, most observers conclude that regardless of whether the government is military or democratic, and regardless of whether television is state owned or in private hands, the content (especially in terms of entertainment and U.S. imports) stays remarkably the same (Horvath, 1988; Sirven, 1988). This content is generally found to be substandard in these evaluations, with an overabundance of violence, sensationalism, and even more stilted gender-role portrayals than is usually found in U.S. television.

TELEVISION IN TAIWAN

In Taiwan, nearly every family owns a television set; it is even more pervasive than in Argentina. However, a different set of political circumstances shaped the development of the Taiwanese broadcasting system. The government of Chiang Kai-Shek sought a degree of overt control of the broadcasting system slightly more restrictive than that seen in Argentina. The system was and is primarily commercial in nature, but government regulation and influence at various stages has been significant.

The Taiwanese government, which conceives itself as a government in exile for all Chinese, has tended to legitimate a greater degree of government restriction of the press and the media than would otherwise be tolerated in most capitalist countries. For many years, a state of martial law was imposed because the government of Taiwan believed they were a nation under siege from the mainland. Under martial law, the military imposed censorship in media materials deemed harmful to the national interest. This legislation was similar to the media laws enacted by the Argentine military governments of the late 1970s, but was not backed up by the same kind of brutal and extensive repression as occurred in Argentina.

The three main television networks are owned by private interests in partnership with various organizations affiliated with the governing Kuomintang party (until recently the only party). Although the model of ownership and programming is essentially commercial, there are program restrictions that at least theoretically prevent an unrestrained market form of television. Officially, radio and television programs cannot contain elements that "disgrace or are harmful to national interests and dignity; violate governmental policies or regulations; incite others to disobey law or to commit criminal acts; harm a child's psychological or mental health; hinder public order or good traditions; spread rumors or evil thinking which confuses the public" (Wu, 1990, p. 77).

These rules, however, perhaps due to their vagueness, are rarely followed. However, the government mandates what percentage of programming must be devoted to various kinds of content, limiting "entertainment" programs to 50% of the schedule (whereas in Argentina, the de facto percentage is about 80%). Although freedom of the press is a precept of the system, the Asian culture and the rigors of living in island exile have meant that the government has been able to act more strongly in the area of program control. In recent years, this has been loosening somewhat, as other political parties have arisen and the reality that Taiwan will not regain control of the mainland sets in.

U.S. influence has never been directly felt in terms of ownership. Historically, imported programming has never exceeded 35% of the total (in Argentina imports have occasionally risen higher than 50%). Still, even local Taiwanese production reflects U.S. influence in terms of style and genre (as is true in Argentina and many other countries).

Thus, the influence of U.S. programs is felt in Taiwan as well, although the greater activism of the government may tend to stifle this impact somewhat. In sum, whereas Argentina is a mixed ownership system that favors unrestrained commercialism (particularly in recent years), Taiwan's is a mixed system that includes a greater direct regulatory role for government, especially with regard to overall program content.

METHODS AND MEASURES

The Argentine and Taiwanese surveys were both designed to deal with issues relevant to cultivation in each country, but they were not designed as part of a single, integrated, comparative research effort. Moreover, the fact that the surveys were given in very different languages (Spanish and Chinese, both adapted from English) and cultural contexts means that there are likely to be subtle and ineffable variations in meanings among the different groups studied. Despite these differences, there is enough overlap to allow for comparative analysis. Both instruments were extensively pretested and revised to be worded in appropriate ways in each country (see Vivoni-Remus, Morgan, & Gorlier, 1990; Wu, 1990).

The Argentine data come from adolescents attending 10 different schools representing a broad variety of socioeconomic contexts, from Buenos Aires and from San Juan province. The data were collected in early-middle 1987, in Argentine autumn soon after the school year began. The process of collecting these data took over a year and involved many procedural, practical, and political problems (see Vivoni-Remus et al., 1990, for a full account of this process). The sample is less than half the size originally planned ($N = 966$) and is heavily dominated by females (almost 70% of the sample). Still, it includes students from 10 very different schools and represents considerable sociodemographic diversity, as indicated by parents' education and occupations. The sample covers grades 8 through 12 (mean age = 16.0). Just over half (52%) of the respondents' fathers did not finish high school; about a third (31%) had at least some university education.

The Taiwanese data come from a single school, of "medium" academic prestige. The data were collected in the middle of the 1988 school year by classroom teachers, who had been given extensive instructions on how to administer the questionnaires. The sample ($N = 1,214$) is split almost exactly between males and females. The Taiwan sample contains students between grades 10 and 12 only (mean age = 17.3), and fathers' education levels are slightly higher than in Argentina; 55% of the respondents' fathers finished high school, and 27% graduated from college.

Overall, the Taiwanese sample is more homogeneous in socioeconomic terms, partly because the data were collected from a single school. Most came from middle-income families; the Argentine sample represents a wider slice of the economic and occupational spectrum.

In Argentina, respondents provided estimates of television viewing hours "on a typical school day between the time you get home and dinner," and "between dinner and the time you go to bed," as well as separate measures of viewing on Saturdays and Sundays. The Taiwan survey asked one question about viewing on "a typical school day," plus separate questions for Saturday and Sunday.

Exposure to U.S. programs was measured indirectly, inasmuch as it is difficult to simply ask respondents how much U.S. programming they view in hours. In Taiwan, respondents were given a list of ten U.S. drama series, and asked how often they watch each. In Argentina, scores are based on the number of U.S. programs named in response to two open-ended questions that asked about respondents' favorite programs and programs seen "yesterday."

Three major dependent areas were examined in both surveys: gender-role stereotypes, interpersonal mistrust ("the Mean World Syndrome" in cultivation studies) and political attitudes (democratic/authoritarian). The specific measures used in each survey are described below.

Gender-Role Stereotypes

The gender-role measures come from previous cultivation studies (Gross & Jeffries-Fox, 1978; Morgan, 1982). Both samples were presented with the following statements:

- By nature, women are happiest raising children and caring for the home.
- It's better if men are out working and women stay home and take care of the family.
- Men have more drive to be ambitious and successful than women.

These were followed by 4-point (in Argentina) or 5-point (in Taiwan) Likert-type response scales from "strongly agree" to "strongly disagree". The difference in the number of points used in the response scales of the two surveys is due only to the fact that the surveys were constructed by different researchers at different times, and not for any specific conceptual or methodological reasons.

Response categories were recoded so that "strongly disagree" = -2, "disagree" = -1, "agree" = 1, and "strongly agree" = 2, to create a scale ranging from -6 to $+6$. (Middle values of "no opinion" were coded as 0 in Taiwan.) When summed, the higher values thus correspond to higher sexism.

Mean World

In both surveys, three standard questions were asked to measure the Mean World Syndrome of interpersonal mistrust:

- In general do you think you can trust most people, or do you think that you can't be too careful in dealing with most people?

- Would most people take advantage of you if they got the chance, or would they try to be fair?
- Do you think that most people try to be helpful, or are they just looking out for themselves?

Both surveys used identical response categories, so the absolute values of the scales are comparable, counting up the number of "mistrustful" responses, and ranging from 0 to 3 (with 3 as the most distrustful index score).

Authoritarianism

Measures of authoritarianism were based on implications of findings from U.S. research (see Gerbner et al., 1982; Morgan, 1989b). Respondents were presented with the following three statements:

- The government should do what it thinks is best, even if it's not what most people want.
- The government's actions should always reflect the will of the majority. (coding reversed)
- People are better off if they do as they are told.

Again, 4-point responses were coded in Argentina, and 5-point responses were coded in Taiwan. As with sexism, responses were recorded to create a scale ranging from −6 to +6, with higher values indicating higher authoritarianism.

RESEARCH QUESTIONS

In U.S. research, television viewing is supposed to be related with the three dependent variables in the following ways:

1. Greater television viewing is associated with more traditional gender-role attitudes. Both the Argentine and Taiwanese cultures tend to be highly "traditional" with regard to gender-role stereotyping, although this is an extremely subjective determination. In Argentina, for instance, women did not get the vote until the 1940s, and there are strong traces of male dominance in the culture and the media today. In Taiwan, the traditional Asian approach to male-female relations holds: males are strongly dominant. Thus, while the specific cultural expressions

of male dominance are highly different, the pattern of the relationship between viewing and traditionalism should be the same for both countries.

2. Greater viewing is associated with perceptions of a more violent and meaner world. Because television presents so much violence, heavy viewers of television should be more mistrustful of others.

3. Greater viewing is associated with more conservative and authoritarian political principles. The idea that television should cultivate authoritarianism may be the least intuitively understood of the three dependent variables. However, research shows that television tends to cultivate conservative political ideologies in the United States, as it draws political extremes into the mainstream and bends that mainstream to the Right. Thus, in countries where the Right happens to be authoritarian, television may be associated with such views.

This research did not presume that these hypotheses would be confirmed in Argentina and Taiwan. In fact, we explicitly did not expect that U.S. relationships would be replicated exactly, because the cultural complexities are too much to comprehend predictively. Rather, our purpose was to explore the data to see what patterns may exist, and to tie these to the structural, social, and cultural factors that may underlie the relationships. These patterns should also suggest further research on international media effects.

FINDINGS

First, overall levels of television viewing in the two samples are strikingly different. Argentine adolescents, on the average, watch roughly twice as much (26.89 hours weekly versus 13.03 in Taiwan). This alone means that we should be advised to look for differences in cultivation; television simply has much more of a place in the Argentine adolescent's world than in the world of the Taiwanese.

Cultural stereotypes about hardworking Asians and lazy Latins notwithstanding, this difference should not be surprising. Taiwan has a comparatively booming economy with a strong work ethic, and the requirements facing the Asian school student are stringent. There is simply less time for television. Conversely, in Argentina, the economy is slack; schools (and many other institutions and services) are frequently closed by strikes. The cultural influence of the United States is also stronger. Therefore, Argentina tends to fall into a more "Western" mode

TABLE 11.1 Television Viewing in Argentina and Taiwan

| | Argentina | | Taiwan | |
	Total	United States	Total	United States
Mean weekly viewing	26.9	1.2[a]	13.0	28.4[b]
Standard deviation	15.3	1.3	7.7	6.9
Range	0-80	0-8	0-84	10-50
Weekly exposure in subgroups				
Sex				
Males	27.1	1.3	13.3	28.7
Females	26.7	1.2	12.8	28.2
Father's education				
No college	28.2*	1.3	13.3	28.4
College	20.9	1.2	12.3	28.8
Grade level				
Youngest	30.4	1.1	14.1	28.7
Middle	26.9	1.4	13.0	29.0
Oldest	24.0*	1.3	12.0*	28.7
Weekend viewing	6.5	——	7.4	——

NOTES: a. U.S. exposure in Argentina based on number of U.S. programs named as "favorites" or "watched yesterday" (open-ended).
. U.S. exposure in Taiwan based on summed scale of frequency of viewing ten U.S. programs, from = "never" to 5 = "almost every episode" for each.
$p < .001$

of leisure time behavior than does Taiwan. For these reasons and others, television is viewed more heavily.

Table 11.1 summarizes the differences in television consumption for local and U.S. programs in the two countries. It should be noted that, in Taiwan, almost half of all viewing is done on the weekend (probably because students are so busy with their difficult school work during the week). In Argentina, much more viewing is done throughout the week, although weekend viewing is heavier in Argentina than in the United States (Morgan, 1990).

Males watch slightly more than females in both countries. The negative relationship between amount of viewing and social class typically found in the United States is also observed in Argentina, in terms of father's education. Viewing by students whose fathers did not attend college is markedly higher than for those whose fathers did attend college. A similar pattern exists in Taiwan, but is not statistically significant. In both countries, viewing decreases as students get older;

because older adolescents are dealing with so many issues of social and interpersonal importance, television becomes a lesser concern. The measures of overall and U.S. exposure are correlated only moderately in Taiwan ($r = .30$, $p < .001$), and even less so in Argentina ($r = .18$, $p < .001$). There are virtually no demographic differences in viewing U.S programs in either country.

In sum, Argentine students watch much more than their Taiwanese counterparts, during the week especially. Taiwanese students watch mostly on the weekends. In quantitative terms, television appears to be much less important to the average Taiwanese adolescent.

Cross-Cultural Cultivation of Attitudes

Table 11.2 presents the findings for the relationship between viewing and sexism in Argentina and Taiwan. The table shows the mean scale scores, broken down by levels of overall and U.S. television exposure (both viewing measures are trichotomized into light, medium, and heavy, at the points that come closest to assigning one third of the sample to each group). The sexism scores range from a low of −6 (least sexist) to +6 (most sexist).

In Argentina, the data show a significant positive relationship between overall exposure and gender-role stereotypes. Although all viewing groups average low (given the −6 to +6 range), the heavy viewers are more likely to give sexist responses. This remains stable in subgroups; for instance although males tend to be much more sexist than females, the strength of the positive association between television exposure and sexism is consistent regardless of gender. Also, those whose fathers have less education are more sexist, but both education groups display similar positive and significant sexism-exposure associations.

All age groups show positive associations between overall viewing and sexism, but the relationship is strongest among the older respondents (even though, as a group, the older students are sharply less sexist). This is a classic case of mainstreaming, in which groups of light viewers who are generally different on some attitude measure tend to be closer together as heavy viewers.

The significant positive relation holds up at all levels of U.S. exposure, but diminishes as U.S. exposure increases. This suggests that U.S programs may exert a mediating influence with respect to gender-role stereotypes, because the positive association for overall amount of viewing is strongest among those who do not report many U.S. programs

TABLE 11.2 Television and Sex-Role Stereotypes in Argentina and Taiwan

	Argentina						Taiwan					
	Overall Viewing Hours			U.S. Programming			Overall Viewing Hours			U.S. Programming		
	Light	Medium	Heavy	Light	Medium	Heavy	Light	Medium	Heavy	Light	Medium	Heavy
Overall	-1.83	-1.17	-0.37***	-1.01	-0.75	-1.34	1.39	1.36	1.14	1.31	1.22	1.37
Sex												
Male	-0.78	0.23	0.64*	-0.35	0.47	-0.05	1.95	2.30	1.91	2.01	2.03	2.13
Female	-2.38	-1.77	-0.90***	-1.29	-1.42	-1.91	0.88	0.43	0.41*	0.69	0.54	0.53
Age												
Young	-0.74	0.02	-0.09	0.00	-0.21	-0.44	1.00	0.93	0.61	1.05	0.78	0.84
Middle	-1.44	-1.06	-0.98	-1.26	-0.49	-1.36	1.53	1.32	1.31	1.22	1.20	1.52
Older	-2.57	-1.82	-0.55***	-1.75	-1.18	-2.09	1.55	1.83	1.76	1.61	1.73	1.78
Father's education												
No college	-1.31	-0.65	-0.08**	-0.59	-0.19	-1.00	1.16	1.20	1.30	1.07	1.17	1.36
College	-2.43	-2.65	-1.69***	-2.18	-2.01	-2.27	1.39	1.26	1.13	1.32	1.10	1.36
U.S. viewing												
Light	-1.93	-1.32	0.03***				1.21	1.53	1.30			
Medium	-1.80	-0.43	-0.28**				1.52	1.02	1.13			
Heavy	-1.69	-1.72	-0.72*				1.63	1.57	1.10			
Overall viewing												
Light				-1.93	-1.80	-1.69				1.21	1.52	1.63
Medium				-1.32	-0.43	-1.72*				1.53	1.02	1.57
Heavy				0.03	-0.28	-0.72				1.30	1.13	1.10

NOTES: Scale range = -6 (least sexist) to $+6$ (most sexist)
$*p < .05$; $**p < .01$; $***p < .001$ (one-way F-test)

among their favorites or among those seen "yesterday." This ma
perhaps be because Argentine television is relatively more stereotypica
than U.S. television, or because U.S. programs may contain at leas
some counter-stereotypical models rarely seen in Argentine programs

But any impact of U.S. exposure (as an independent variable) o
sexism is less apparent. Heavy viewers of U.S. programs are the leas
sexist, and the relationship is not monotonic across viewing levels. I
different subgroups (i.e., older viewers, low-socioeconomic-status view
ers, and others), there are some scattered associations that suggest tha
U.S. exposure cultivates less sexism. Again, this may indicate that U.S
programs (or those who watch them) are more progressive than Argen
tine programs in terms of gender-roles. In any case, and in contrast t
the strong patterns observed for overall viewing, there is essentially n
relationship between sexism and exposure to programs imported fror
the United States.

The Taiwanese data are far less clear. The Taiwanese students are
by these same measures of gender-role stereotypes, more sexist than th
Argentines, across the board. However, exposure to Taiwanese televi
sion actually goes with less gender-role stereotyping, although th
relationship is not significant. The only significant subgroup relation i
for females, who are much less traditional than their male counterparts
and who are even more "progressive" if they watch more television.

Controlling for age produces a similar cross-current. Younger an
middle students show negative associations between viewing and sex
ism, but older students (who are most traditional) show a positive one
These patterns are all nonsignificant, but they are the exact opposite o
mainstreaming; greater viewing goes with an increase, not a reduction
in the attitude differences of Taiwanese students within sex and ag
subgroups. There are also nonsignificant mainstreaming patterns unde
controls for father's education and U.S. exposure.

U.S. television exposure itself as an independent variable has negli
gible impact. Among those who watch relatively little television over
all, more viewing of U.S. programs means slightly higher sexism
whereas the relationship is negative among those who do watch a lo
overall. On the whole, however, frequency of watching U.S. program
is essentially unrelated to sexism scores in Taiwan, overall and withi
subgroups.

Thus, for sexism, the association with television is far greater i
Argentina than in Taiwan, where sexism is greater and more consisten
across subgroups. U.S. viewing has little-to-no apparent impact i

ither country, except perhaps to reduce the positive contribution of
verall viewing in Argentina and to increase the negative contribution
f overall viewing in Taiwan.

In terms of the "Mean World Syndrome," the data show no relation-
hips with television exposure in the Argentine sample. Table 11.3
resents the data on this construct (scores range from 0 to 3, indicating
ie number of "Mean World" answers given on the three items). The
:ale values are essentially clustered around the median, and there is
o real deviation across viewing levels in any subgroups.

Similarly, there is no evidence that U.S. exposure contributes much
) Mean World beliefs for Argentine students. In fact, such beliefs are
lightly less evident among heavy U.S. viewers. The largest difference
)r U.S. viewing is found among those who watch little television in
eneral, who are actually less mistrustful if they watch more U.S.
rograms. The other controls reveal very small relationships and no
onsistent trends. We conclude that there is no cultivation of a Mean
/orld Syndrome in this Argentine sample.

The situation is different in Taiwan, however, where mistrust scores
re lower than in Argentina, but more related to television exposure.
he relationships are positive in all subgroups, as would be typically
ypothesized by cultivation analysis, although they are not always
ignificant or monotonic. Moreover, the relationship between overall
xposure and the Mean World Syndrome is strong within the group that
; more heavily exposed to U.S. television, which is something that
ultivation would predict.

As an independent variable, however, U.S. television makes no
ifference in Mean World scores. Counter to expectations, heavy U.S.
iewers in Taiwan are slightly less likely to give Mean World answers,
1 almost all subgroups. Thus, overall exposure to television may
ultivate Mean World beliefs in Taiwan, but watching U.S. television
oes not.

Finally, Table 11.4 presents the data on authoritarianism. In Argen-
na, the evidence is quite strong that television cultivates authoritarian
iews. Although all respondents, on the average, score on the non-
uthoritarian end of the scale, the heavy viewers score significantly
igher than the light viewers. This is especially noticeable in the
otherwise" less authoritarian groups: females, older students, and those
'hose fathers attended college. All three demographic controls produce
iainstreaming. As with sexism, the association is strongest among
iose who watch less U.S. television, and weakest among those who

TABLE 11.3 Television and Mean World Beliefs in Argentina and Taiwan

	Argentina						Taiwan					
	Overall Viewing Hours			U.S. Programming			Overall Viewing Hours			U.S. Programming		
	Light	Medium	Heavy	Light	Medium	Heavy	Light	Medium	Heavy	Light	Medium	Heavy
Overall	1.97	2.05	2.01	2.03	1.96	1.98	1.48	1.37	1.59*	1.53	1.49	1.45
Sex												
Male	1.93	1.94	1.97	2.02	1.88	1.93	1.52	1.40	1.58	1.52	1.63	1.42
Female	1.98	2.10	2.04	2.04	2.01	2.00	1.46	1.35	1.60	1.54	1.38	1.50
Age												
Young	2.03	1.95	2.05	2.00	1.96	2.01	1.44	1.52	1.57	1.52	1.56	1.51
Middle	2.05	1.93	2.12	2.03	1.93	1.95	1.42	1.23	1.50	1.43	1.42	1.32
Older	1.86	2.12	1.92*	2.03	1.95	1.95	1.57	1.41	1.74*	1.62	1.51	1.55
Father's education												
No college	2.04	2.04	2.01	2.05	2.05	1.98	1.54	1.41	1.65	1.69	1.49	1.53
College	1.86	2.14	1.98	2.00	1.75	1.98	1.48	1.32	1.58	1.33	1.49	1.47
U.S. viewing												
Light	2.12	1.97	2.17				1.52	1.49	1.62			
Medium	1.89	2.09	1.90				1.50	1.38	1.65			
Heavy	1.82	2.09	1.97				1.47	1.31	1.58*			
Overall viewing												
Light				2.12	1.89	1.82*				1.52	1.50	1.47
Medium				1.97	2.09	2.09				1.49	1.38	1.31
Heavy				2.17	1.90	1.97				1.62	1.65	1.58

NOTES: Scale range = 0 (no Mean World responses) to 3 (3 Mean World responses)
*$p < .05$ (one-way F-Test)

TABLE 11.4 Television and Authoritarian Attitudes in Argentina and Taiwan

| | Argentina | | | | | | Taiwan | | | | | |
| | Overall Viewing Hours | | | U.S. Programming | | | Overall Viewing Hours | | | U.S. Programming | | |
	Light	Medium	Heavy	Light	Medium	Heavy	Light	Medium	Heavy	Light	Medium	Heavy
Overall	-2.90	-2.34	-1.93**	-2.38	-2.34	-2.37	-1.14	-1.26	-1.25	-1.08	-1.30	-1.21
Sex												
Male	-2.52	-1.80	-2.03	-2.39	-1.93	-2.07	-1.21	-1.36	-1.34	-1.06	-1.39	-1.34
Female	-3.10	-2.60	-1.87**	-2.36	-2.57	-2.50	-1.07	-1.17	-1.14	-1.09	-1.20	-1.07
Age												
Young	-2.23	-2.32	-2.37	-2.22	-2.08	-2.34	-1.17	-1.55	-1.37	-1.10	-1.48	-1.36
Middle	-2.96	-2.05	-1.98	-2.47	-2.22	-2.35	-1.08	-0.88	-0.97	-0.84	-1.12	-0.98
Older	-3.19	-2.43	-1.70**	-2.73	-2.75	-2.19	-1.16	-1.43	-1.37	-1.25	-1.25	-1.33
Father's education												
No college	-2.58	-2.33	-1.88*	-2.12	-2.33	-2.27	-1.02	-1.36	-1.12	-1.18	-1.25	-1.09
College	-3.38	-2.41	-1.93**	-2.90	-2.58	-2.57	-1.13	-1.17	-1.30	-0.95	-1.40	-1.13
U.S. viewing												
Light	-3.09	-2.15	-1.78**				-1.22	-0.92	-1.02			
Medium	-2.76	-2.47	-1.90				-1.09	-1.44	-1.36			
Heavy	-2.74	-2.39	-2.05				-1.20	-1.26	-1.16			
Overall viewing												
Light				-3.09	-2.76	-2.74				-1.22	-1.09	-1.20
Medium				-2.15	-2.47	-2.39				-0.92	-1.44	-1.26
Heavy				-1.78	-1.90	-2.05				-1.02	-1.36	-1.16

NOTES: Scale range = -6 (least authoritarian) to +6 (most authoritarian)
*$p < .05$ **$p < .001$ (one-way F-Test)

watch more; that is, as with sexism, U.S. viewing appears to diminish, and not to intensify, the contribution of overall exposure.

On the other hand, when U.S. exposure is treated as an independent variable, there is simply no relationship. Only for those whose fathers attended college is there even a marginally significant (positive) association ($p < .10$). Those who do not watch much television overall are the least authoritarian, but are more likely to express authoritarian views if they watch more U.S. programs; conversely, those who are generally heavy viewers are the most authoritarian, but are less so if they are heavy viewers of U.S. programs. As with sexism, exposure to U.S. television seems to moderate the extreme views cultivated by Argentine television, while it cultivates those same views among those who do not watch much and would "otherwise" not hold them.

In Taiwan, scores on the authoritarian scale are on the average higher than in Argentina. There are, however, no relationships between overall television exposure and authoritarianism. Subgroup patterns are small and inconsistent, and may simply reflect random fluctuations. U.S. exposure in Taiwan is associated with lower authoritarianism, but not significantly so. In most subgroups, the heavy viewers of U.S. programs are less authoritarian than the light viewers U.S. programs, but none of the relationships are statistically significant, and there are no significant interactions. Thus, amount of viewing (overall or U.S.) appears to be unrelated to authoritarianism in Taiwan.

CONCLUSION

First, we must note that these analyses were done without the benefit of an important foundation of cultivation analysis, namely the empirical analysis of the television message system in Argentina and Taiwan. For this reason, it is especially important to recall some of the qualitative differences in the television systems that were discussed early on in this chapter. Overall, the Argentine system is arguably closer to that of the United States than is the case for Taiwan. Given this alone, one might expect cultivation patterns to be more similar to the United States in Argentina than in Taiwan. The fact that Argentina is in some ways more dependent culturally upon the United States than is Taiwan also reinforces this notion.

For the most part, the data lend support to this view. In Argentina, television exposure clearly relates to students' attitudes, especially in the areas of gender-role stereotypes and authoritarianism. The overall cultivation patterns and instances of mainstreaming are highly congruent with what is often found in U.S. research. Argentine television, like U.S. television, appears to reinforce notions of traditional gender-roles and authoritarianism.

The interesting "cross-current" relationships seen with U.S. and Argentine television exposure suggest that Argentine television may be even more sexist and more authoritarian than U.S. television, or is interpreted to be such by local viewers. The frequency, consistency, and intensity of sexist images disseminated by Argentine television are arguably even higher than in the United States, which would explain why the cultivation relationships (with overall viewing) decrease at higher levels of U.S. television exposure. The same observation would apply in terms of authoritarianism. For Argentine youth who see few U.S. programs (and who are most sexist/authoritarian), greater overall viewing goes with less sexism/authoritarianism; for those who see more U.S. programs (and who score lowest on these measures), greater overall viewing goes with higher scores.

With respect to the data about mistrust, the cultivation of the Mean World Syndrome was supported in Taiwan, and especially among those who also see more U.S. programs, even though such exposure itself is not associated with these beliefs. In the context of the lack of relationships with other variables in Taiwan, and the weakness of the relationship, this association should not be overinterpreted.

Generally, the important thing to note about Taiwan is the lack of overall cultivation. Compared to both Argentina and the United States, television appears to be relatively less important in terms of adolescents' conceptions of social reality. The most important statistic in this regard is the simple amount of television exposure, which is much less in Taiwan than any Western countries that have been studied. Given this, to find strong cultivation patterns in Taiwan might have been something of a shock. Except for the Mean World measures, there appear to be few substantial or consistent relationships with television viewing in Taiwan. One possibility is that Taiwanese students do not watch enough television to manifest any real "effect." Also, the simple lack of variation in the answer categories suggests a greater cultural homogeneity in Taiwan than in Argentina. Argentina has been torn by divisive cultural and political rifts, while Taiwan has lived under single-party rule for a significant time. This may partially explain the lack of variation in the Taiwanese data.

Another possible inference is a kind of mainstreaming between the two countries. Adolescents in Argentina score lower than adolescents in Taiwan on both sexism and authoritarianism, yet viewing is related to those attitudes only in Argentina. Conversely, the Taiwanese students are less mistrustful than the Argentines, and the cultivation of the Mean World Syndrome is observed only in Taiwan. Thus, the heavy viewers of the two countries are more similar in their attitudes than are the light viewers.

Although overall amount of viewing in each country does show some relationships that replicate U.S. findings, there is little evidence for much impact of exposure to U.S. television itself. This is striking given the concerns of many about the impacts of U.S. television abroad. In most cases, relationships with U.S. exposure in both countries are either weak and inconsistent or actually opposite to those found in the United States.

Some implications for the cross-cultural study of media effects are fairly clear. Cultivation theory argues that television messages are important in direct proportion to two factors: the extent to which they are consistent, and the extent to which they are consumed. Thus, the greater consistency of messages in Argentina (where 80% of screen time consists of entertainment) compared to Taiwan (where only 50% is entertainment) and the greater consumption of messages in Argentina (at twice the rate of the Taiwanese) might help explain why cultivation would be more pronounced in Argentina.

Of course, there are everyday cultural particularities that may be important for mass media effects as well. Different people (and cultures) have different ways of attending to television, and different contexts for interpreting its content. This study, attending to the macrolevel and systemic differences between the two countries, has not dealt with these issues. Other studies have begun to focus on the different practices involved in watching television in different national contexts (e.g., Lull, 1988), although they are not explicitly linked to cultivation research. A challenging but fruitful area for future research would be to explore the links between microlevel cultural practices and macrolevel media effects, especially within a comparative framework.

In sum, when the models and methods of cultivation analysis are applied to countries in which television's portrayals are less repetitive and homogeneous, the findings will tend to be more inconsistent. Imported (U.S.) programs can augment, diminish, or be irrelevant to these dynamics. The cross-cultural "effects" of television are complex and nonmechanical and involve far more than the technology alone.

Different historical, political, social, economic, and cultural contexts, and different mixes of messages and exposure patterns, produce different consequences.

REFERENCES

Antola, L., & E. M. Rogers. (1984). Television flows in Latin America. *Communication Research, 11*(2), 183-202.

Bonfadelli, H. (1982). Der Einfluss des Fernsehens auf die konstruktion der sozialen Realitat: Befunde aus der Schweiz zur Kultivierungshypothese. *Rundfunk und Fernsehen, 31*(3-4), 415-430.

Bouwman, H. (1984). Cultivation analysis: The Dutch case. In G. Melischek, K. E. Rosengren, & J. Stappers (Eds.), *Cultural indicators: An international symposium* (pp. 407-422). Vienna: Verlag der Osterreichischen Akademie der Wissenschaften.

Bouwman, H., P. Nelissen, & U. Meier. (1987). Culturele indicatoren 1980-1985. *Massacommunicatie, XV*(1), 18-35.

Bouwman, H., & N. Signorielli. (1985). A comparison of U.S. and Dutch programming. *Gazette, 35*, 93-108.

Bouwman, H., & J. Stappers. (1984). The Dutch violence profile: A replication of Gerbner's message system analysis. In G. Melischek, K. E. Rosengren, & J. Stappers (Eds.), *Cultural indicators: An international symposium* (pp. 113-128). Vienna: Verlag der Österreichischen Akademie der Wissenschaften.

Daddario, G., Kang, J. G., Morgan, M., & Wu., Y. K. (1988). Les programmes américains de télévision et les transformations culturelles en Corée et à Taiwan. *Tiers-Monde, 3*, 65-74.

Doob, A. N. & G. E. Macdonald. (1979). Television viewing and fear of victimization: Is the relationship causal? *Journal of Personality and Social Psychology, 37*, 170-179.

Ford, A. (1987). Aproximación al tema de federalismo y comunicación. In O. Landi (Ed.), *Medios, transformación cultural y política*. Buenos Aires: Editorial Legasa.

Gerbner, G. (1958). On content analysis and critical research in mass communication. *AV Communication Review, 6*(2), 85-108.

Gerbner, G. (1969). Toward "cultural indicators": The analysis of mass mediated message systems. *AV Communication Review, 17*(2), 137-148.

Gerbner, G. (1977). Comparative cultural indicators. In G. Gerbner (Ed.), *Mass media policies in changing cultures* (pp. 199-205). New York: John Wiley.

Gerbner, G., & Gross, L. (1976). Living with television: The violence profile. *Journal of Communication, 26*(2), 173-199.

Gerbner, G., Gross, L., Morgan, M., & Signorielli, N. (1982). Charting the mainstream: TV's contribution to political orientations. *Journal of Communication, 32*(2), 100-127.

Gerbner, G., Gross, L., Morgan, M., & Signorielli, N. (1986). Living with television: The dynamics of the cultivation process. In J. Bryant & D. Zillman (Eds.), *Perspectives on media effects* (pp. 17-40). Hillsdale, NJ: Lawrence Erlbaum.

Gross, L., & Jeffries-Fox, S. (1978). What do you want to be when you grow up, little girl? In G. Tuchman, A. K. Daniels, & J. Benet (Eds.), *Hearth and home: Images of women in the mass media* (pp. 240-265). New York: Oxford University Press.

Gunter, B. (1987). *Television and the fear of crime*. London: Libbey.

Hawkins, R. P., & Pingree, S. (1982). Television's influence on social reality. In D. Pearl, L. Bouthilet, & J. Lazar (Eds.), *Television and behavior: Ten years of scientific progress and implications for the 80's: Vol. II. Technical reviews* (pp. 224-247). Rockville, MD: National Institute of Mental Health.

Hedinsson, E., & Windahl, S. (1984). Cultivation analysis: A Swedish illustration. In G. Melischek, K. E. Rosengren, & J. Stappers (Eds.), *Cultural indicators: An international symposium* (pp. 389-406). Vienna: Verlag der Österreichischen Akademie der Wissenschaften.

Horvath, R. (1987). *La trama secreta de la radiodifusión Argentina: Los dueños de la información electronica y el largo brazo de su poder* (2nd ed.). Buenos Aires: Ediciones Unidad.

Horvath, R. (1988). *Los medios en la neocolonización.* Buenos Aires: Editorial Rescate.

Kang, J. G., & Morgan, M. (1988). Culture clash: Impact of U.S. television in Korea. *Journalism Quarterly, 65,* 431-438.

Landi, O. (Ed.). (1987). *Medios, transformación cultural y política.* Buenos Aires: Editorial Legasa.

Lull, J. (Ed.). (1988). *World families watch television.* Newbury Park, CA: Sage.

Melischek, G., Rosengren, K. E., & Stappers, J. (Eds.). (1984). *Cultural indicators: An international symposium.* Vienna: Verlag der Österreichischen Akademie der Wissenschaften.

Morgan, M. (1982). Television and adolescents' sex-role stereotypes: A longitudinal study. *Journal of Personality and Social Psychology, 43*(5), 947-955.

Morgan, M. (1989a). Cultivation analysis. In E. Barnouw (Ed.), *The international encyclopedia of communications* (pp. 430-433). New York: Oxford University Press.

Morgan, M. (1989b). Television and democracy. In I. Angus & S. Jhally (Eds.), *Cultural politics in contemporary America* (pp. 240-253). New York: Routledge & Kegan Paul.

Morgan. M. (1990). International cultivation analysis. In N. Signorielli & M. Morgan (Eds.), *Cultivation analysis: New directions in media effects research* (pp. 225-247). Newbury Park, CA: Sage.

Piepe, A., Charlton, P., & Morey, J. (1990). Politics and television viewing in England: Hegemony or pluralism? *Journal of Communication, 40*(1), 24-35.

Pingree, S., & Hawkins, R. (1981). U.S. programs on Australian television: The cultivation effect. *Journal of Communication, 31*(1), 97-105.

Reimer, B., & Rosengren, K. E. (1990). Cultivated viewers and readers: A life-style perspective. In N. Signorielli & M. Morgan (Eds.), *Cultivation analysis: New directions in media effects research* (pp. 181-206). Newbury Park, CA: Sage.

Schement, J. R., & Rogers, E. M. (1984). Media flows in Latin America. *Communication Research, 11*(2), 305-320.

Signorielli, N., & Morgan, M. (Eds.). (1990). *Cultivation analysis: New directions in media effects research.* Newbury Park, CA: Sage.

Sirven, P. (1988). *Quien te ha visto y quien TV.* Buenos Aires: Ediciones de la Flor.

Stappers, J. G. (1984). De eigen aard van televisie: Tien stellingen over cultivatie en culturele indicatoren. *Massacommunicatie, XII*(5-6), 249-258.

Straubhaar, J. D., & King, G. (1987). Effects of television on film in Argentina, Brazil, and Mexico. In B. A. Austin (Ed.), *Current research in film: Audiences, economics, and law* (Vol. 3, pp. 52-71). Norwood, NJ: Ablex.

Tamborini, R., & Choi, J. (1990). The role of cultural diversity in cultivation research. In N. Signorielli & M. Morgan (Eds.), *Cultivation analysis: New directions in media effects research* (pp. 147-180). Newbury Park, CA: Sage.

Tan, A. S., Li, S., & Simpson, C. (1986). U.S. television and social stereotypes of Americans in Taiwan and Mexico. *Journalism Quarterly, 63,* 809-814.

Tan, A. S., & Suarchavarat, K. (1988). U.S. television and social stereotypes of Americans in Thailand. *Journalism Quarterly, 65,* 648-654.

Tan, A. S., Tan, G. K., & Tan, A. S. (1987). U.S. television in the Philippines: A test of cultural impact. *Journalism Quarterly, 63,* 537-541.

Varis, T. (1984). The international flow of television programs. *Journal of Communication, 34*(1), 143-152.

Vivoni-Remus, C. A., Morgan, M., & Gorlier, J. C. (1990). Problems in conducting survey research on the effects of television in Argentina: A case study. In U. Narula & W. B. Pearce (Eds.), *Practical problems in field research.* Hillsdale, NJ: Lawrence Erlbaum.

Weimann, G. (1984). Images of life in America: The impact of U.S. T.V. in Israel. *International Journal of Intercultural Relations, 8,* 185-197.

Wober, J. M. (1978). Televised violence and paranoid perception: The view from Great Britain. *Public Opinion Quarterly, 42*(3), 315-321.

Wober, J. M. (1984). Prophecy and prophylaxis: Predicted harms and their absence in a regulated television system. In G. Melischek, K. E. Rosengren, & J. Stappers (Eds.), *Cultural indicators: An international symposium* (pp. 423-440). Vienna: Verlag der Österreichischen Akademie der Wissenschaften.

Wober, J. M. (1990). Does television cultivate the British? Late 80s evidence. In N. Signorielli & M. Morgan (Eds.), *Cultivation analysis: New directions in media effects research* (pp. 207-224). Newbury Park, CA: Sage.

Wober, J. M., & Gunter, B. (1988). *Television and social control.* New York: St. Martin's Press.

Wu, Y. (1989). *Television and the value systems of Taiwan's adolescents: A cultivation analysis.* Unpublished doctoral dissertation, University of Massachusetts, Amherst.

III

MEDIA ACROSS CULTURES
AND THE FUTURE

12

Media Networking
Toward a Model for the Global
Management of Sociocultural Change

L. RIPLEY SMITH ● *University of Minnesota*

World cooperation will require sociocultural change; change in the way we think, the attitudes we possess, and the behaviors we manifest. The following chapter presents an interdisciplinary theoretical model for managing global ecological resources, and the ensuing sociocultural change, interculturally. It explores the role of media in network formation and the promotion of transsocietal cooperation, cross-cultural coordination, and "institutionalizing ecological interdependence." The creation of empathy through vicarious interaction experience is posited as a key process in the necessary cognitive restructuring for international cooperation. Achieving cooperation at the global level requires certain levels of shared cultural meaning, a method for managing that meaning and its consequences, and an integrated plan for management sharing. A model describing the use of media to transmit empathy-generating messages that link local level networks in a process of global network formation is defined and illustrated. The chapter concludes with a challenge to focus future research and practice on local-level networks and their efforts to instill geocentric perspective and globalize their communities.

There are many problems confronting the world today, such as preventing nuclear war and slowing the arms race, stopping global warming and deforestation, restructuring debt-ridden and failing economies, and supporting the earth's burgeoning population on finite resources. In view of all of these problems it seems that what is needed most of all is a vision for world cooperation. World cooperation across local, regional, ethnic, cultural, political, and ideological borders will require sociocultural change: change in the way we think, the attitudes we possess, and the behaviors we manifest. The recognition of the need for trans-societal

AUTHOR'S NOTE: The author wishes to express his thanks to Dr. Luther Gerlach for helpful criticism on an earlier draft. The responsibility for inaccuracies, however, remains solely that of the author.

cooperation, cross-cultural coordination, and "institutionalizing ecolog ical interdependence" regarding what are essentially common resource: has been crescendoing for some time, until recently it hit a forte (Bennett, 1987; Gerlach, 1989, in press; Gerlach & Radcliffe, 1979) Now models are being sought and solutions are being discussed. Unfortunately, it may take a fortissimo in order to reach a state of action Events and changes taking place in the environment, Eastern and Western Europe, and the Middle East may provide the necessary impetus for that action. President Eisenhower's words of 1959 ring with increased poignancy today:

> What we call foreign affairs is no longer foreign affairs. It's a local affair Whatever happens in Indonesia is important to Indiana. Whatever happens in any corner of the world has some effect on the farmer in Dickinson County, Kansas, or on a worker at a factory. . . . The world must learn to work together—or finally it will not work at all. (p. 2)

In response to a lack of specific intercultural models to follow, the present chapter will develop a working model for the initiation and coordination of sociocultural change that must accompany interdependence. Specifically, this chapter will focus on managing sociocultural change resulting from recognition of interdependence on environmental or ecological resources. By combining complementary theories and paradigms in a critical realist, or pluralistic fashion, a holistic picture of the processes necessary for transsocietal cooperation and management is presented. Ideally, the model presented will result in an increase in ecological awareness, intercultural interaction, and sensitivity to the ramifications of collective actions among and between societies. Following a brief discussion of interdependence and an overview of the proposed model, the chapter will focus on the underlying assumptions, theoretical constructs, and propositions set forth.

RESOLVING INTERDEPENDENT TENSION

The problem of global interdependence has received extensive attention from multiple disciplinary perspectives (Arcury et al., 1986; Bennett, 1987; Cotgrove, 1982; Durning, 1989; Gerlach, 1989, 1990; Gerlach & Radcliffe, 1979; Gerlach & Rayner, 1988; Large, 1981; Lerner, 1966; Mulford, 1984); however, the insight afforded from a communication perspective has yet to be substantially offered. Gerlach and Radcliffe (1979) delineate the growing tension between concerns over independence and movements toward interdependence. They allude to the need for answers that can only be derived from a "higher consciousness" and "vision." Cotgrove (1982, citing Bell, 1976) provides a beginning point to the search for answers, stating that "change[s] in consciousness—in values and moral reasoning—is what moves men to change their social arrangements and institutions" (p. 110). Such a beginning point requires a process of cognitive restructuring, that is, a reformation of social schemata that dictate action.

Large (1981) suggests that "the starting point of social ecology is respect for and clear understanding of the phenomena of life: in the organic realm, and in man and society" (p. 7). He further argues that the physical consciousness that enabled the opening up of our planet and its resources must be replaced by a new life consciousness concerned with the maintenance of the biosphere, in terms of the natural environment, the life of the atmosphere, and social concerns. A life consciousness indicates an empathetic disposition toward, and appreciation of, all forms of life; it is in contrast to a narcissistic attitude and disrespect for the needs and concerns of others, and a disregard for the rest of the system to which one belongs. The development of a "life consciousness" in turn, "gives rise to holistic thinking appropriate to the understanding of the development of human and social forms in time" (Large, 1981, p. 10). Similarly, Arcury, Johnson, and Scollay (1986) associate changes in environmental worldview with increased effort to comprehend the nature of the human-ecology relationship.

To manage interdependence, several processes must work in concert. Interdependence must be recognized, mutual understanding and respect established, and cooperation and coordination must be institutionalized. These processes involve a multitude of complex issues, including defining the social and biophysical parameters of the common resource and identifying its uses and users. Transnational or transsocietal agreements must be established regarding priorities of use, obligations, and privileges, in order to satisfy any conflicts of prima facie ownership or rights. A system for organizing the evaluation of sociocultural change must also be developed as well as a means of enforcing agreements. As a result of what Gudykunst and Kim (1984) refer to as "technological connectedness," a condition exists in which the earth's societies have been forced to construct a superculture to accommodate the interaction of diverse worldviews in an emerging global society (Mowlana, 1983).

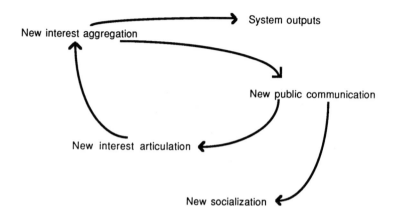

Figure 12.1: Modification of Lerner's (1966) Modernization Cycle

That same superculture must begin to accommodate recently recognized ecological interdependence as societies realize the need to share the earth.

The proposed model is based in part on Lerner's (1966) cycle of modernization (see Figure 12.1). Lerner described the social change process as beginning "with new public communication—the diffusion of new ideas and new information which stimulate people to want to behave in new ways, . . . new public communication leads directly to new articulation of private interests . . . simultaneously—new public communication activates new modes of socialization" (p. 241). Table 12.1 presents the core components of the media-networking model that suggests a process for the management of global resources whereby media are used to link local level networks to issues of global concern. The operational task can be thought of as forming, or utilizing existing, local networks, which are connected to the global network via mass media. The mass media serve to expose new populations with information, which motivates public interest and raises consciousness, increasing the size of, and interaction within, the global network. The audience is presented with a vicariously experienced universe through mediated messages, theoretically resulting in an increase in empathy for the cultural other. The generation of empathy consequently ties the individual to a subjective, global network, which finds its outworking in local networks. The global network's structure is created by social relationships consisting of sharing information and ideas with a common purpose.

TABLE 12.1 Media-Networking Model Outline

Assumptions
1. A sociocultural system emerges as environments, resources, and patterned flows of those resources are defined and operationalized.
2. Societies are interdependent for ecological security to the degree they share the same social and biophysical environment.

Theoretical Constructs
1. Media effected consciousness raising as a means for generating empathy through vicarious experience.
2. Network convergence as a means for sharing symbols and meanings.
3. Cooperative network modality as means for network organization and interaction.
4. Empathy as means for developing cooperation.

Propositions
1. Intercultural management of sociocultural change requires a degree of shared cultural meaning effected by mediated consciousness raising.
2. Intercultural management of sociocultural change requires an integrated networking strategy for cooperation to exist.
3. Intercultural management of sociocultural change requires a commitment to macrolevel egalitarianism and microlevel autonomy for purposes of coordination and efficiency.

Central to the efficacy of the model is the state, or modality of the interconnected networks; it is essential that networks operate within a cooperative rather than a competitive modality. These network patterns not only produce new socialization patterns, but also system outputs affecting the environment in positive ways. Given increased ecological awareness, and a more geocentric cosmology, people will attempt to ascertain the limits to which the natural environment can be pushed, and the optimal state and function of human biosphere interaction. One might also infer that people will come to recognize that the "care of the natural environment is a socially shared activity" (Large, 1981, p. 9).

FOUNDATIONS OF THE MODEL

Assumption 1: Sociocultural Systems

As environments, resources, and patterned flows of those resources are defined and operationalized, a social system emerges. Much of the literature surrounding sociocultural change on a global scale views the world's societies as participating in a system where the interdependent parts are linked together in relationships that serve to define a much larger, inclusive society that has distinguishing properties apart from those of the individual units that comprise it. Ruben (1983) proposes that "individuals are members of a social system—as opposed to a simple social aggregate, when: (1) the unit they are a part of is definitionally distinct from and greater than the sum of the individuals; and (2) the individuals are organized in relationship with one another such that the actions and reactions of one individual will have potential consequences for other individuals and for the social unit as a whole, and vice versa" (p. 139). If we view the world's societies as comprising a system where the individuals in each subsystem are linked to the larger system through resource relationships, then the social definition of resources and interaction within that system create patterned flows of resources that define the larger system and produce repercussions on each subsystem. Embracing this assumption leads to two further suppositions regarding culture and the media.

First, managing sociocultural change within a global system necessitates a systemic understanding of the levels of culture, and the extent participants in the system must share in these levels in order to effectively cooperate in the management of global resources (Gerlach, 1990, personal communication). First, a systemic perspective views culture as a complex phenomenon, consisting of various levels upon which individuals may operate (Hofstede, 1984; Spindler, 1977). Secondly, a systemic view suggests that participation in a culture is not a discrete or dichotomous relationship, but operates on a continuum, allowing individuals multiple degrees of involvement on those various levels. Finally, the systemic nature of cultural entities involves interrelationships between external and internal influences, both acting and reacting in a process of mutual (recursive) definition. Viewing the management of sociocultural change as a quest for a global vision that facilitates cooperation, culture becomes a cognitive construct that must be shared in order to come to a consensus on meaning. D'Andrade (1984) notes that anthropologists from the cognitive paradigm argue that "culture consists not of behaviors, or even patterns of behavior, but rather of shared information or knowledge encoded in systems of symbols" (p. 88). In essence, cultures are shared systems of meaning, and "one of the basic things that meaning systems do for individuals is to guide their reactions and behavior" (p. 109). The term *culture* "designates a cognitive system, that is, a set of 'propositions' both descriptive . . . and normative . . . about nature, man, and society that are more or less embedded in interlocking higher-order networks and configurations" (Spiro, 1984, p. 323). Similarly, other anthropologists, such as Goodenough and Geedz, treat culture not as "things or behavior, but rather 'the forms of things that people have in mind, their models for perceiving, relating, and otherwise interpreting them' . . . as an ordered system of meanings and of symbols, in terms of which social interaction takes place and develops" (Barnett & Kincaid, 1983, p. 172).

Second, increasing technological interconnectedness within the global system indicates that media as human extensions produce effects that intersect social and cultural boundaries. Yaple and Korzenny (1989) conclude that even though media messages might undergo a great degree of distortion where transmitted between cultures, "some effect must take place" (p. 309). Media affect social arrangements, symbols, and meanings with their pervasiveness, tying societal systems together. D'Andrade (1984) sees the concept of social structure as pertaining to the coordinated use of systems of meaning (culture): "Social structure is one aspect of the organization of culture—the achievement of systematicity across persons through meanings" (p. 110). It is media's ability to create and coordinate a sense of shared meaning that the present model will emphasize as the instrument that serves to bond diverse groups together.

Assumption 2: Interdependence

Societies are interdependent for ecological security to the degree they share the same social and biophysical environment. This assumption suggests that each system and subsystem operates in an environment containing resources. The realm, or setting, of a system is considered an environment that consists of physical and/or symbolic space and a set of conditions identifying its boundaries and rules of operation. Mulford (1984) expands on the notion of environment, delineating several modes (technological, political, economic, demographic, ecological, and cultural), and proposes two distinct ways of conceptualizing it. He suggests that the environment may be seen as "a pool of needed resources" or "as information" (p. 9). Conceptualizing the environment as resources emphasizes the notions of dependence, exchange, relative power, control over sources of support, and the impact of transactions on structure. Conceptualizing the environment as information results in an emphasis on the acquisition of information on external elements, the means of that acquisition, perception, and uncertainty. In either conceptualization, a resource can be understood as "socialized/culturized environment . . . a resource is a functional relationship between an aspect of the biophysical environment and culturally valued goals and the means of manipulating this aspect" (Gerlach, 1989, p. 6). Resources, then, can be either informational or instrumental, tangible or intangible.

COMPONENTS OF THE MODEL

Media Effects

In conceptualizing a framework for utilizing media to facilitate sociocultural change, the focus is on media as an adaptive tool. The notion of media serving adaptive purposes is not new; thoughtful researchers have spoken of human "extensions" in the past and their place in human ingenuity, inventions, and scientific breakthroughs (Hall, 1976; Mcluhan, 1967; Yaple & Korzenny, 1989). These human extensions are fundamental to meeting environmental challenges and comprise a unique strategy for promoting international cooperation. The pervasive influence of media enables it as an extension to "permit man to solve problems in satisfactory ways, to evolve and adapt at great speed without changing the basic structure of his body" (Hall, 1976, p. 29). As an externalization, the media can be used as a tool for transmitting cultural visions and accelerate the adjustment process so that humankind is not forced to alter its basic structure—social, political, or biophysical—for ecological reasons.

Lerner (1966) demonstrated the role of global communication as a key factor in socialization. Many of his conceptualizations of communication as "enlightenment" are relevant to the issue of intercultural resource management. Lerner speaks of enlightenment as "the communication of information that affects the preference models of peoples" (p. 227). Mass media, with their extensive global coverage, play a very important role in disseminating information and modifying preferences. Social institutions that reinforce values can be molded and shaped so that new preferences are formed. Syme, Seligman, and Macpherson (1989) suggest that management of environmental resources be approached via the dynamic formation of values, rather than fitting a solution to a set of known preferences. In a sense, the management of ecological interdependence becomes a process of consciousness raising,

d as Large (1981) points out, "the media are increasingly involved in
e 'management of consciousness' " (p. 24).

Media are used for more than just raising consciousness, however.
indy and Matabane (1989) indicate that people are dependent on the
iss media for their link to the economic and political systems. The
imary purpose of the mass media is to supply viewers with "the raw
iterials from which they may construct an image of the 'lives, mean-
gs, practices and values for other groups and classes'. The media rank
d arrange these images as preferred meanings and interpretations that
produce and extend the dominant ideology" (Gandy & Matabane,
'89, p. 319). Others have suggested that in the international arena,
iages are the primary means by which nations communicate (Edelstein,
84). However, the extent of power or effectiveness of those media
iages to create consciousness and influence public opinion is vigor-
isly debated. Some research appears to indicate that people uncriti-
lly internalize media content and thus it shapes their consciousness;
her research characterizes the audience as a remediating, reinterpret-
g receiver of messages (Peck, 1989). Still other research seems to
lvocate a media effect that lies somewhere in between (Yaple &
brzenny, 1989). The following media effects theories recognize a
rtain degree of influence on individual and collective perception and
eference.

ultivation Hypothesis

This perspective associates the "common and recurring patterns of
ents and outcomes in television content to the social perceptions of
dividuals. . . . The cultivation hypothesis simply argues that the more
ie is exposed to a particular construction of reality, the more one will
>me to perceive that reality in similar terms" (Gandy & Matabane,
)89, p. 338). Exposure to various themes and content is thought to
irture the central patterns of a culture's institutions, attitude, value,
id belief systems, and interaction conventions (Gandy & Matabane,
)89). Cultivation produces a cumulative effect on an audience as the
idience is subjected to repeated exposures of a certain content. As
erbner (1969) has pointed out,

The creation of both the consciousness and the social structure called public
is the result of the "public-making" activity appropriately named publication. . . . Publication . . . is the creation and cultivation of shared ways of

selecting and viewing events and aspects of life. Mass production and distr
bution of message systems transforms selected private perspectives into broa
public perspectives, and brings mass publics into existence. . . . Publicatic
is thus the basis of community consciousness and self-government amon
large groups of people too numerous or too dispersed to interact face-to-fac
or in any other personally mediated fashion. (pp. 125-126)

Gerbner further suggests that mass media open up new avenues for th
formation of collective thought and action across difficult boundarie
of time, space, and culture. Closely associated with the cultivatio
hypothesis is the idea of "mainstreaming" (Gandy & Matabane, 1989
it refers to the idea of media as an instrument of social consensu
formation. Consistent and repeated cultural messages are eventuall
assimilated by the audience and commonalities are formed due to th
subtle effect of inundation.

Agenda Setting

This theory proposes that media "help produce the symbolic aren
within which are formed people's perceptions, knowledge, and belief
about the world. . . . Media's power reside in their ability to set certai
parameters on the symbolic realm within which we fashion a picture c
reality" (Peck, 1989, pp. 159-160). Agenda setting suggests that ther
is not an explicit causal connection between images transmitted throug
media and the construction of meaning on an individual level; howeve
consciousness is affected by a general constraining process. It is simila
to the popular phrase, "the media don't tell us what to think, but wha
to think about." Peck (1989) notes that studies have shown a relation
ship between people's perception of reality and the representations c
reality generated by mass media.

Symbolic Convergence

Yet another approach to mass media's influence in the creation c
meaning is that of symbolic convergence. Specifically, within th
symbolic convergence paradigm, the theory that is most informative t
the intent of the present model is that of fantasy theme/rhetorical visio
Breen and Corcoran (1986) suggest that "alternative approaches t
media research which place more emphasis on the symbolic capacity c
audience members" stress the interactive nature of the media-audienc
relationship, "an interactive process in which the symbolic worlds c

rticipant come closer together, particularly through the dynamic ocess of sharing group fantasies" (p. 197). Bormann's (1972) fantasy eme/rhetorical vision theory consists of the notion that participants teract in a particular scenario, assuming specific roles, and act out llective fantasy themes that are guided by an encompassing rhetorical sion. It is assumed that as the participants interact, they will experi- ce a convergence upon shared symbols and meanings, thus develop- g a common fantasy theme and perpetuating the rhetorical vision. is theory is enlightening to the network process as it relates to the ediated construction of meaning. As the media transmit the rhetorical sion, each local network adapts their local fantasy theme to the rpose of the vision and in a sense share in the symbols of the global etorical vision. These ideas appear to work in concert with Mead's ncept of the "significant symbol," in that commonality is developed rough the social construction of symbolic consciousness (Yaple & orzenny, 1989).

etwork Convergence

Systems, such as the global network described, are distinguished by their ique configuration of components, their relationships among units, their vironment, and the level upon which symbols and meanings are shared. e units within these systems, and the relationships that link them gether, can be understood as forming a regular pattern of exchange. ese patterns, or networks, are defined as "a specific set of linkages ong a defined set of persons with the additional property that the aracteristics of these linkages as a whole may be used to interpret the cial behavior of the persons involved" (Mitchell, 1969, p. 2). Network- sed theory assumes that "the ways in which nodes are connected to one other, both directly and indirectly, influence the behavior of particular des and the system as a whole" (Mulford, 1984, p. 136).

Networks can be driven by exchange, which emphasizes the notion reciprocity in relationships. Within a social network the relationships rve as channels for resources. The flow of these resources between des may be either unidirectional or bidirectional. For the proposed odel, the links must consist of mutual exchanges in order to be nctional. The existence of bidirectional exchange will most often dicate cooperation and participation. Another driving source for net- orks is that of action. Action suggests manipulation and goal attain- ent. It is perhaps inevitable, given the human condition, that whenever

personal interests are at stake there will be a certain degree of manip
lation involved in order to attain goals. Within and between networl
relations will be manipulated as individuals and groups seek to ma
mize their gain and minimize their loss in the pursuit of goals. For t
purposes of the present model, manipulation is something to be mi
mized. A third driving process within networks is that of convergen
We have discussed convergence as it relates to symbols and the forn
tion of a shared vision or reality, in essence it is the adhesive of t
network. Convergence theory posits that "mutual understanding p
vides the basis for mutual agreement and collective action" (Kinca
1987, p. 210). As exchange relations of information and other resour
are formed, the exchange provides the basis for mutual understandi
and consequently a convergence of cooperative interest, reducing t
manipulation which is a product of competition. Yum (1988) sugge
that the network-convergence paradigm offers a basic theorem that
"a prerequisite for self-organization and cultural evolution" (p. 243)

The function of networks then, both micro and macro, is to facilita
communication and information sharing in order to achieve empathe
cooperation and consensus in problem resolutions. Networking is id
for this purpose because it provides "an opportunity for broad pub
participation in policy development and program implementation, a
developing a true sense of 'community' " (Gilray & Swan, 1984, p. i

Cooperative Modality

Mulford (1984) suggests that networks may be characterized by o
of two different modalities (competitive or cooperative), where mod
ity "describes the general normative context permeating a network"
137). Mulford compares these modalities to the notion of "instituti
alized thought structures" in local communities that define acceptat
bases for relationships. The distinction is comparable to that of t
dichotomous relationship in interpersonal communication in whi
behaviors may either be complementary or symmetrical (in oppositio
As Barnett and Kincaid (1983) note, "once the participants reach sor
level of mutual understanding they may or may not agree with o
another's respective points of view" (p. 174). For that reason, t
present model suggests that interdependencies between communicate
need to be emphasized in a manner that promotes cooperation. A pivo
construct in the whole model is that of empathy. It is by means
creating empathy that cooperation is achieved.

Empathy

In a system as large as the posited global network, the only way to come to a point of convergence and shared understanding is by generating intercultural empathy via vicarious experience provided through mass media. Research has shown that cooperation and competition can be predicted based on expectations of a like response from "other." Lanzetta and Englis (1989) demonstrated that even through vicarious experience, expectations of cooperation resulted in empathetic responses while expectations of competition produced counterempathy. They associate empathy not with certain personality characteristics, but with expectations of situation outcomes and specific history influences. Empathy has been defined in a number of different manners and has been shown to serve many functions (Redmond, 1989). It will be used in a broad sense here to understand the process of identification needed in order to align one's interests with those of another and the consequent recognition of interdependence that allows optimal, mutually beneficial action. That means empathy may include perspective taking, emotional responses, concern for other, fantasy, and other cognitive responses that produce an attitude of cooperation toward the other.

PROPOSITIONS OF THE MODEL

The delineation of model constructs suggests several propositions regarding the management of sociocultural change that accompanies interdependence. A global network links the world's societies together. Even though at the level of the individual one may not perceive an inclusion in a global network, because of ecological resource involvement every individual represents a node in the network system. The media-networking model suggests that local networks, operating in a cooperative modality, articulate environmental/ecological resource concerns via media that effectively link them to other local-level networks with common concerns; presumedly the local networks become more cognizant of their place in a global social network, producing an increase in empathy for cultural others. The aggregate of concerns within the global network are bound together by an underlying vision to solve common problems, in this case ecological.

To begin to understand how a change in consciousness might be effected, transforming an out-of-awareness infrastructure into a participative global network, we need to see the management of interdependence as involving three simultaneous processes: the construction of shared cultural meanings, a means of global management, and a commitment to management sharing.

Sharing Meaning for Intercultural Interdependence

Intercultural management of sociocultural change requires a degree of shared cultural meaning effected by mediated consciousness raising. Communication is the process that integrates and ties a social system together. Many communication theorists have suggested that communication functions in everyday life as a means of coping and organizing social reality (Albrecht & Adelman, 1987; Brislin, 1981; Church, 1982; Dinges, 1983; Gudykunst, 1977; Gudykunst & Hammer, 1988; Gudykunst & Kim, 1984; Hanvey, 1976; Kim, 1978, 1987, 1989). The theoretical train of thought can be summarized as follows: When examining a social process, such as sociocultural change, adapting to that process requires knowledge; and acquiring that knowledge requires communication. From a convergence theory perspective, communication is "a process in which information is created and shared by two or more individuals who converge over time toward a greater degree of mutual understanding, agreement, and collective action" (Kincaid, 1987, p. 210). Media as extensions of natural human communication systems provide the channel for convergence and the process of sharing culture on a global level by sharing information through media.

The process of sharing meaning through media can be conceived of as occurring on three separate levels (see Figure 12.2): (a) an individual consciousness level of cultural meaning where problem recognition and interdependent awareness occur; (b) a local cooperative level of cultural meaning and symbol convergence where local solutions are planned and coordinated; and (c) a global management level where problem formulation occurs and crises are defined, consisting of shared symbols and a vision that guides local-level cooperative efforts. The media function to communicate a vision that guides future thought structures and institutions, which in turn cultivate new levels of global consciousness. Once a global vision is in place and local efforts to publicize "life consciousness" are institutionalized, the entire system becomes self-sustaining. The media serve the system by creating and sustaining the interdependent "village," becoming the means of interacting with the transmitted image of cultural others.

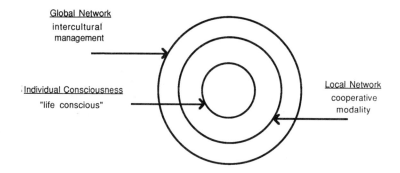

Figure 12.2: Sociocultural Levels of Conscious Interdependence

All of the media effect notions reviewed, cultivation and mainstreaming, agenda-setting, and fantasy theme/rhetorical vision are consistent with the goal of the present model in developing a means of linking sociocultural units to a global culture in which shared understandings pave the way toward cooperation. As the individual local units recognize their interdependence in the larger system, information flow through media outlets will serve to form a global level of culture where collective action is possible due to a convergence of symbols and meanings. Meaning is negotiated between communicators as they proceed via a feedback loop to approach mutual understanding of one another and a shared perception of reality. As the participants interact with one another on the same "logical level" they converge toward social relationships that facilitate collective action through an emergent organizational structure.

As with most any campaign, the level of public interest and involvement will be directly proportional to the degree that they perceive the communication is relevant to their situation. In other words, public commitment is a function of communication impact. It is not enough to just have communication; the communication content must be such that it generates cross-cultural empathy. In fact the principle underlying the ideal global community may be as simple as "Do unto others (neighbors, cultures, ethnic groups, enemies) as you would have them do unto you." Empathy then becomes a construct for managing social change and global issues. Because empathy must be generated on a global basis, focusing on diverse issues and incorporating multiple interests, the most efficient manner in which to generate it is through mediated, vicarious experience. The media function to present new network audiences with a vicariously experienced universe (information/images) resulting in an increase in intercultural empathy. Global management means global action, however, cooperation must often be achieved in the absence of face-to-face interaction. In other words, everyone must take part in the convergence process, but everyone cannot possibly interact directly in order to achieve the level of mutual understanding necessary to truly coordinate action and manage the global problems that confront the system as a whole. The communication necessary for global management, then, must stimulate cooperation through vicarious interaction. The mediated, vicarious interaction experience must produce in the communicators an empathic response toward the other, such that they recognize their interdependence with one another. In addition, because empathy is associated with expectations of cooperative situation outcomes and history influences, the mediated messages will have to reflect a cooperatively dependent attitude on the part of the sender; this may require that certain images be broken down and replaced by favorable images if two local networks have historically been at odds. One of the central propositions of the proposed model is that cooperation in managing global problems can be achieved on the local level by developing interdependency through empathy, generated via mediated, vicarious interaction experience.

An illustration of consciousness raising via media can be found in the work of Tom Sine (1981), a Christian futurist who has published a book titled, *The Mustard Seed Conspiracy*. Sine communicates to a specific class of local networks using a form of media to link them to other existing networks, involving the network members in the global regime and its broader vision. Sine develops a theme in his book, using Christian symbolism and meanings, which effectively relates the Christian culture of local networks to the broader culture of the global network. His chapter and subject headings lay out the framework whereby he develops a sense of empathically produced responsibility (Awakening from the Western dream—a world in trauma; Awakening from the American dream—a nation in transition; Awakening to the globalization of planet earth; Awakening to the future of the global poor; and Awakening to a shrinking pie). This is one example of linking networks in the globalization process by using already existing structures. A number of relevant global problems are dealt with in Sine's book, including poverty, scarcity of resources, environmental degradation issues, and world population problems.

Another example of mediated empathy is found in the work relief organization, Compassion International. Compassion's focus is on providing physical, financial, educational, and spiritual resources worldwide, primarily for needy children. As a network concerned with individuals realizing their responsibility to social, ethnic, and cultural "others," Compassion spends a great deal of time and energy communicating their concerns through various media. Not only do they publish pamphlets, attract endorsements from popular figures within target audiences, sponsor speakers and concerts, and conduct direct mail campaigns, but they also produce professional videos, which they offer to network members who can then show them to dispersed local networks and conduct discussion sessions on the local level. These videos embody the essence of the present model's notion of creating empathy and cooperation via mediated, vicarious experience. The videos graphically represent the conditions of these "others" and emphasize the local network member's responsibility in solving these problems of managing "common resources." One can scarcely view the videos and still dispute the fact that the distribution and misuse of various resources requires some form of global coordination and management, or that actions of one society have inevitable consequences for other societies, either in the short run or the long.

Recently major television networks have provided additional examples of the consciousness raising (agenda setting, or reinforcing, cultivation, convergence) capability of media. ABC television network, via the *Good Morning America* program, aired a series on preserving the earth's natural environment during the broadcast week of February 12-16, 1990. The program related the effects of industrialization and "progress" to the deterioration of the biosphere, and made it clear that each individual's ecological relationship was influential. Turner Broadcasting System has created special programming like "Network Earth" to feature important global issues such as environmental degradation. In like manner, many local public stations have devoted programming time to a similar series of topics under the theme "operation earth" (KTCA, Minneapolis, MN, 1990). Special interest groups and prominent international businesses like the Sierra Club and IBM are conducting advertising campaigns, featuring popular movie and television personalities discussing environmental problems and making available resources for combating these problems (i.e., IBM's Global Resource

Information Database). These types of mediated experiences serve to cultivate a new consciousness in the audience, a consciousness of cooperation, conservation, and responsibility to the global community. One could argue that an agenda was being set and empathy created through the discussion of these topics in the media. These examples serve to illustrate the diversity that can exist in this model at the local level. Obviously it will take different approaches to link different communities to the global network. The local articulation of interests and concerns will undoubtedly be diverse, as will the means of developing cooperation. Developing interdependencies then, or linking diverse individuals and groups together, means developing multiple levels of social networks.

Networking for Intercultural Cooperation

Intercultural management of sociocultural change requires an integrated networking strategy for cooperation to exist. Mowlana (1983) suggests that growth in technology, economies, and sophistication of business and political institutions have made distribution the key factor in the media effect chain: "Control of the distribution process is the most important index of the way in which power and values are distributed in a communication system, which may be the global community, a country, or some smaller cultural unit" (p. 158). The social architecture within which media messages travel then is of crucial importance to cooperative management of interdependence.

Many systems of global management have been proposed. Syme, Seligman, and Macpherson (1989) offer a planning approach. They argue that there needs to be a conscious interaction between the political process, planners, and diverse special interest groups in communities in the management of the environment. By incorporating interaction among diverse interests in the management process, satisfaction can best be maximized for all concerned.

Bennett (1987) takes a convergence position, suggesting that the world is experiencing a convergence of cultural frameworks which will result in a dominant global culture, or one that is "universal." He cites indicators of an emerging order as advanced communications technology and the international propensity toward English as a lingua franca; a heightened sensitivity of the use and benefit of societal manipulation and planning; the integration of local and sublocal cultures; and the appearance and increasing import of internationally coordinated and controlled financial institutions. Others have also noted the structural interdependencies of global economic relations and its foundation on dependencies created by necessary economic exchanges that could substantiate an argument for convergence and an emerging world order (Breiger, 1981).

Gerlach (1989) assumes a middle ground between the two previous approaches, understanding the globalization process, in part, as consisting of "groups cutting across social boundaries." He is correct in that many of the local networks form in an effort to articulate their interest and/or concerns to other groups that do not occupy similar geographic, ethnic, social, or political realms. These local level networks serve to connect individuals to the broader global network, or in Gerlach's terms, they serve the general globalization process. Of particular interest is his description of noncentralized coalitions: they have "segments, each of which can be self-governing, none of which yields authority to a single center, but all of which in fact or potential cooperate or at least work in the same direction. . . . They cooperate through a variety of integrating mechanisms such as shared culture, shared umbrella organization, shared challenges and foes, cross-cutting and overlapping participation and membership" (p. 5). These coalitions have been previously described as segmentary, polycentric, ideologically integrated networks (SPIN) (Gerlach, 1990; Gerlach & Hine, 1970). Gerlach suggests that these coalitions emerge "as the nations of the world slowly build a variety of often informal and implicit arrangements to work together to manage common environmental, economic, and other problems" (p. 5). Gerlach (1990) expands the notion of coalition, using the political term *regime*. He understands a regime to consist of loose participatory networks based on shared principles: "A regime, in short, is a transnational social network coordinated by shared designs for action and interaction and shared interpretations of a problem to be solved" (p. 328). It is through these interactive regimes, he suggests, that a culture of interdependence is being constructed that will enable further development and institutionalization of cooperative efforts in the management of global resources and problems. Gerlach's SPIN/regime model offers a useful means by which we may understand how the management of shared meaning occurs.

Networking has recently grown in popularity according to the bestselling book by John Naisbitt, *Megatrends,* in which the development of informal networks are described as likely to be one of the most influential forces to shape society in the future. Informal networks are often formed and utilized in a reactionary manner to various key social issues like conservation and will be founded on a common ideological theme (d'Abbs, 1982). They are, to some extent, a rebellion against large formal, bureaucratic social institutions. The network synergy is crucial to intercultural management of global issues. Naisbitt characterizes the "network style of management" as informal, egalitarian, interdisciplinary, and communicatively lateral, diagonal, and bottom-up (see also Gilray & Swan, 1984). Naisbitt's characterization is consistent with much of the research on favorable intercultural contact (Gudykunst 1977). There are other reasons for the rapid increase in affinity for the idea of networks. Some of the more popular aspects are (a) they maximize the full potential of individual and small-group innovation while minimizing the consequences of failure; (b) they promote maximum penetration of ideas across sociocultural boundaries while preserving diversity; (c) they are flexible enough to quickly adapt to changing conditions and circumstances; and (d) they put a premium on egalitarian interaction and personal relationship skills, unlike large bureaucracies (Gilray & Swan, 1984). In sum, networks provide a means of decentralizing authority and increasing involvement on the local level where implementation must occur, thus allowing the networks to function in the cooperative modality, rather than the competitive.

Alan Durning (1989) from the WorldWatch Institute, provides examples of local networks working to communicate concerns consistent with the vision of the global network, although they do not necessarily involve the direct media support that the present model advocates. The local networks do lucidly point out some of the tangible results of environmental degradation, such as hunger, thirst, sickness, disease, and shortage of many basic resources. These consequences are communicated in such a way that diverse and widely dispersed groups can associate their own actions with the outcomes in these local communities from where the local networks arise. To some degree these local networks often fulfill the globalization function without a superpresent conscious awareness of what they are accomplishing. What may be motivated by a NIMBY (not in my back yard) consciousness may often result in a globally shared life consciousness.

Other network movements have a definite awareness of their purpose and goals, as well as the means by which they will attain those goals. The California Environmental Network (CEN) is an example of a consciousness-motivated network. The CEN was formed by aggregating and linking together multiple, diverse groups. It disseminates information using many forms of media including computerized bulletin boards, published lists of experts and speakers, a news service, and data banks with information on pertinent and current issues (Gilray & Swan, 1984).

A similar network motivated by a consciousness-raising agenda is that of the World Future Network (WFN). This network's stated purposes are as follows:

> 1) The development of a World Future Network that will serve as a communications system for people everywhere who are seriously concerned about our common global future. 2) The encouragement of new visions of a better future world, so that people will be motivated to achieve an improved world. 3) The dissemination of the futurist perspective, so that more people will accept responsibility for the building of a better world. (Cornish, 1980, p. 15)

The WFN is a developed network in that they employ a variety of media to facilitate the globalization process and are highly aware of the purpose they must serve and the problems they will encounter. Cornish (1980) points out that the network will not be feasible on a global scale "until there is agreement, and we can't have global agreement until we have the means of communication with each other so that we can work out an agreement" (p. 17). Cornish illustrates the role of publication and the media and their integration with the network when he states that "the Network would facilitate the communication, information-gathering, opinion-formation, and consensus that could eventually lead to joint action on collective problems" (p. 17). The WFN also serves to exemplify the fantasy theme theory. One of the goals of the World Future Society is to develop global visions of a better world and inculcate local networks with these visions. Each local network would of course maintain its own unique emphasis, or fantasy theme, but the collective vision would drive and coordinate actions.

Sharing Management Responsibilities for Intercultural Coordination

Intercultural management of sociocultural change requires a commitment to macrolevel egalitarianism and microlevel autonomy. It is important to remain aware of the fact that the type of networks that participate at the local level are not those of bureaucrats, intellectuals, and corporate strongmen only, but cross-class networks in which there is a concurrent sharing and shaping of power. As mentioned earlier in the discussion of convergence theory, participants communicate on the same logical level. It is that breadth of participation and egalitarian approach to communicated interest that makes the network efficacious. Mere participation in intercultural interaction does not necessarily generate favorable impressions. Certain conditions must exist to enhance the positive potential in intercultural interaction. Amir (1969) and Amir and Garti (1977) confronted the issue of influencing positive outcome in cross-cultural contact (see Gudykunst, 1977, for a review). Synthesizing the work of these contact hypothesis researchers, a set of factors necessary for positive interaction has been developed that mirrors many descriptions of optimal network interaction. These factors are as follows:

1. Equal status communication—the interactants must perceive each other as existing on the some level, or at least respecting the other's level as equal to their own.
2. Common purpose—the communication must unite the two interactants in some form, or focus on an issue of common concern.
3. Intimate—the communication must be of an intimate rather than casual nature.
4. Cooperatively dependent—the communication must demonstrate an attitude of cooperation and mutual reliance.
5. Supportive social/authoritative climate—the communication must take place in an atmosphere of positive support from law and custom.

Providing these conditions exist, the interaction might be considered "effective" and would most likely produce an increase in the ability of the interactants to cope with the problematic situation (i.e., sociocultural change).

Gerlach and Radcliffe (1979) note that interdependence must be balanced and voluntary. In order for cooperative management to be effective, it must consist of somewhat autonomous action at the local level. Interdependence is very much a cross-level problem, spanning societies from micro to macro social structures. Actors on the local level must perceive that their concerns are recognized at the global level, and experience the autonomy and authority to implement policies that are the most suitable, and often more effective, in their localities. As Gerlach and Radcliffe (1979, citing Soedjatmoko, 1978) point out, "the building of a participatory society requires freedom as an essential condition to develop the capacity of a society to organize itself. Local autonomy, self-reliance and effective social participation at the village level are inalienable parts of that freedom" (p. 183). Undoubtedly there will be culturally influenced differences in problem interpretation and management strategies; these differences should be welcomed. Particular cultures possess unique methods of adaptation that allow for the expression of the most efficient and satisfactory coping strategies to deal with sociocultural change in their societies (Spindler, 1977). Increased involvement in tangible and intangible expressions of interdependence in a global system will only become a reality under circumstances of autonomous local expression.

CREATING LIFE CONSCIOUSNESS

The process of actually forming a global community with a common vision can be accomplished following a number of different strategies, such as how each local network will use media resources to respond to each exigency will depend on the cultures and/or networks involved, the salient issues, the availability of various media technologies, and the urgency of the problem situation. There are constants, however, amid the flexibility in the process. Interdependence must be recognized, empathy, mutual understanding, and respect established, and cooperation and coordination must be institutionalized. Only after these processes are engaged will a consciousness of ecological interdependence begin to produce tangible evidence in our shared biosphere. Several of these processes are illustrated in the recent effort to preserve Antarctica.

Will Steger (1990), speaking about his recent Antarctic trek, suggested that he intended to influence international cooperation and shape public opinion via the media that followed his expedition in order to preserve the Antarctica resource. The first action taken in this effort to manage sociocultural change was creating an awareness of interdependence. He purposefully formed an international team, comprised of scientists, explorers, and educators from nations including France, the People's Republic of China, the United States, and the USSR, to promote the concept of international cooperation. The second action taken in the Antarctica program was a sophisticated media campaign publicizing the expedition and its goals. A media team accompanied the expedition on the trans-Antarctica trek capturing moving images of the "resource" and the team's unity. Not only was media coverage planned for the expedition itself, additional materials were created for educational purposes. Maps and computer programs were developed for school children to enable them to "participate" in the expedition. Teaching seminars and colloquia were offered prior to the journey to build a base of support in the educational community. Finally, following the expedition, a documentary film was created and Steger is co-authoring a book written for the lay-person entitled, *Saving the Earth*. These tools, combined with a policy tour that followed the expedition, produced immediate results in France, China, and Australia. These nations pledged themselves to the preservation of Antarctica by signing the International Antarctica Treaty. The Antarctica effort "started with a dream," said Steger, a vision for international cooperation in managing the world's "last uninhabited continent." Steger sees the Antarctica treaty as a beginning point for the institutionalization of cooperation, a "world constitution for the environment which will set rules for international resource use." The Steger Antarctica expedition is an excellent example of linking networks through media to raise consciousness and keep an issue in the public arena.

An interdependent society requires the incorporation of new roles, values, ideologies, and responsibilities, identifying "personal values with public issues, individual demand with institutional supply" (Lerner, 1966, p. 228). Lerner describes the interdependent society as one that must "function by consensus" through "high empathic capacity" in order to cooperate in a system of common resources and governance; the global network functions to form and shape a truly "world public opinion" (p. 224). Lein (1983) suggests that "the social network is the arena in which social life occurs" (p. 13). The goal is to get people to broaden their "arenas" and recognize their individual responsibility for global consequences. Essentially, private interest must be "translated" to public policy via new interest aggregation. Cotgrove (1982) referred to sociocultural structure as the "clue to cosmology" (p. 43). Social structures constrain behavior and shape cosmologies; therefore, the key is to change and expand social structures to accommodate and facilitate a concomitant change in ecological cosmologies. If the structure is the "clue," then the commonality constructed through communication (empathy) is the "glue" that gives the structure its integrity. Blair, Roberts, and McKechnie (1985) state that "communication is the social glue that ties organizations together" (p. 55). The glue holds regardless of the members involved and yields a certain "synergy," described as "doing more with less" (Gilray & Swan, 1984). The network, and the communicative empathy which is its glue, aids and increases collaboration. Through the formation of vicarious relationships, empathy is developed nd managing on a global scale becomes conceivable. Once the system s in place and the process of creating a new consciousness underway, "networks" of rules and procedures to sustain patterned behavior begin o stabilize, generating a congruent "regime" with special kinds of ociocultural institutions (Gerlach, 1990, personal communication). It s a quality of regimes that they act to manage problems across sover-ign borders, producing a convergence of expectations around an issue, nd hence patterned action (Gerlach, 1989, 1990; Lipschutz, 1989).

This chapter has presented an initial formulation of a theoretical ramework for sociocultural change. The challenge for future research nd practice is to search out existing networks and grass-roots move-nent that are attempting to broaden the social arenas of their audience y means of mediated, vicarious experience. What types of empathy enerating mechanism, or other means of cooperation stimulation, are mployed? At what level of culture are the networks attempting to reate a convergence of symbols and meanings? What sorts of symbols re effective? Which forms of media are most effective with specific udience types? With specific cultures? What are the effect of remedi-tion in different cultures? Are there differences in the mechanics of etwork formation and distribution of mediated messages? There are nany other important questions that could be posed, utilizing empirical nd ethnographic methods for investigation. Following Yaple and Korzenny 1989), future investigations need to consider environmental and cul-ural factors, message content, distribution effects, and the influence hese factors have on message interpretation. It is a new era in interna-ional cooperation requiring immediate attention by researchers from nultiple disciplines within the social sciences. In the final analysis, the eal, bottom-line management that occurs on an everyday, hourly basis nust be a bottom-up, interaction of multiple communication networks Gerlach & Radcliffe, 1979). As individuals become more aware of their elationship to the ecological stability of the globe, in conjunction with an ncrease in empathy for cultural others, a new 'life-consciousness' will merge and unite the world in a global network with a cultural vision e can all live with.

REFERENCES

lbrecht, T. L., & Adelman, M. B. (1987). *Communicating social support*. Newbury Park, CA: Sage.

Amir, Y. (1969). Contact hypothesis in ethnic relations. *Psychological Bulletin, 71,* 319-342.

Amir, Y., & Garti, C. (1988). Situational and personal influence on attitude change following ethnic contact. *International Journal of Intercultural Relations, 1*(2), 58-75.

Arcury, T., Johnson, T., & Scollay, S. (1986). Ecological worldview and environmental knowledge: The "new environmental paradigm." *Journal of Environmental Education, 17*(4), 35-40.

Barnett, G. A., & Kincaid, D. L. (1983). Cultural convergence: A mathematical theory. In W. B. Gudykunst (Ed.), *Intercultural communication theory: Current perspectives* (pp. 171-194). Beverly Hills, CA: Sage.

Bennett, J. (1987). Anthropology and the emerging world order: The paradigm of culture in an age of interdependence. In K. Moore (Ed.), *Waymarks: The Notre Dame inaugural lectures in anthropology.* Notre Dame, IN: University of Notre Dame Press.

Blair, R., Roberts, K., & McKechnie, P. (1985). Vertical and network communication in organizations. In R. McPhee & P. Tompkins (Eds.), *Organizational communication: Traditional themes and new directions* (pp. 55-77). Beverly Hills, CA: Sage.

Bormann, E. G. (1972). Fantasy and rhetorical vision: The rhetorical criticism of social reality. *Quarterly Journal of Speech, 58,* 396-407.

Breen, M., & Corcoran, F. (1986). Myth, drama, fantasy theme, and ideology. In B. Dervin & M. Voigt (Eds.), *Progress in communication sciences* (Vol. VII, pp. 196-223). Norwood, NJ: Ablex.

Breiger, R. L. (1981). Structures of economic interdependence among nations. In P. M. Blau & R. K. Merton (Eds.), *Continuities in structural inquiry* (pp. 353-375). Beverly Hills, CA: Sage.

Brislin, R. (1981). *Cross-cultural encounters: Face to face interaction.* New York: Pergamon.

Church, A. (1982). Sojourner adjustment. *Psychological Bulletin, 91,* 540-575.

Cornish, E. (1980, October). Creating a better future: The role of the World Future Society. *The Futurist,* 15-19.

Cotgrove, S. (1982). *Catastrophe or cornucopia: The environment, politics, and the future.* New York: John Wiley.

d'Abbs, P. (1982). *Social support networks.* Melbourne: Globe.

D'Andrade, R. G. (1984). Cultural meaning systems. In R. A. Shweder & R. A. LeVine (Eds.), *Culture theory: Essays on mind, self, and emotion* (pp. 88-119). Cambridge, UK: Cambridge University Press.

Dinges, N. (1983). Intercultural competence. In D. Landis & R. Brislin (Eds.), *Handbook of intercultural training, Vol. 1* (pp. 176-202). New York: Pergamon.

Durning, A. B. (1989, July/August). Grass-roots groups are our best hope for global prosperity and ecology. *The Utne Reader,* 40-49.

Edelstein, A. A. (1984). Comparative communication research. In B. Dervin & M. Voigt (Eds.), *Progress in communication sciences, Vol. IV.* Norwood, NJ: Ablex.

Eisenhower, D. D. (1959, December 20). Words to live by. *The Denver Post,* p. 2.

Gandy, O. H., & Matabane, P. W. (1989). Television and social perceptions among African Americans and Hispanics. In M. K. Asante & W. B. Gudykunst (Eds.), *Handbook of international and intercultural communication* (pp. 318-348). Newbury Park, CA: Sage.

Gerbner, G. (1969). Toward "cultural indicators": The analysis of mass mediated public message systems. In G. Gerbner, O. Holsti, K. Krippendorf, W. Paisley, & P. Stone

(Eds.), *The analysis of communication content: Developments in scientific theories and computer techniques* (pp. 123-132). New York: John Wiley.

Gerlach, L. (1989). *Cooperating for ecological interdependence: A study of wetlands and wildfowl management from Canada, through the U.S.A. to Mexico.* Proposal submitted to the North American Waterfowl Management Plan.

Gerlach, L. (1990). Cultural construction of the global commons. In R. Winthrop (Ed.), *Culture and the anthropological tradition* (pp. 319-342). Lanham, MD: University Press of America, Inc.

Gerlach, L., & Hine, V. H. (1970). *People, power, change: Movements of social transformation.* Indianapolis: Bobbs-Merrill.

Gerlach, L. & Radcliffe, B. (1979). Can independence survive interdependence? *Futurics, 3*(3), 181-206.

Gerlach, L. & Rayner, S. (1988). Culture and the Common Management of Global Risks. *Practicing Anthropology, 10,* (3-4), pp. 15-18.

Gilray, N. T., & Swan, J. (1984). *Building networks: Cooperation as a strategy for success in a changing world.* Dubuque, IA: Kendall Hunt.

Blessing, R., & White, W. (1973). *Mass media: The invisible environment.* Chicago: Science Research Associates.

Gudykunst, W. B. (1977). Intercultural contact and attitude change: A review of literature and suggestions for future research. In N. C. Jain (Ed.), *International and Intercultural Communication Annual, Vol. IV.* Falls Church, VA: Speech Communication Association.

Gudykunst, W. B., & Hammer, M. R. (1988). Strangers and hosts. In Y. Y. Kim & W. B. Gudykunst (Eds.), *Cross-cultural adaptation.* (pp. 106-139). Newbury Park, CA: Sage.

Gudykunst, W. B., & Kim, Y. Y. (1984). *Communicating with strangers: An approach to intercultural communication.* New York: Random House.

Gudykunst, W. B., & Nishida, T. (1989). Theoretical perspectives for studying intercultural communication. In M. K. Asante & W. B. Gudykunst (Eds.), *Handbook of international and intercultural communication* (pp. 17-46). Newbury Park, CA: Sage.

Hall, E. T. (1976). *Beyond culture.* Garden City, NY: Anchor Press/Doubleday.

Hanvey, R. (1976). *An attainable global perspective.* New York: Center for Global Perspectives in Education.

Hine, V. (1977, April/May). The basic paradigm of a future socio-cultural system. *World Issues.*

Hofstede, G. (1984). *Culture's consequences.* Beverly Hills, CA: Sage.

Kim, Y. (1978). A communication approach to the acculturation process: A study of Korean immigrants in Chicago. *International Journal of Intercultural Relations, 2*(2), 197-224.

Kim, Y. Y. (1987). Facilitating immigrant adaptation: The role of communication. In T. Albrecht & M. Adelman (Eds.), *Communicating social support* (pp. 192-211). Newbury Park, CA: Sage.

Kim, Y. Y. (1989). Intercultural adaptation. In M. K. Asante & W. B. Gudykunst (Eds.), *Handbook of international and intercultural communication* (pp. 275-294). Newbury Park, CA: Sage.

Kincaid, D. L. (1987). The convergence theory of communication, self-organization, and cultural evolution. In D. L. Kincaid (Ed.), *Communication theory: Eastern and Western perspectives* (pp. 209-221). San Diego: Academic Press.

Lanzetta J., & Englis, B. (1989). Expectations of cooperation and competition and their effects on observer's vicarious emotional responses. *Journal of Personality and Social Psychology, 56*(4), 543-554.

Large, M. (1981). *Social ecology.* Stroud, Gloucester: B. P. Hawkins.

Lein, L. (1983). The ties that bind: An introduction. In L. Lein & M. Sussman (Eds.), *T ties that bind: Men's and women's social networks.* New York: Haworth Press.

Lerner, D. (1966). Enlightenment and communication. In H. W. Peter (Ed.), *Comparati theories of social change* (pp. 221-225). Ann Arbor, MI: Foundation for Research Human Behavior.

Lipschutz, R. D. (1989, August). *Bargaining among nations: Culture, history, & perce tions in regime formation.* Paper prepared for the workshop on managing the glob commons, Knoxville, TN.

McLuhan, M. (1967). *The medium is the message: An inventory of effects.* New Yo Bantam.

Mitchell, J. C. (1969). The concept and use of social networks. In J. C. Mitchell (Ed *Social networks in urban situations* (pp. 1-50). Manchester, UK: Manchester Unive sity Press.

Mowlana, H. (1983). Mass media and culture: Toward an integrated theory. In W. Gudykunst (Ed.), *Intercultural communication theory: Current perspectives* (pp. 14 170). Beverly Hills, CA: Sage.

Mulford, C. (1984). *Interorganizational relations: Implications for community develo ment.* New York: Human Sciences Press.

Peck, J. (1989). The power of the media and the creation of meaning. In B. Dervin & Voigt (Eds.), *Progress in communication sciences, Vol. IX* (pp. 145-182). Norwoc NJ: Ablex.

Redmond, M. (1989). The functions of empathy (decentering) in human relations. *Hum Relations, 42*(7), 593-605.

Ruben, B. D. (1983). A system-theoretic view. In W. B. Gudykunst (Ed.), *Intercultur communication theory: Current perspectives* (pp. 131-145). Beverly Hills, CA: Sag

Sine, T. (1981). *The mustard seed conspiracy.* Waco, TX: Word.

Spindler, L. (1977). *Culture change and modernization.* New York: Holt, Rinehart Winston.

Spiro, M. (1984). Some reflections on cultural determinism and relativism with spec reference to emotion and reason. In R. A. Shweder & R. A. LeVine (Eds.), *Cultu theory: Essays on mind, self, and emotion* (pp. 323-346). Cambridge, UK: Cambrid University Press.

Steger, W. (1990). *Saving the earth: Meeting challenges through international cooper tion.* Hubert H. Humphrey Institute of Public Affairs, Carlson lecture series, Univers of Minnesota.

Syme, G., Seligman, C., & Macpherson, D. (1989). Environmental planning and manag ment: An introduction. *Journal of Social Issues, 45*(1), 1-15.

Yaple, P., & Korzenny, F. (1989). Electronic mass media effects across cultures. In K. Asante & W. B. Gudykunst (Eds.), *Handbook of international and intercultur communication* (pp. 295-317). Newbury Park, CA: Sage.

Yum, J. O. (1988). Network theory in intercultural communication. In Y. Y. Kim & B. Gudykunst (Eds.), *Theories in intercultural communication* (pp. 239-258). Newbu Park, CA: Sage.

13

The Ethics Behind the Effects
A Comparison of National Media Codes of Ethics

THOMAS W. COOPER ● *Emerson College*

*This chapter reviews the major studies of international and national approaches
media ethics and describes the various academic and global contexts for
ternational media ethics study. Methodology is suggested for helpful, if em-
·yonic, comparison and for accurate pattern recognition. The question of
·hether there are universals—common ethical values or guidelines—in national
·d cultural approaches to media ethics is explored. Three such universals are
·pothesized based upon areas of common ground within available media ethics
·des, guidelines, and similar documents.*

When contemplating mass media effects across cultures, one discovers
that there are differing national and cultural ethical systems. Effects
deemed "ethical" in one society may be deemed "unethical" in another.
Accordingly, this research investigated whether some mass communication practices might be deemed "ethical" in all societies.

One way of framing such research is by posing the question: "Is there
global mass communication ethic?" In this essay, representative
attempts to answer that question prior to 1991 will be investigated.

THE QUEST FOR UNIVERSALS

To date research reveals at least three major areas of worldwide
concern within the field of communication ethics. The first could be
called "the quest for truth," which includes a global concern with media
"objectivity" and "accuracy." The second could be described as the
"desire for responsibility" among social (cf. professional) communicators. This concern includes differing regional emphases upon professionalism, accountability, justice, equality, loyalty priorities (to government, public, peers, personal integrity), adherence to social mores

229

(e.g., cultural notions of secrecy, privacy, source protection, etc.), ar
ultimate motivation issues (such as conflict of interest, bribery, ar
self-promotion). The third, which might be called the "call for fre
expression," includes differing regional emphases upon free flow ‹
information, censorship, regulation, freedom of the press and of speec‹

Although these three areas can be categorized in numerous oth‹
ways, and are suggestive, not conclusive, they are each, based upon t‹
research available to date, candidates for "universal" status. That ‹
each of the three concerns (and perhaps others) may prove to ‹
common to human beings as individuals or to collective forms such ‹
societies, cultures, or nations.

DEFINING UNIVERSALS

Throughout the scholarly literature dealing with "universals" is t‹
underlying assumption that the phenomenon in question (i.e., universa
pervades, transcends, or includes all elements within its universe. If t‹
astrophysical universe (of stars) is chosen as an example, then t‹
statement "It is a universal trait of stars to be gaseous," if true, wou‹
hold that all stars in the universe are currently gaseous. A small
universe could be specified, for example, Australians, in which case t‹
statement "It is a universal characteristic of Australians to wear hat
would mean, if true, that each Australian wears a hat.

A "growing literature on the subject of 'ethical universals and a unifi‹
theory of human nature' " springs from sociology (e.g., Selznick's "Natur
Law and Sociology"), anthropology (e.g., Linton's "Universal Ethic
Principles: An Anthropological View"; Mead's *Continuities in Cultur*
Evolution), and philosophical ethics itself (e.g., Brandt's *Ethical Theor*
The serious discussion of universals is both broad and ancient.

The more embryonic "discipline" of communication or particular
the subdiscipline of mass communication ethics has not yet develop‹
a sizable literature defining universal tendencies. However, from o‹
perspective, the early attempts of Americans (such as Shannon, Weave
Schramm, and others) to construct simple models of communicati‹
was an attempt to distill simple universal essences from a complex
situations and technologies. The Canadians Innis and McLuhan look‹
for universal "laws of media," although Innis described these in hu‹
bler, more tentative terms. European critical thinkers, structuralis‹
hermaneuticists, and others have shown important tendencies in dev‹

oping an approach to the philosophy of communication, in which more social elements (structures, class relations, languages) may be seen as central, if not universal, to communication's essence.

Nevertheless, a precise attempt to determine specific universals within media ethics is needed. The following definitions, although embryonic, grow out of that necessity:

1. Universal: phenomenon or quality currently extending to an entire selected universe of elements.
2. Absolute: phenomenon or quality extending to an entire selected universe of elements throughout history.
3. Representative Universal: phenomenon or quality extending to the entire subset of representative elements within a selected universe.
4. Subconscious Universals: intangible essences, thoughts, instincts, and feelings thought to be common throughout all elements within a selected human universe.
5. Overarching (Conscious) Universals: concrete, verifiable, articulated phenomena common to all elements within the selected universe.
6. Representative Subconscious Universals: combine definitions 3 and 4.
7. Representative Overarching (Conscious) Universals: combine definitions 3 and 5.

Such definitions are meaningful only to the degree that they provide useful distinctions. In the forthcoming description of international communication ethics, these terms will serve as helpful categories. It is empirically impossible to determine a pure global absolute for communication ethics. All people, living and dead, may not be successfully interviewed about the moral role of mass media within society. However, representative instruments—international declarations and communication law, national press codes, press council documents—may be inspected as conscious statements intended to represent institutions and populations. These are different from subconscious universals, which are more difficult to codify.

ARE CONSCIOUS UNIVERSALS AN ILLUSION?

Kaarle Nordenstreng and various co-authors have sought to amass and discuss different types of national, multinational, and global instruments that treat international media regulation, policy, ethics, and guidelines.

In one instance, Nordenstreng and Alanen analyzed 44 international community documents:

> the so-called instruments of international law (the Charter of the United Nations, international conventions, etc.), as well as other instruments of less legally binding nature such as declarations and resolutions of the UN and its various specialized agencies, above all UNESCO, which has a particular mandate in the field of culture and communication. The instruments analyzed here include 12 conventions, 14 declarations, and 18 resolutions. (1981, p. 233)

In a much larger work, in which Nordenstreng and Hannikainen (1984) primarily inspect the Mass Media Declaration of UNESCO, they provide an "Inventory of Codes of Ethics" in which a "crude content analysis" of 50 national and multinational codes reveals patterns to be discussed later within this chapter. Although common sense itself offers hunches about why universal international agreement would be difficult to obtain and maintain, the research of Nordenstreng may qualify him to be a leading voice for articulating the key difficulties in the conscious charting of a universal media ethic.

As Nordenstreng explained at the International Organization of Journalists in his presidential address (Paris, 1977), even among a specialized profession of communicators, such as journalists, there are significant difficulties in reaching global consensus:

> It is very problematic to construct a code of conduct which would be clear both in conceptual and practical terms and, furthermore, applicable under different socio-political circumstances of journalists themselves. And secondly, we know from experience—for example considering the debate around UNESCO's Draft Declaration on the use of mass media—that these kinds of issues easily turn into controversies among non-professional political ambitions, in which the original substance gets easily lost. (1978, p. 15)

The example used by Nordenstreng, the Mass Media Declaration of UNESCO, is an excellent case in point. Instead of collective wisdom emerging regarding a pannational communication ethic, three proposals for an alternative text to the Declaration were drafted.

The proposal for a "Socialist Alternative" text represented 12 countries; the proposal for a "Western Alternative" text represented 10 countries; the proposal for a "Non-Aligned Alternative" text represented member states of UNESCO belonging to the Group of Non-Aligned Countries and to the

Group of Seventy-Seven. Prevailing political differences are not unrelated to the more recent withdrawal of the United States and England from UNESCO and continuous debate within the organization about the role and regulation of communication worldwide.

The expectation that international law might provide a universal standard for professional communicators is also unrealistic. As Nordenstreng and Alanen indicate:

> Under close scrutiny international law is not found to set many direct standards on journalists. Setting standards on the contents of communication is, according to the principles of international law, the duty of states, which may, within their power of legislation and administration control the information media in a country. Besides, only a few of the most authoritative instruments, those namely of the international conventions, treat explicitly of the communication media and the journalists. (1984, p. 238)

Nor do more informal gatherings, such as conferences among media "experts"—whether academic, professional, or policy delegates—necessarily achieve a state of Utopian agreement. As Clifford Christians, delegate to the Brikeland Conference in Norway, noted, representatives were as interested in conflicting points of view as in overlapping causes:

> The International Mass Media Institute of Kristiansand, Norway, played host to a conference on media ethics last May. One hundred delegates were invited from seventeen different countries, including Austria, France, Holland, India, Sri Lanka, Singapore, Finland, Uganda, Nigeria, England and Switzerland. . . . The three most prominent ethical positions which appeared were Marxist, secular humanist and Judeo-Christian. Rather than work toward a bland consensus or avoid ultimate questions, the delegates saw their role as struggling to understand opposing perspectives while defending and articulating their own. (1981, p. 16)

Possibly the greatest concern among those working within the field of international relations is implementation of paper agreements. As Dutch scholar Cees Hamelink has written in "Toward an International Code of Ethics": "There are numerous obstacles on the road to such a code and . . . there ought to be sufficient skepticism vis-à-vis its implementation" (Bruun, 1979, p. 5). If international political law is consistently violated, why would international communication codes be more likely to remain inviolate?

Beyond the problems of negotiation, compromise, political maneuvering, and implementation are the deeper questions relating to authority, control, homogenization, and imposition. Would a universal ethics law truly unite people or simply expand the division between those who are regulated and those who regulate? Would national and cultural differences be preserved or homogenized by such legislation? Would such "universals" be imposed, and thus not truly universal, or "discovered" (cf. "revealed") to be already subconsciously present?

Many fears and areas of resistance surface when uniform regulation, even gentler "guidelines" and "codes" are suggested. There is much evidence to suggest that conscious universals, if manufactured, to the degree that they must be imposed, are not in fact universal, but involve the consensus of a majority imposed upon at least one minority, or the consensus of at least one minority imposed upon the majority.

If conscious universals are not manufactured (through negotiation, compromise, etc.), but rather recognized in the course of discussion (as at an international convention of musicians who discover the same folk melody, with different words, common to their heritage), there is no longer the problem of imposition and control, nor of negotiation compromise. Such discoveries, however, usually pertain more to the discovery of a common subtext, or hidden subconscious, than to the forging of paper agreement. Such subconscious overlap is interesting, but is it concrete?

ARE SUBCONSCIOUS UNIVERSALS TANGIBLE?

The psychologist Carl Jung (1875-1961) posited a collective subconscious, in which all human beings touch the horizon of a collective race memory. It does not necessarily follow that all human beings therefore subconsciously love truth, responsibility, and freedom. To be sure, the line of thought is provocative; the quest to find common dreams, subconscious desires (as in the Freudian tradition), symbols, and essences has been no less the province of philosophy and anthropology, than of sociology, and of psychology. Nor have there been a scarcity of archaeologists, scientists, and theologians who have posited some common "homing" instinct in which human beings innately but vaguely perceive a lost Motherland, Eden, Atlantis, or indecipherable déjà vu sensation—which is translated in other modes (e.g., religion, ritual, the quest for "roots") or suppressed entirely.

In the field of communication it would seem that certain other subconscious impulses could be labelled primary, if not primal. For example, "the longing for self-expression" might be suggested as universal. Who could argue conclusively that monks who take vows of silence do not nevertheless communicate or that autistic children have never experienced at least the "longing" for self-expression? Could not "the longing for self-expression" be common to all human beings, at least hypothetically?

If one suggests, however, that the longing for truthful communication is a subconscious compulsion, there may be an intuitive resonance with the assertion, but where is the weight of evidence? Magicians, political scientists, advertisers, and cosmeticians, among others, have all argued that in various ways human beings enjoy being deceived, not shown the truth. Data proving the presence of subconscious universals must be more indirect than evidence of conscious universals and thus involves inference and deduction, not observable evidence. If subconscious universals exist, an element of Kierkegaard's "leap of faith" is necessary to unconditionally accept their presence, let alone their identity. One may leap as easily to the hypothesis that "human beings wish to be deceived" as to the hypothesis that "human beings wish to be told the truth." From an empirical standpoint, more tangible and specific evidence must be investigated. However, subconscious universals are neither useless nor imaginary, as will be discussed later.

ARE CODES OF ETHICS VALID EVIDENCE OF CROSS-NATIONAL PATTERNS?

Possibly the most useful evidence of representative conscious communication ethics is the media code. Ideally (and this ideal will be later cross-examined), the media code's value is fivefold.

1. A code of ethics is concrete. However much interpretations of a code differ, the code itself is, even when revised, fixed. It is tangible, written (in the vast majority of cases), reproducible, historically dated, and available for study.
2. The ideal code is representative: it may represent the professional, government, or people of a country, institution, or group of countries or institutions.
3. Ideally, a code of ethics is focused. Unlike a charter of international relations, national constitution, or multinational trade law, the mission of

a code of ethics is specifically to delineate some measure of universal ethical principles and practices consistently throughout the universe to which it applies. Communication ethics are usually central, not peripheral, to its particular purpose.

4. A code of ethics is intentional. Whatever its relationship to subconscious universals, a code is consciously, and often laboriously, conceived. It may be the product of hours, days, even years of conscious thought, revision, collective negotiation, and critical scrutiny.

5. A code carries some degree of meaning. Many codes are strictly symbolic, others nominal, still others inspirational. Nevertheless, whatever weight a code carries in the actual influence of human behavior, it is suggestive of either altruistic ideals or self-interested buffers that reflect upon the authors and, to some degree, those they represent.

For this reason media codes of ethics, not the reports of Press Councils nor declarations of international organizations, nor theories of subconscious universals, have been chosen for the empirical instruments to be used in the studies explained below. Nevertheless, as data for research, and as meaningful statements, codes have numerous weaknesses that are worthy of specific consideration:

1. Global Representation? As Clement Jones pointed out in 1980, there are more countries without than countries with Codes of Ethics.

2. Clear Meaning? Although the word *code* may mean "law of prescriptive principles," it may also mean a "system of secret writing or signals." Codes of ethics are not always merely the former and may require cryptographers, of a sort, to determine their exact meaning.

3. Spatio-temporal Translation? Codes do not easily compare across national, media, and date boundaries. A Tanzanian Press Code of 1957 might be three steps removed (time, nation, medium) from a French Television Entertainment Code of 1986.

4. Democratic Representation? A code may not be truly representative of its country or institution. It may have been adopted by a minority elite, a figurehead assembly, or an overthrown political regime. Thus it may be obsolete, impotent, doctored for appearances, or politically abridged.

5. Superficial Similarities? Codes, by virtue of a tendency toward telegraphic compression, may lend themselves to false similarities.

6. Hollow Facades? Codes are often rhetorical, rather than genuine. Codes sometimes are camouflaged, meaningless, and impotent.

7. Committee Compromises? Codes are often group mosaics written for posterity, if not prosperity. Like the elephant (intended to be a horse)

created by a committee, codes may be the result of compromises and negotiations.

8. Superimposed Values? Codes are not always indigenous, and thus not purely representative. A code that is copied by a developing country or imported from a colonial power may not be supported by the local majority.

9. Genuine Ideals? Codes are written for audiences. An individual within a committee may wish to please peers on the committee and thus revise views or wording. Moreover, the committee may wish to please a larger body that will not ratify the code beyond anticipated parameters. The ratifying body or its representatives in turn may be seeking approval by a higher body or government, inspection agency, regulatory power, and so forth.

To this list must be added the general problems of research such as Robert Rosenthal's caution that researchers often "discover what they are looking for," rather than making sense of the totality of favorable and unfavorable data. In an even more self-reflexive mode, Krippendorff asks the researcher/scholar to "draw others like yourself," that is, as an ethical imperative, "when involving others in your constructions, always grant them (those addressed/studied) the same autonomy you practice in constructing them" (1985, p. 1). Such a line of thought reminds one of the larger ethnocentric problems of cross-cultural and cross-national research in which "foreign" peoples (cf. codes) are studied through one's own bias, language, and methods, not seen through native eyes. Comparing codes involves comparing cultures.

THREE CONTENDERS

Within a framework of such qualification, the available evidence suggests that, within the universe of intranational, national, multinational, and global codes available for comparative research, at least three principles emerge as leading contenders for consensus. To support this claim, quantitative evidence is readily obtained through the combined studies of H. Leppanen (*Jounalistien Kansaliset ja Konsainvaliset Saannostot*, 1977), C. Jones (*Mass Media Codes of Ethics and Councils*, 1980), and Nordenstreng, Hannikainen, and Alanen (Alanen research thesis, University of Tampere, 1979).

Although he does not mention the exact number of codes he has examined, Clement Jones describes codes from 50 countries. Virtually all of the codes assembled mention "Journalism" or "Press" in their title or within the title of the sponsoring organization. Exceptions (such as Tanzania) suggest that the scope of media and content covered may extend beyond journalism.

Harry Leppanen focused his study upon journalistic codes and enumerates 59. These include multinational codes such as the International Federation of Journalists' 1954 Declaration of Principles and the Draft International Code of Ethics adopted by the United Nations Economic and Social Council (EOSOC) in 1952.

There is admitted overlap between the codes studied by Jones, Leppanen, and Bruun and those studied by Nordenstreng, Hannikainen, and Alanen. For example, The International Federation of Journalists' Declaration of 1954 listed above is used by both Bruun and Nordenstreng. Nordenstreng et al., however, use 50 codes (cf. Leppanen, 59 codes; Jones, 50 countries), 42 (possibly 44 depending upon category scheme) of which they list by country and the others by multinational association.

Because the comparison between international standards (documents) with professional manifestations of ethics (codes) influenced their categorization, Nordenstreng et al.'s 7 categories are considerably different from Bruun's 18. Jones, rather than use subject headings for categories, lists 5 "factors of difference" among the codes. Thus, each comparative scheme is significantly different.

Despite the differing methodologies, types of codes, purpose of the research, and depth of scholarship, a comparison of the studies reveals interesting overlap. In survey I (Leppanen), the "theme which is represented more than any other topic is the theme of honest and true dissemination of news," which appears in 53 of the 59 codes. In survey II (Nordenstreng et al.), the theme mentioned most is "objectivity, veracity, honesty," which appears in 49 out of 50 codes. Jones, who does not quantify his findings, leads his five "elements which are commonly to be found" with "the emphasis upon the integrity, truth and objectivity of all forms of news collection and dissemination" (Bruun, p. 28).

Thus, in survey I, approximately 90% of 11 codes, in survey II, 98% of all codes, and in survey III, a very high, if not the highest percentage (figures not given) of all codes, focus upon the general theme of "truth, truthfulness, objectivity, honesty, accuracy, etc." Further research might well reveal that a high percentage of these codes also places the theme of truthfulness as the most important one within journalism, if not within communication.

There can be no pretense that any or all of these codes directly and literally mention "the quest for truth." As Bruun indicates, the National

Association of Hungarian Journalists may call more for "verification" and accuracy "in conformity with reality" while the Japanese Nihon Shinbun Kyodai's Code calls for news reporting to "convey facts accurately and faithfully" (Bruun, p. 28). The Code of Ethics adopted by the U.S. Society of Journalists, Sigma Delti Chi, and also adopted by the Journalists' Association in Columbia, "believes the duty of the journalist is to serve the truth. . . . Truth is our ultimate goal" (Merrill & Odell, pp. 172-174). Thus codes categorized together may vary considerably in language, emphasis, and in the aspects of truthfulness articulated. The "quest for truth" is simply a collective superobjective.

Truth itself, however translated, cannot be said to have monolithic objective (and this word is used paradoxically) meaning. Merrill and Odell, for example, list five levels of truth—"transcendental, potential, selected, reported, perceived." Moreover, there are numerous philosophical and other texts that question the existence, meanings, and levels of "truth," "objectivity," "accuracy," "verification," and so on. What can be said is that based upon available representative research, "the longing for the communication of truth," particularly by journalists, but also by social communicators in toto, tends most toward conscious global universality. It has already been carefully demonstrated that social contexts, linguistic factors, and many other considerations provide many levels of interpretation to the notions of truth and truthfulness.

In one sense it is extremely difficult to distinguish "the desire for responsibility among social communicators" from most other categories. Tautologically, one of the primary responsibilities particularly of journalists (in many countries, entertainers are offered forms of "poetic license") is to be truthful; a journalist who is deliberately deceptive to both his public and his "employers" is considered irresponsible. Moreover, because for many codes, "responsible" is equated with, or closely related to, "professional," and because many codes seek to define professional behavior, a second tautology appears—to disobey a professional code is thus, by definition, to behave irresponsibly. At one level then many codes define "responsibility," or at least ethical responsibility.

That the word and notion *responsibility* is a key concept cannot be easily refuted. Hans Jonas's entire book *The Imperative of Responsibility* (1979) is written in response to the question "Why is responsibility brought to the fore as the key principle of the 20th century?" In 1986, 52 groups of media professionals and enthusiasts in 19 countries affirmed the central significance of "responsibility" to communication in a 90-minute teleconference. "The Responsibilities of Journalism" conference at Notre Dame University in Indiana in 1982 spawned Robert Schmuhl's useful book by that name (1984). These are only a few important examples.

A major discussion area within codes might be called "responsibility to . . . " For example, Jones's third representative universal candidate, "professionalism," reflects responsibility to the profession. His "commonly found element" number 4 mentions responsibility (cf. loyalty) to one's country, which, in turn, is closely related to the notion of social responsibility (cf. responsibility to society). About half of the categories advanced by Bruun relate directly to the theme of social responsibility—professional secrecy (42 codes), following the objectives of mass communication (42 codes), respecting right to privacy (39 codes), not accepting personal benefits (37 codes), avoiding plagiarism and slander (33 codes), and many others.

Nordenstreng et al. provide a system of categories in which global responsibility is measured (responsibility to international law or global requirements). By this larger definition of social responsibility (toward the maintenance of global peace and security, for example), 28% mention the communicator's responsibility toward the maintenance or establishment of peace and security; 24% are concerned with the responsibility for friendship and cooperation among nations, and 36% are concerned with racial equality and discrimination. The majority of codes do not reach to such international scope and many codes may represent journalists who do not sense that the responsibilities listed above are specific to journalists, or mass media.

It is significant to note, however, that, as previously stated the notion of the responsibility to the truth or truthfulness is held in 98% of all codes. "Other obligations" (cf. responsibilities) are mentioned in 94% of all codes. The notion of social responsibility is inherent within the Nordenstreng schema, and thus does not appear as an official category.

The important overall unifying ingredient of virtually all codes is the expectation that the communicator be accountable or responsible to, if not for, people other than himself or herself. Such people are described in differing orders of magnitude—"employers," fellow workers, all professionals, all members of the institution, and so forth. There is the implicit or explicit expectation that such people, or the ideals that serve such people (justice, fairness, truth, equality, etc.) will be acknowledged through behavior. Such behavior is "socially responsible." Depending upon how this "social responsibility" is defined, roughly

85%-100% of the codes examined in all three surveys call for or assume social responsibility.

"Freedom of expression" has many interpretations and contexts. For example, the Hungarian code previously cited mentions "In the spirit of the Freedom of the Press laid down in the Constitution of the Hungarian People's Republic." Bruun and Leppanen, from whom these codes are quoted, note 33 citings of "freedom of information" in 59 codes (56%), which is a lower ratio than Nordenstreng et al. listings under "Free Flow of Information," which includes 34 codes (68%). It should be noted that "free flow of information" has specific meanings, literature, and ongoing debate about its interpretation and implementation. Jones uses this phrase within his second "elements commonly to be found" and defines the flow as "from governments to those whom they govern, and from those who are governed to governors" (1980, p. 63).

Jones's listing to the contrary, the 56% and 68% listings of the other two surveys does not prove universal status. However, because "freedom of the press," "freedom of speech," and similar phrases are already specified in most national constitutions, and since the responsibility for maintaining that freedom is often given to governments or courts, the notion is often inferred "between the lines" of a code. Thus the third candidate for universal status, "call for freedom of expression," must, on the basis of this research, maintain borderline status. Such a "universal" can only be inferred.

Moreover, "freedom" has vastly different implications in different codes. A common interpretation of Marxian usage of the term "freedom of the press" emphasizes the freedom of the poor, enslaved, or otherwise oppressed to publish and broadcast, not just those who can afford (cf. control) media institutions and technology. In many more "libertarian" type codes, "freedom" has the emphasis of freedom from government control or interference. Thus, at one level, this is a "surface" representative universal, fixed by language, if not rhetoric. However, "the call for free expression" may in fact be indigenous to human beings, and thus transcendent of its many interpretations. At some level communication ethics focuses upon the concern that organisms (whether individuals, institutions, governments, classes, minorities, and the media they use) should not be muzzled. However, there is no widespread agreement about whose voices should be heard, to what extent, and through which media.

Like larger philosophical and political systems, codes may call for freedom, responsibility, and truth, but not examine the consequent contradictory implications. Some codes do account for potential contradictions within their principles and wording; most ignore larger political, philosophical, and linguistic contexts in which contradiction occurs.

SUMMARY

The most dominant essence is the quest for truthfulness, if not truth. Empirically, the theme of truth and truthfulness is most pervasive. The second most dominant theme, that of responsibility, particularly social responsibility, and its subthemes—professionalism, loyalty, and accountability—is inherent within a vast majority (85% to 100%) of codes. It is specified within almost as many. The theme of "freedom of expression,"—and the subthemes "free flow of information," "freedom of press," and so on—are articulated less frequently than "truth" or "responsibility," and empirically is a "borderline" representative universal. However, the contexts of codes, the constitutions of nations, and the subtexts within codes, point toward the universality of concern with "freedom."

These three "ideals" have been carefully entitled candidates for the status of conscious representative universal. "Candidates" is a necessary qualification because three studies and less than 100 codes are not globally universal. It is possible that the methodologies, translations, and materials within any (or all) of the three studies conceal more than they reveal. It is also evident that the three themes isolated within this essay could be recategorized, subcategorized, or renamed in a variety of manners. However, this simple rank-ordering of theme frequency may give evidence of what could be discovered in larger, more current studies of consistent methodology. It may, with the necessary leap of faith, point toward thoughts and feelings within the minds and hearts of human beings worldwide.

REFERENCES

Altschull, J. H. (1984). *Agents of power*. New York: Longman.
Barney, R., & Black, J. (1985). "The case against mass media codes of ethics." *Journal of Mass Media Ethics, 1*(1), 7-9.
Bertrand, C-J. (1985). "Ethics in international communication." *Intermedia, 13*(2), 9-13.
Bohn, T. W., Herbert, R. E., & Ungurait, D. F. (1985). *Mass media IV*. New York: Longman.
Brislin, R. W. (1981). *Cross-cultural encounters*. New York: Pergamon Press.

Brislin, R. W., Lonner, W. J., & Thorndike, R. M. (1973). *Cross-cultural research methods.* New York: John Wiley.

Bruun, L. (Ed.). (1979). *Professional codes in journalism.* Prague: International Organization of Journalists.

Christians, C. (1981). "Ethics abroad." *Journalism Ethics Report,* 16.

Curry, J. L., & Uassin, J. R. (1982). *Press control around the world.* New York: Praeger.

Gerbner, G., & Siefert, M. (1984). *World communication.* New York: Longman.

Hartley, E. L., & Ruth, E. (1959). *Fundamentals of social psychology.* New York: Knopf.

Head, S. (1985). *World broadcasting.* Belmont, CA: Wadsworth.

Johannesen, R. (1983). *Ethics in human communication.* Illinois: Waveland Press.

Jonas, H. (1984). *The imperative of responsibility.* Chicago: University of Chicago Press.

Jones, C. (1980). *Mass media codes of ethics and councils.* Paris: UNESCO.

Kroeber, A., & Kluckhohn, C. (1952). *Culture.* Cambridge, MA: Papers of the Peabody Museum, 47, 1.

Martin, L. J., & Chaudhary, A. G. (1988). *Comparative mass media systems.* New York: Longman.

Merrill, J. C., & Odell, C. J. (1983). *Global journalism.* New York: Longman.

Merrill, J. C., & Odell, C. J. (1983). *Philosophy and journalism.* New York: Longman.

Nordenstreng, K. (1978). "International Organization of Journalists presidential address." In *Presidium de L'IOJ.* Prague: International Organization of Journalists.

Nordenstreng, K., & Alanen, A. (1981). "Journalism ethics and international relations." *Communication, 6,* 225-254.

Nordenstreng, K., with Hannikainen, L. (1984). *The mass media declaration of UNESCO.* Norwood, NJ: Ablex.

Powell, J. T. (1972). "Broadcast advertising of medical products and services: Its regulation by other nations." *Federal Communications Bar Journal, XXV*(2), 144-175.

Powell, J. T. (1974). "Protection of children in broadcast advertising: The regulatory guidelines of nine nations." *Advertising Law Anthology, II,* 253-267.

Rivers, W., Schramm, W., & Christians, C. (1980). *Responsibility in mass communication.* New York: Harper & Row.

Saulberg, H. (1973). "The canons of journalism. XXX: A fifty-year perspective." *Journalism Quarterly, 50*(4), 731-734.

Schmuhl, R. (1984). *The responsibilities of journalism.* Notre Dame, IN: University of Notre Dame Press.

UNESCO. (1977). "Meeting of experts on contribution to an ethic of communication" (UNESCO document SS-77/Conf. 803.17). Paris: Author.

UNESCO. (1980-1981). *A New World Information and Communication Order: Toward a wider and better balanced flow of information.* Paris: Author.

Van Der Meiden, A. (1980). *Ethics and mass communication.* Utrecht: State University of Utrecht.

Varis, T. (1984). "The international flow of television programs." *Journal of Communication, 34*(1), 143-152.

Weaver, D. H., Buddenbaum, J., & Fair, J. E. (1985). "Press freedom, media, and development, 1950-1979: A study of 134 nations." *Journal of Communication, 35*(2), 104-117.

EPILOGUE

14

Mass Communication and Culture
An Epilogue

FRED L. CASMIR ● *Pepperdine University/Seaver College*

The study of mass mediated communication is only part of our overall societal endeavor to understand human interactions. Because of its cultural bases in Greek logic, rationalism, and the Enlightenment, that effort has been based on assumptions of order, and cause and effect relationships that have not always proven adequate. That is especially the case if one realizes that cultural bases and individual needs and perceptions have often been neglected in favor of statist, politically oriented perceptions of mass media. Recent changes in political entities throughout the world and the reemergence of cultural/national concerns should make it easier to consider a model of mutuality, interdependence, and interaction. That could help avoid a continuation of concerns with traditional transactional models, which resulted primarily in the use and abuse of media in accordance with the needs and interests of elites.

The conflicts, confusion, and misinterpretations that result when scholars attempt to use old models in order to deal with emerging cultural and societal changes in perceptions is repeatedly illustrated in this volume. At the same time it is also evident that many of the scholars whose essays are included in this volume are struggling to gain more adequate insights based on new paradigms.

INTRODUCTION

Most of us have experienced the mixed emotions and even confusion related to mass communication research and criticism in the United States. Such reactions are also possible as one reads the pages of this volume. The cause, at least in part, can be traced to the love-hate relationship that citizens of many democratic societies have with their media. Peters (1989) makes my point very well in his essay "Satan and Savior: Mass Communication in Progressive Thought." However, the

AUTHOR'S NOTE: The author gratefully acknowledges the contributions of his graduate assistants, Joy Swenson and Linda Santucci, to the library research supporting this essay, and the editing of the final manuscript.

challenges scholars face as they study the impact of mass mediated communications are based on more than feelings of ambivalence.

Consideration of the cultural foundations of our scientific inquiries represents one of the more central issues. The assumptions made about logic and cause-effect relationships, evolved by Greek philosophers and rationalists, as well as Enlightenment scholars and thinkers that have strongly influenced all of us in the United States (Aristotle, 1954; Bredvold, 1961; Descartes, 1941; Locke, 1760) illustrate that point. To some extent those of us working in various areas of communication studies share the difficulties that had to be faced by physicists. Scholars in that field came to realize that simplistic cause and effect models used in the natural sciences had to give way to the much more complex paradigms that emerged out of their understanding of a universe whose basic law appears to be one of chaos. As Jaki (1978) put it, "the turbulence of all that is, is governed by the order of law; but that turbulence is a law of disorder" (p. 362).

In the pages of this volume a number of authors, most notably Witte, struggle with such complexities and the resulting necessity of dealing with more than simple models of order and logical structures based on them. In spite of her Western orientation and focus on persuasion, she nevertheless provides important insights into the importance of choosing the correct target variables, as well as a variety of applicable means of communication. Her specific focus on media as only one of the variables to be considered in our attempts to prevent AIDS is very helpful in that regard. If we concede that media effects are inseparable from message recipients, her point is truly significant.

MASS MEDIA STUDIES: COMPLEXITY VERSUS SIMPLIFICATION

The fact that we continue to confuse the basic differences between states or political entities, and nations or cultural groupings, further complicates our task (Casmir, 1991). In the United States critical concern with and challenges to the role of government have become almost a sacred tradition. Therefore, statist emphases, or confusion over the use of the terms "nation" and "state" in our research and writing, seems curious. The significance of that confusion becomes clear when we read in one of the preceding essays that many "cultures" are represented on what is called "national" television. What the author needed to emphasize is that many political entities, or "states," are faced with the necessity to accommodate a diversity of cultures in their television programming. As a result, the use of multiple cultural themes on any one country's or state's television requires of scholars a multi-, cross-, or inter-cultural orientation in much of their work. That fact cannot be simply ignored by lumping together cultural diversity under the term "national television."

Even the use of the term *media* occasionally illustrates the confusion discussed here. Not only grammatically incorrect, the use of the term *media* as a singular (i.e., "media is") indicates an attempt to bring simplistic order and unity to a complex subject. At the same time, such usage is difficult to bring into congruence with our insistence that a "multiplicity" of voices is vital to a democratic society, and the fact that we understand how different the impact of various media can be.

MASS MEDIA, STATES, CULTURES, AND INDIVIDUALS

No greater challenge is faced by us than the necessity to somehow bring global or even international problems into some congruent and nondestructive relationship with individual human needs and perceptions. Many of the authors in this volume have had to face that most basic problem of all. In part that requires reconsideration of some of our earlier models, concepts, and approaches. For instance, initial attempts by Hall (1959) to identify cultural specifics in the area of proxemics, were largely inadequate. Both the categories and their measurement, and the attempt to identify German or Arab (or any other) universals, are problematic. The statist/political identifications used by Hall indicate little of the rich cultural diversity they mask. Even recent work by such scholars as Hofstede (1984) suffers from similar problems. The use of a highly select sample of individuals from business and industry, and the subsequent identification of "typical cultural" norms for states, certainly suffers from a number of methodological and conceptual difficulties. What has passed, in many instances, for societal or state norms, was often developed in an attempt to provide some common ground for the citizens of culturally diverse countries. Truly intercultural research thus becomes the exception rather than the rule. In addition, studying highly specific, subcultural groups, such as university students, makes generalizations to a total culture even more difficult.

Smith, if you recall the essay in this volume, bases his work on the conviction that his highly idealistic, futuristic use of media networking will result in the global orientation of media users. In that framework there appears to be little room for individual cognitive processes studied by Chaffee, and the need for transformations in cross-border media use considered by Cohen and Roeh in this volume. Recent history, and especially events in such countries as the Soviet Union and Yugoslavia, has reminded us that the central role of a culture (or nation) still influences many human interactions.

Consider contemporary events in the Soviet Union. They have once again made it apparent that in spite of almost total state control over communication media and technologies, human beings make use of what is offered them for their own purposes and the fulfillment of their own needs, within specific cultural and social settings. Madden's chapter in this volume, on Inuit broadcasting, is one of many possible examples supporting that claim. Significant to her overall approach is the fact that she uses a rhetorical textual analysis because she correctly identifies the subject matter of her work as rhetorical exigency. In light of the additional insights on third-culture building in this chapter, it is worth noting that the Inuit appear to have merged Western program structures with traditional Inuit cultural content. Some other third-culture developments are emerging as well in the acceptance by Inuit of "Southern" (Canadian and American) entertainment programs.

We can conclude that in many instances specific types of media consumption or use result, regardless of the intentions of those who present material to their viewers, readers, or listeners. What that suggests is that our focus needs to be not so much on institutions or systems, but rather on negative and positive, successful and unsuccessful interactions between individuals and the media available in their societies. Greenberg and his co-authors examine one specific instance of the many that help us to focus on media use by individuals. How parents mediate behavior of their children, however, will require even more detailed study of the total cultural setting if we are to adequately understand how mass media behaviors fit the total cultural context. Admittedly that is a much more complex and difficult subject than can be accomplished in a survey.

My emphasis on such interactions, as contrasted with transactions, is quite deliberate. The former requires participatory, mutually agreed upon, and developed processes that are considered beneficial not only by representatives of political entities, as models for contemporary mass communication. The latter is much more concerned with the completion of a task. Such an emphasis on transactions lends itself well to concerns for development and mass media use from a strictly technological orientation.

TECHNOLOGY AND MASS MEDIA AS VALUE SYSTEMS

For years the impact of mass media was discussed by various governmental or political entities primarily from the standpoint of their technology or hardware (Cherry, 1971; Schramm, 1964). It was common to think that technological improvement, and thus more and better communication hardware, indicated both change and progress. Technological progress, in turn, had already been labeled as a social "good." However, questions concerning this simplistic, linear, or circular argument, especially in intercultural or cross-cultural communication, have been raised during recent years (Grunig, 1978; Mowlana, 1986; Yaple & Korzenny, 1989).

It is significant that vigorous debates about the role of mass media calling for a new world communication or information order, very quickly and consistently addressed fundamental issues beyond the narrow confines of technology, communication hardware, or even software (Ansah, 1986; Nordenstreng & Kleinwachter, 1989). Ultimately, the intrinsic rights or natural abilities of human beings to determine their own ways of life became central issues (Meyrowitz, 1985; Schramm, 1980).

Once we recognize the interconnectedness of these central issues, the question would appear to be: Can we guarantee social benefits and the maintenance of cultural values to all human beings while using mass media? Additionally, can we avoid control over or domination of human beings by those using these media systems? Smith, in this volume, assumes that we have a beneficial superculture already in existence. He uses Lerner's model, which stipulates that public communication stimulates individuals to behave in new ways, but fails to prove the vital causal relationship between media existence or use and societal change. In effect, Smith's concerns with "enforcing agreements" and "organizing the evaluation of sociocultural change" are major hindrances to achieving the proposed networking effects. His insistence that manipulation would have to be minimized in such an approach has to be evaluated in light of our past experiences and the common human inability to overcome temptations to manipulate others. One major

factor considered in this epilogue chapter also is ignored in suc
networking proposals. The interactive needs of cultures and individual
may not be any better accommodated by a global system than has bee
true of international or "national" (one-country) attempts to serv
diversified interests.

The basic questions in the 1970s (Ellul, 1973; Toffler, 1970) wer
as they are today, whether or not all change is progress and whether c
not all progress is desirable from a human survival standpoint. You ma
recall that Chaffee, in this volume, reminds us that besides enormou
problems with correlational research, the study of change requires mor
than laboratory settings. Chaffee also stresses the necessity of unde
standing cognitive individual human processes, in addition to thos
related to the supposed causal impact of mass media technology an
messages. Consideration of contemporary economic, political and cu
tural changes appears to reflect a widespread re-evaluation of the need
and the future of human beings worldwide, who are living in pos
industrial societies. Human needs rather than those of science an
technology have thus taken on a new significance (Lowrance, 1985).

It would seem unnecessary to make the following point, but Toffle
(1970) felt otherwise: the end of development is not perfect technolog
(and, the end of culture is not the survival of institutions), because th
desired end of cultural efforts is the development and the survival c
human beings. If we are to take Ellul's (1973) challenge seriously, w
need, at the very least, to closely link the needs of human beings wit
the institutions, systems, organizations, and states they have develope
An up-to-date reevaluation of human cultural needs for survival appea
to be required. The emerging paradigm would undoubtedly be signif
cantly different from those based on developmental models of the pas
which tended to separate technological change from cultural and huma
needs.

TECHNOLOGY, ECONOMICS, IDEOLOGIES, AND COMMUNICATION: A COMPLEX MIX

As scholars, we need to make certain that our assumptions or presu
positions do not result in inevitable findings that provide little insig
into existing situations. To cite just one example, we need to understar
more about the impact of American television programs, such as Micke
Mouse cartoons or Westerns, beyond references to the use of slic

marketing strategies. At this point we can only guess what universal human needs are being met by such effective intercultural communication efforts.

One specific chapter in this volume makes it possible for me to illustrate the complexity of mass media studies, and the need to integrate or interrelate a variety of insights. Straubhaar and his co-authors share with us the results of their study of newscasts, accepting translations for their research texts. It seems important, however, to relate their efforts to the arguments made by Hobb and Frost or Cohen and Roeh who indicate that tone and treatment are fully as important as the translatable text.

The use of strongly Western values in Straubhaar et al.'s research might cause us to question whether the conclusions drawn by Chaffee about individual cognitive aspects and causality, in relationship to mass media use, are compatible with their findings. That is especially the case if we remember that Straubhaar et al. point to significant differences within the blocs they studied, and the fact that news coverage has changed in the Soviet Union since glastnost emerged. These and other factors indicate the importance of considering more than media related aspects such as the formats of newscasts. Understanding what represents news in different situations for different people is more complex than discovering similarities or differences in formats of newscasts.

I have discussed the influence of cultural or societal norms and values on communication elsewhere (Casmir, 1991). One conclusion reached is that in the West or North, our norms have tended to include concepts like influence, control, controlled change, and persuasion (Howell, 1979). Within that kind of framework, strategies evolved that were perceived by some as a desire to dominate others. Others saw them as attempts to produce change by bringing individuals and cultures in line with the values held by a communicator, or in mechanistic terms, a sender. Closed, mechanical systems tend to occupy or take over territory rather than adapt or flexibly interact with their environments in a process of mutual change. Earlier Western or Northern communication models, based on technological or mechanical assumptions thus were frequently perceived by others as "imperialistic" or as "neocolonialist," especially when they were internationally and interculturally applied (Fejes, 1982; Nordenstreng & Schiller, 1979). The perception of how human communication works and how it is allowed or expected to function is a chief consideration in the development and maintenance of any society or culture. Models of conjoint human interaction have been discussed by several authors (Blakar, 1985; Casmir, 1978; Casmir & Asuncion-Lande, 1989). These paradigms illustrate that communication is not merely a tool, but a survival mechanism, comparable in biological terms, to the functions of metabolism.

Political and ideological presuppositions of all kinds have limited our ability to study media impact objectively. Cohen and Roeh's work, included in this volume, is indicative of our recent willingness to consider more critically what impact texts have in cross-border communications. Their findings indicate that messages identified as news often undergo more transformations than fiction, because of the role assigned to news and information by contemporary social and political institutions. At the same time, these authors make it clear that context is vital to interpretation and that we exist in a post-Babel world in which people do not speak with one tongue.

During the last two decades it has become evident to students of intercultural and international communication, especially with regard to study of the mass media, that all applicable social, economic, ideological, political, and cultural implications of contemporary conflicts have to be considered (Giddens, 1979; Habermas, 1984). Earlier discussions often centered too readily and easily around questions relating to the negative impact of multinational companies, the evils of capitalism, socialism, and media imperialism, because sociopolitical rather than individual or cultural needs were considered to be primary. Unfortunately, few books or articles, including those by Schiller (who has supported a Socialist/Marxist approach that is opposed to the role of multinational firms and the capitalistic system), provided basic, objective data based on the careful testing of underlying assumptions and value judgments (Ansah, 1986; Schiller, 1969a, 1969b). In such efforts, "cultural imperialism" was readily identified only with the influence of foreign states or economic interests, rarely with internal suppression of cultural minorities.

Fundamental questions in this area remain, which need to be answered through careful research. Does technology—in the societies in whose formation it plays a major role—become a dominating force that challenges philosophies, religious concepts, and all other basic cultural and societal value systems? Does control of media technology structure all political points of view and all societal institutions (Ellul, 1964; Stanley, 1978; Volti, 1988)? If media technology can become such a dominant force, it behooves us to find out if political, cultural, and social systems are inevitably changed by the use of technology and science, and how. If media dominance and control and imposed change are inevitable, it might be much more sensible to submit quickly, in the way in which at least one social scientist has suggested (Skinner, 1971).

As of now, we have insufficient understanding of the control media technology exerts. For instance, we are not sure how it creates its own organizational structures, ethics, and values (Jassem & Desmond, 1985; Williams, Rice, & Dordich, 1985). A fundamental question is whether or not it makes any difference what our cultural background is once we become part of a technological growth model. Some indicate that the social and economic strategies of apparent opponents in today's geopolitical struggles are really very similar as long as they are driven by models of technological change and development (Ellul, 1973; Volti, 1988). All such paradigms developed by various political or ideological systems certainly allow for population growth, and economic expansion. They also encourage rising demands that result in ecological and population problems.

MASS MEDIA AND INTERCULTURAL COMMUNICATION

In contemporary intercultural and international communications, mass media (or so-called mass communications) play a vital role. Today's mass media are the products of highly developed technologically oriented states. As a result, important questions emerge: Do the mass media, as presently constituted, provide a setting for or engender mutuality in intercultural and international interactions? Do they assist in maintaining communication subcultures, thus facilitating a process that avoids domination by majorities or the most powerful? Are technological societies and their tools actually counterproductive to that process? Some contemporary authors believe that technological societies and mass communication hinder rather than facilitate the development of interactive, adaptive communication subcultures or third cultures that could facilitate mutuality on an interpersonal level (Casmir, 1978). Clearly, it is important to determine if mass media, and those who manipulate them for their own political, philosophical, or economic power and gain, negatively influence the survival needs of other human beings or even those of entire societies.

Smith and Cooper offer us two related approaches in this volume that deal with media use. Smith has great faith in the impact of media networks, which would cause all of us to think and act in new, global ways. Cooper supplements that with his confidence in our ability to discover cultural universals (in contrast to attempts to manufacture them). His approach is considerably more interactive than Smith's, and focuses on the importance of discussion, responsibility, and freedom of expression. In fact, Cooper is impressed with Clifford Christian's emphasis on struggling to understand opposing perspectives. The central question remains, however, whether or not mass media are designed, or capable to serve as facilitators in that process.

Do we acknowledge the possibility of media use for purposes of massifying audiences in order to unify political entities for the use of their leaders? If so, what is the solution to any attempt to "globalize" audiences for the primary purpose of easier centralized manipulation within and between states? Behind much of our research is an assumption that bigger is better, or that a unified global approach somehow will overcome the problems human beings have had to face on a local, state, or national level. It would appear that such an assumption requires more proof—especially considering the past history of humankind. It can be argued that changes in technology and its use need to be increasingly researched from the standpoint of human concerns, instead of attempting to tailor humans to existing technologies (Bahr, 1981; Fischer, 1985; Schumacher 1981). Only recently have some scholars in the field of mass communication taken steps in the direction of understanding the relationship of individual needs as they relate to interactions with mass media (Gumpert & Cathcart, 1986; Reeves & Garramone, 1983).

It is important, however, to distinguish between the instruments technology provides and their actual use by human beings. As a result we should avoid automatically transferring the already uncertain social effectiveness or positive impact of mass media and mass technology to leaders or individuals who use them for their own purposes. Only if the complex interrelationships between media, cultures, individuals, ideologies, and states can be better understood, will we be able to make mass media nondominant, efficient, effective partners in the evolution of new, mutually accepted processes of interaction.

Berger's chapter is representative of contemporary scholarly concerns related to these issues. Especially significant is Berger's insight into countries that attempted to use the media for unification, and where cultures and subcultures were maintained in spite of that fact. Obviously, significant distinctions need to be made between media, content, and perception, because different people in different societies read messages differently. Once again it must be stressed that both media and cultures are much more complex than much of our past scientific research has indicated.

MODIFYING OUR SEARCH FOR UNDERSTANDING

The following three modifications of our earlier approaches would appear to be beneficial in light of what has been discussed so far:

1. We need to re-examine communication and the impact of mass media. The use of new models can assist us in that effort. One example would be to ask: Who selects what from among the resources available for communication to meet individual needs—resulting in a feeling of balance that leads, in turn, to a greater perceived chance for individual and cultural survival? Of course, "survival" in this context is more than mere biological survival. It includes also aesthetic, moral, and spiritual aspects.

2. Mass media may be more meaningfully studied as having been primarily developed or maintained as part of the attempts by various internal or external elites to exert influence and control. Their most important roles thus may not be those of progressive, revolutionary agents of change, nor as means for serving the needs of their receivers for information, education, entertainment, or progress (Curran, 1982; Gonzalez-Manet, 1988).

3. The impact or power of mass media to direct and control needs to be studied and understood in relation to local, national, or international leaders and their institutions. These powerful individuals see the media as their best opportunity to exert a unifying, conservative influence over an increasingly diversified and complex world (Hornik, 1984; Pye, 1980). Mass media thus become primarily politically unifying institutions. Interactive processes, taking into consideration cultural end individual needs, or attempts to develop mutuality, are easily neglected in such settings.

Gozzi, in his chapter, attempts to cut through some of our confusion, misperceptions, and our inability to address individual and cultural differences by using Hall's concepts of sparse/dense and high/low contexts. However, Gozzi almost immediately falls into the common trap of using state/political entities to illustrate these concepts rather than cultures or subcultures. Although he intimates that other than "whole culture" contexts are worthy of our study, he never follows through on that more difficult task. Gozzi's realization that the so-called "Third World" actually consists of a great variety of countries and cultures never comes to full fruition. As a result, he, like many other scholars, ultimately faces the challenge posed by terms of great generality related to phenomena of great variability.

It may be fortunate for human beings that "power is under the necessity of becoming absolute and totalitarian," as Ellul (1970) writes: "After a certain period of pressure, institutions and sociological phenomena do in fact lose their vigor, fall into decay, and thus cease to constitute necessities." In spite of dramatic changes in their environment, human beings, on the other hand, do survive. Individuals are more flexible, more adaptive, more selective than their institutions—as long as their model for survival is metabolic rather than mechanistic, open rather than closed, interactive rather than dominance-oriented—and based on mutuality.

It would seem that scholars in the field of communication have the special credentials, preparation, and interests to respond to the challenges outlined here—something that may not be true for members of many other disciplines. In this volume, the work of Morgan and Shanahan, among others, supports that claim. Their concern with an unintentional but implicitly ethnocentric view of media effects represents a growing and important awareness that the symbolic environment of any culture helps to perpetuate the basic assumptions and cultural ideologies of the institutions and societies that produce them. They indicate that on the microlevel there is little evidence that exposure to American television produces much cultivation. In effect, cultivation may be highly culture specific. Whether or not their insights will stand up under further scrutiny is not the most significant point. Rather, the fact that their challenge requires us to take another look at the relationship of microlevel cultural practices and macrolevel media effects is of primary concern.

SUMMARY

What I have sketched in the preceding pages suggests the traces of a pattern. Individuals build societies; they create cultures. To assist them in maintaining these vital structures humans form institutions. Eventually the people who are part of such institutions become more concerned with maintaining their own positions—positions that are actually characteristic of the controlling elites. In other words, they do not serve the needs of individuals outside their organizations. The value systems of these elitists then become all-encompassing, demanding, authoritarian.

Mass media, as is true of all communication systems, are vital to the perpetuation of any new value systems. Yet as the total system becomes unresponsive to human needs for individual freedom, expression, and mutuality, people begin to challenge it and provide alternatives. The cycle continues, speeded up by technological tools, but persisting by virtue of the nature of humans as adaptive, metabolic, interactive beings. After all, the human ability to accept, reject, and modify institutions in order to survive is almost limitless.

Culture is both objective and subjective (Stewart, 1978; Tokarev, 1977). It is the subjective, individualistic part of culture that presents us with the greatest contemporary challenges. The reader who has carefully considered the essays in this volume has seen examples of that fact in many of the contributions as their authors strive to gain a better understanding of the role of mass media. Hobbs and Frost, for instance, make it clear to all of us that the cognitive apparatus used by individuals in making sense of their world requires careful study. Much of what appears to be true for African tribes that need translation of arbitrary editing conventions undoubtedly applies to the rest of us. At the same time, Hobbs and Frost's work makes it evident that a brief exposure to other cultures is not enough if we are to truly understand the cognitive foundations of their perceptions, as well as the measurement biases we may bring as scholars to the study of other cultures.

A model for the study of communication and mass media that is based on individual experience and that makes diversity the aim of its findings seems at this point to be difficult to imagine even for any one cultural system. In an intercultural, international, or global scenario that becomes more difficult yet. A major "cultural" change in our scholarship appears to be one of the required modifications if we are to adequately face our challenges. At least, that seems desirable, if our understanding and use of mass media in intercultural and international communication are to be improved. Only then can we move from dominance and persuasion-oriented models, to cooperative, interactive systems better suited to both the needs of individual human beings and, in the long run, their political, social, economic, and media institutions in today's world.

If, as scholars, we are to deal more effectively with future challenges, three efforts would be helpful. First, we need to consider the lessons of history. Second, we must lay new foundations for studying and learning from existing situations; in that search for understanding it is vital to let our insights emerge out of the societies and cultures we study. To achieve the best results we need to identify and understand the assumptions and ideological inclinations we bring to our work. Combining initial qualitative research used to discover factors that are relevant to the societies or cultures we attempt to understand, with intensive quantitative research to verify what we have learned, may be the most meaningful procedure. Finally, we need to actively explore the possibilities provided by developmental models based on mutuality and nonthreatening interactions in an interdependent world.

REFERENCES

Ansah, P. A. V. (1986). The struggle for rights and values in communication. In M. Traber (Ed.), *The myth of the information revolution: Social and ethical implications of communication technology* (pp. 64-83). London, UK: Sage.

Aristotle (1954). *The rhetoric and the poetics of Aristotle.* W. R. Roberts & I. Bywater (Transl.). New York: Random House.

Bahr, F. R. (1981). The man-machine confrontation. In L. Hickman & A. Al-Hibri (Eds.), *Technology and human affairs* (pp. 30-55). St. Louis, MO: C. V. Mosby.

Bredvold, L. I. (1961). *Brave new world of enlightenment.* Ann Arbor, MI: University of Michigan Press.

Casmir, F. L. (Ed.) (1978). *Intercultural and international communication.* Washington, DC: The University Press.

Casmir, F. L. (Ed.) (1991) *Communication in development.* Norwood, NJ: Ablex.

Casmir, F. L., & Asuncion-Lande, N. C. (1989). Intercultural communication revisited: Conceptualization, paradigm building, and methodological approaches. In J. A. Anderson (Ed.), *Communication yearbook 12* (pp. 278-309). Newbury Park, CA: Sage.

Cherry, C. (1971). *World communication: Threat or promise?* New York: John Wiley.

Curran, J. (1982). Communications, power and social order. In M. Gurevitch, T. Bennett, J. Curran, & J. Woollacott (Eds.), *Culture, society and the media* (pp. 202-235). London, UK: Methuen.

Descartes, R. (1941). *A discourse on method.* Berkeley: University of California Press.

Ellul, J. (1973). *Propaganda: The formation of men's attitudes.* New York: Alfred A. Knopf.

Ellul, J. (1964). *The technological society.* New York: Alfred A. Knopf.

Fejes, F. (1982). Media imperialism, An assessment. In D. C. Whitney & E. Wartella (Eds.), *Mass communication review yearbook, Vol. III* (pp. 345-353). Beverly Hills, CA: Sage.

Fischer, C. S. (1985). Studying technology and social life. In M. Castells (Ed.), *High technology, space & society* (pp. 284-300). Beverly Hills, CA: Sage.

Giddens, A. (1979). *Central problems in social theory.* Berkeley: University of California Press.

Gonzalez-Manet, E. (1988). *The hidden war of information.* Norwood, NJ: Ablex.

Grunig, J. E. (1978). A general system theory of communication, poverty and underdevelopment. In F. L. Casmir (Ed.), *Intercultural and international communication* (pp. 72-104). Washington, DC: The University Press.

Gumpert, G., & Cathcart, R. (Eds.). (1986). *Intermedia: Interpersonal communication in a media world.* New York: Oxford University Press.

Habermas, J. (1984). *The theory of communication action.* Boston, MA: Beacon Press.

Hall, E. T. (1959). *The silent language.* Garden City, NY: Doubleday.

Hofstede, G. (1984). *Culture's consequences.* Beverly Hills, CA: Sage.

Hornik, R. C. (1984). Communication as complement to development. In G. Gerner & M. Siefer (Eds.), *World communications: A handbook* (pp. 330-345). New York: Longman.

Howell, W. S. (1979). Theoretical directions for intercultural communication. In M. K. Asante, E. Newmark, & C. A. Blake (Eds.), *Handbook of intercultural communication* (pp. 23-42). Beverly Hills, CA: Sage.

Jaki, S. L. (1978). *The road of science and the ways of God.* Chicago: University of Chicago Press.

Locke, J. (1760). *An essay concerning human understanding.* London, UK: D. Brown.

Lowrance, W. W. (1985). *Modern science and human values.* New York: Oxford University Press.

Meyrowitz, J. (1985). *No sense of place.* New York: Oxford University Press.

Mowlana, H. (1986). *Global information and world communication.* New York, Longman.

Nordenstreng, K., & Kleinwachter, W. (1989). The new international information and communication order. In M. K. Asante & W. B. Gudykunst (Eds.), *Handbook of international and intercultural communication* (pp. 87-113). Newbury Park, CA: Sage.

Nordenstreng, K., & Schiller, H. I. (1979). Communication and national development: Changing perspectives. Introduction. In K. Nordenstreng, & H. I. Schiller (Eds.), *National sovereignty and international communication* (pp. 3-8). Norwood, NJ: Ablex.

Peters, J. D. (1989). Satan and savior: Mass communication in progressive thought. *Critical Studies in Mass Communication, 6,* 247-263.

Pye, L. W. (1980). Communication, development and power. In H. D. Lasswell, D. Lerner, & H. Speier (Eds.), *Propaganda and communication in world history: Emergence of public opinion in the West* (pp. 424-446). Honolulu, HI: University Press of Hawaii.

Reeves, B., & Garramone, G. M. (1983). Television's influence on children's encoding of personal information. *Human Communication Research, 10,* 257-268.

Schiller, H. I. (1969a). *The mind managers.* Boston, MA: Beacon Press.

Schiller, H. I. (1969b). *Mass communications and American empire.* New York: A. M. Kelley.

Schramm, W. (1980). The effects of mass media in an information era. In H. D. Lasswell, D. Lerner, & H. Speier (Eds.), *Propaganda and communication in the world history: A pluralizing world in formation* (pp. 295-345). Honolulu, HI: University Press of Hawaii.

Schramm, W. (1964). *Mass media and national development: The role of information in the developing nations.* Stanford, CA: Stanford University Press.

Schumacher, E. F. (1981). Technology with a human face. In L. Hickman & A. Al-Hibri (Eds.), *Technology and human affairs* (pp. 426-438). St. Louis, MO: C. V. Mosby.

Skinner, B. F. (1971). *Beyond freedom and dignity.* New York: Alfred A. Knopf.

Stanley, M. (1978). *The technological conscience: Survival and dignity in an age of expertise.* New York: Free Press.

Stewart, E. C. (1978). Outline of intercultural communication. In F. L. Casmir (Ed.), *Intercultural and international communication* (pp. 265-344). Washington, DC: The University Press.

Toffler, A. (1970). *Future shock.* New York: Random House.

Tokarev, S. A. (1977). The segregative and integrative functions of culture. In B. Bernardi (Ed.), *The concept and dynamics of culture* (pp. 165-177). Paris, France: Mouton Publishers.

Volti, R. (1988). *Society and technological change.* New York: St. Martin's Press.

Yaple, P., & Korzenny, F. (1989). Electronic mass media effects across cultures. In M. K. Asante & W. B. Gudykunst (Eds.), *Handbook of international and intercultural communication* (pp. 295-314). Newbury Park, CA: Sage.

Index

About the Editors

FELIPE KORZENNY is Professor of Communication and Coordinator of Graduate Studies in the Department of Speech and Communication Studies at San Francisco State University. He received his B.A. in 1973 from Universidad Iberoamericana in Mexico City and his M.A. in 1975 and Ph.D. in 1977 from Michigan State University. He has served as Chairperson of the Intercultural and Development Communication Division of the International Communication Association. His publications have appeared in many major communication journals. His work includes a book on Mexican Americans and the mass media as well as research articles and projects on communication discrimination, communication with strangers, drug communication across cultures, effects of international news, sociopolitical communication, and communication and new technologies. His most recent books are *Communicating for Peace* and *Cross-Cultural Interpersonal Communication* (coedited with Stella Ting-Toomey).

ELIZABETH SCHIFF is Training Officer at the Management Development Unit, San Francisco City and County, Civil Service Commission. She received her B.A. in 1975 from Colorado College, Colorado Springs, and her M.A. in 1986 from San Francisco State University. Her research work has focused on the effects of communication discrimination on Chinese Americans and Hispanics. She is coauthor of the *Culturgram* series on Morocco. She has served as an officer for the Intercultural Interest Group of the Western Speech Communication Association.

STELLA TING-TOOMEY is Associate Professor of Speech Communication at California State University, Fullerton. Her research focuses on identity negotiation, face work, and conflict styles across cultures. Her most recent books include *Culture and Interpersonal Communication* (with William B. Gudykunst) and *Language, Communication, and Culture* and *Communicating for Peace* (both coedited with Felipe Korzenny). Her work has appeared in *American Behavioral Scientist,*

Communication Monographs, Human Communication Research, and *International Journal of Intercultural Relations,* among others. She has served as the Chairperson of the Speech Communication Association's International and Intercultural Communication Division. She is currently writing a textbook on intercultural communication patterns.

About the Contributors

ARTHUR ASA BERGER is Professor of Broadcast Communication Arts at San Francisco State University. He is the author of many books and articles on popular culture, the mass media, and related concerns. Among his recent books are *Media Research Techniques* (Sage) and *Reading Matter: Multidisciplinary Perspectives on Material Culture* (Transaction).

FRED L. CASMIR received his Ph.D. from Ohio State University in 1961. He is presently Professor of Communication at Seaver College, Pepperdine University. He has served as Developer and Coordinator of International Studies at Pepperdine from 1988 to 1991. In 1991, he headed the first Pepperdine-Japan Semester Overseas Program and toured East Germany and Austria as a lecturer in communication. His time at Pepperdine is spent teaching communication courses, such as "Intercultural Relations and Mass Media."

STEVEN H. CHAFFEE (Ph.D., Stanford University, 1965) is Janet M. Peck Professor of International Communication at Stanford University. He is a past President and Fellow of the International Communication Association. His research has included such topics as family interaction, political communication, adolescent socialization, interpersonal coorientation, health and prevention campaigns, and survey research methods. His publications include *Political Communication* (1976), *Television and Human Behavior* (with George Comstock and others, 1978), *Handbook of Social Science* (with Charles Berger, 1987), and *Communication Concepts 1: Explication* (1991).

AKIBA A. COHEN is the Danny Arnold Professor of Communication and Chair of the Department of Communication at the Hebrew University of Jerusalem. His current research interests are content analysis and perception analysis of television news in the cross-cultural and cross-national context.

267

THOMAS W. COOPER received his B. A. from Harvard University and his Ph.D. from the University of Toronto. Author of 20 articles and 3 books on media ethics, he published *Communication Ethics and World Change* (Longman, 1989) with contributing scholars from 14 countries. He is a former assistant to Marshall McLuhan and assistant speech writer in the White House. He has taught at the University of Maryland, Temple University, Harvard University, and is now at Emerson College.

LEONARDO FERREIRA currently teaches at the University of Miami, Coral Gables.

RICHARD FROST is Associate Professor of Sociology at Babson College in Wellesley, Massachusetts. He received his Ph.D. in sociology from Boston University in 1968.

RAYMOND GOZZI, Jr. received his Ph.D. in 1987 from the University of Massachusetts, Amherst. He currently is Associate Professor in the Division of Communication at Bradley University in Peoria, Illinois.

BRADLEY S. GREENBERG is University Distinguished Professor of Telecommunication and Communication at Michigan State University.

CARRIE HEETER is a faculty member in the Department of Telecommunication at Michigan State University.

RENÉE HOBBS is Assistant Professor of Communication at Babson College in Wellesley, Massachusetts, and Lecturer on Education at Harvard University. She received her Ph.D. in Education from Harvard University in 1985.

LINLIN KU is a Ph.D. candidate at Michigan State University.

TUEN-YU LAU received his Ph.D. from Michigan State University. He is Assistant Professor in the Department of Communication at Purdue University. He teaches courses in print and broadcast journalism, international communication, and telecommunication technologies and policy. He has a special research interest in mass media development in China and telecommunication development in Asia.

HAIRONG LI is a Ph.D. candidate at Michigan State University.

KATE MADDEN is Assistant Professor in the Department of Communication at the State University of New York, Geneseo. She received her Ph.D. from Pennsylvania State University in 1989.

MICHAEL MORGAN received his Ph.D. from the University of Pennsylvania in 1980. He is Associate Professor in the Department of Communication, University of Massachusetts, Amherst.

ITZHAK ROEH is Senior Lecturer in the Department of Communication at the Hebrew University of Jerusalem and a Visiting Professor at Columbia University. His current research focuses on news as storytelling, the coverage of the Intifada in the Israeli press, and the globalization of television news.

JAMES SHANAHAN received his Ph.D. from the University of Massachusetts in 1991. He is Assistant Professor in the College of Communication at Boston University.

L. RIPLEY SMITH received his M.A. in 1990 from the University of Minnesota. He currently is a Ph.D. candidate in the Department of Speech Communication at the University of Minnesota. His present research interests include structural constraints on interpersonal and intercultural relationships.

JOSEPH D. STRAUBHAAR is Associate Professor in the Department of Telecommunication at Michigan State University.

ROBERT H. WICKS is Assistant Professor at Indiana University.

KIM WITTE received her Ph.D. from the University of California. She is Assistant Professor in the Department of Speech Communication at Texas A&M University. Her primary research interests are in the area of public health campaigns and persuasion, with a special emphasis on the role of culture as it relates to these areas. She has authored papers on topics of intercultural communication, health communication, communication theory, and research methods.